A Worldbuilder's
Guide to Societies

ALSO BY BRENT A. STYPCZYNSKI
AND FROM McFARLAND

*A Worldbuilder's Guide to Magic:
Essentials for Writers, Game Developers
and Dungeon Masters* (2021)

*The Modern Literary Werewolf:
A Critical Study of the Mutable Motif* (2013)

A Worldbuilder's Guide to Societies

Essentials for Writers, Game Developers and Dungeon Masters

BRENT A. STYPCZYNSKI

McFarland & Company, Inc., Publishers
Jefferson, North Carolina

Library of Congress Cataloguing-in-Publication Data

Names: Stypczynski, Brent A., 1977– author.
Title: A worldbuilder's guide to societies : essentials for writers, game developers and dungeon masters / Brent A. Stypczynski.
Description: Jefferson, North Carolina : McFarland & Company, Inc., Publishers, 2023. | Includes bibliographical references and index.
Identifiers: LCCN 2023040434 | ISBN 9781476693637 (paperback : acid free paper) | ISBN 9781476651095 (ebook) ∞
Subjects: LCSH: Fantasy fiction—Authorship. | Imaginary societies—Authorship. | Fantasy games—Design. | Creation (Literary, artistic, etc.)
Classification: LCC PN3377.5.F34 S79 2023 | DDC 808.3/8766—dc23/eng/20230901
LC record available at https://lccn.loc.gov/2023040434

British Library cataloguing data are available

ISBN (print) 978-1-4766-9363-7
ISBN (ebook) 978-1-4766-5109-5

© 2023 Brent A. Stypczynski. All rights reserved

No part of this book may be reproduced or transmitted in any form or by any means, electronic or mechanical, including photocopying or recording, or by any information storage and retrieval system, without permission in writing from the publisher.

Front cover image by Next Mars Media (Shutterstock)

Printed in the United States of America

McFarland & Company, Inc., Publishers
Box 611, Jefferson, North Carolina 28640
www.mcfarlandpub.com

Table of Contents

Introduction   1

1. Concept   9
2. History   21
3. Governments   41
4. Religion   57
5. Magic   79
6. Technology   100
7. Education   112
8. Species   126
9. Language   141
10. Sex and Gender   152
11. Organizations   161
12. Geography   171
13. Places   191
14. Finishing Touches   202

Appendix A: Divine Spheres of Influence   211
Appendix B: Recommended Resources   213
Appendix C: Selected Primary Texts and Series   217
Chapter Notes   219
Bibliography   229
Index   233

Introduction

Beyond characters, societies and cultures may be the most recognizable elements of the fantasy genre and its many subgenres. Fictitious societies are built in all the fantasy genres, from sword and sorcery to epic fantasy, urban fantasy to comedic. They are an integral part of any worldbuild, unless the entire world and story have only a single person who was born, grew up, and lived with no other living beings around them—this is unlikely, though, as even Mowgli had a society of jungle animals. It is part of the nature of humanity, by and large, to come together in groups and those societies shape who people are and how they interact with the world.

The specific fantasy subgenre, of course, has an impact on the type of societies that the builder creates to populate the world. Some are open societies, visible to all. This type appears in most secondary world (not Earth) fantasies and open magic primary world (Earth) settings. Others are hidden from outsiders, concealed by location, tradition, magic, veils of secrecy, or some combination thereof. These are mostly primary world, hidden magic settings, but can also be elements of secondary worlds, whether as secret societies (ex. criminal societies, some magic societies, some religious societies), isolated communities (due to choice, geography, or history), or remnants of supposedly lost societies.

A pause seems appropriate here, to clarify terminology and scope.

As used in this work, the term society can range from nations to cities to villages to monastic communities. It can include international organizations and residential schools, even neighborhoods. Ultimately, a society is "a unified tribe, city-state, or nation with a shared culture, language, and traditions."[1] Additionally, M.K. Tod defines society as a confluence of environment, religion, technology, language, economy, politics, and family.[2] As such, a society can be all inclusive (a nation) or built around a single group (ex. the Jesuit Order or the Mafia). It can cover a single world or multiple worlds, such as the Otherworld in Roshani Chokshi's *Aru Shah* (or *Pandavas*) series or the multiverse of Robert Asprin's *MythAdventures* series. A society can be comprised of one species (ex. Lothlórien in

Middle Earth) or multiple species (ex. Waterdeep in the Forgotten Realms or post-Shift Atlanta in the *Kate Daniels* series).

Some notable examples include:

> Nations: Ravka and Kerch (Grishaverse); Solamnia (*Dragonlance*); The Empire (*Warhammer*).
> Cities: Ankh-Morpork (Discworld); Waterdeep (*Forgotten Realms*); Ketterdam (Grishaverse).
> Smaller Locales: Diagon Alley and Hogwarts (Potterverse); Camp Half-Blood (Riordanverse); Unseen University (Discworld); Shaolin Monastery (real history and Marvelverse); Yale University (*The Ninth House*, Leigh Bardugo).

In all cases, the level of depth of development is important to consider, something that will be revisited throughout this book. In large part, depth depends on the purpose and centrality of the society to the world and any story written in it. A focal society requires more depth and detail, while a side society that is barely mentioned may only need a couple of sentences to describe it.

Regardless of the purpose and the depth, creating societies can be a fun exercise, as well as a rewarding element of worldbuilding. The act of building a society defines a character's resources and background,[3] and, as some authors have noted, "if you know the culture of your characters' homeland, you understand your characters and why they think the way they do."[4] The society provides language, religious context, political identity, skills, traditions (about mating, magic, harmony), laws, structure, and ethics.[5] The process adds depth to the setting and creates room to explore socio-cultural ideas in the safe place that is fiction, including taking our own world and extrapolating along different axes of possible development.

Scope and Intent

Due to space and other concerns, the scope of this work is necessarily limited. The decision to focus on the fantasy (F), urban fantasy (UF), and paranormal romance (PNR) genres of fiction and games rather than any sort of fictional society was made for these reasons. Attempting to cover society creation in all worldbuilding genres is impossible in a reasonably sized book. Even limiting the scope to the "conscious" worldbuilding genres—fantasy, UF, PNR, science fiction (SF), post-apocalyptic, alternate history, and others—is too varied in factors and elements. However, despite clear differences, F and UF/PNR are similar enough to be

Introduction   3

reasonably covered in a decent level of detail in a not overly large book. For these purposes, UF and PNR are considered effectively the same genre, the difference being merely a question of marketing and possibly the ratios of fantastic to romance elements. In any event, the three (or two) genres share enough of a foundation of species, magic, magical creatures, and other elements to be connected well. They also share a firm grounding in myth, legend, and traditional romances (of the medieval era, or its equivalent in non-European cultures) though often used somewhat differently. Incorporating SF introduces aliens—similar to fantasy's species, but with different issues and less "standardization"—and ultra-tech space travel (admittedly not too far from dimensional travel's effects), and other such factors, including planet and/or space station creation. Even so, there is some crossover on social elements, so some of the following chapters may be applicable to SF societal worldbuilding as well.

Another limit to scope is that I have chosen to focus on an overview with occasional details rather than covering every single possible detail. In part, not every detail may be helpful or necessary for every society. Also, there are limits to space and a desire to be more inspirational rather than prescriptive or limiting—to say, "Here are possibilities and examples" rather than to say, "You must do this." As Kevin J. Anderson states, "Questions often spark more imagination and more ideas than straightforward answers do."[6] The idea is to provide and discuss many major elements and considerations in the creation of societies. This can include such issues as Eurocentrism in the genre and issues of species. The question of detail is also an important part of the decision here, as it is not necessary to know the location of every single tree or dwelling in a given society, or a detailed history of every minor resident, usually.

Another aspect of the intent is to provide enough overview to suggest other interesting factors to consider and explore. With a general discussion, we can explore the application with examples, both from various authors and hypotheticals. This approach shows how the social factors might be, or have been, addressed by others as inspiration. Such inspiration can lead to new twists—seeing an idea in film or text and thinking "I could do better" or "What if?" It helps to recall that our most notable and famous authors and worldbuilders were inspired by others (Shakespeare, for instance, had few, if any, original plots, but took those of others and gave them his own unique spin). Inspired by such people, we bring a host of other knowledge, experiences, and familiarity with even more creators to create a synthesis that is new and different.

Thus, a major percentage of the intent behind this piece is to explore applying society building to the three genres. To do so, I will provide brief examples of aspects and subtopics in published work.

Issues in Building Societies

Every field of art, scholarship, or endeavor has issues unique to its focus, some more minor or major than others. Most such issues that develop in worldbuilding, particularly the creation of societies, such as race and "historical realism," will be covered in their appropriate chapters. However, a couple do not fit neatly into chapters, so will be addressed here, since they should be mentioned and accounted for.

What to Include

On one level, determining what to include is a major question and issue in that it determines the workload for the project as well as the level of detail. On another level, it is a minor issue in comparison to others that arise.

Some people suggest that every detail should be known, even if only 1 or 2 percent is shown (arguably, Harry Turtledove is in this camp). Others hold the view that less is more, that the broad strokes are the important part and details can be filled in by the writing or over time. The latter is usually true for novels and stories, but often appears in the interactive storytelling of tabletop roleplaying games (TTRPGs), where the society building gamemaster (GM) often incorporates the feedback and ideas of the players. Examples of both directions are easy to find, for instance, Tolkien fits in the former category while Steven Brust seems to be in the latter. However, in good hands, it can be difficult to tell the difference, since the broad strokes approach can be made to look like the detailed approach. In this question, it is important to remember that the world and its societies can and should evolve over time, as seen in Dragaera (Brust), the Forgotten Realms (*D&D*), Krynn (*D&D*), Discworld (Pratchett), Azeroth (*Warcraft*), Tamriel (*Elder Scrolls/Skyrim*), and Eberron (*D&D*).

Some, such as M.R. Johnson, argue that worldbuilding is "a question of sociological realism" in which the goal is to determine whether the world, or society, could "actually exist and function as depicted, or would it collapse under its own weight?"[7] Johnson further claims that the world must "function on … the complex interactions between … society, culture, economy, politics, people, places, geography, [and] history."[8] Conversely, Emily Temple argues that worldbuilding's "primary function is to give yourself enough knowledge about the [society] that you have the authority and ability to tell it to somebody else."[9] In short, for Temple, the world is "the existence of an internal logic, mood, or yes, set of descriptions that gives [the builders'] world a sense of context."[10] Temple and Johnson do not necessarily disagree, but Temple's discussion suggests a less complex worldbuilding than Johnson's.

Rather than taking one of the extremes, a happy medium generally seems the best approach in most cases. This may not be true in the realm of video games, for instance, due to the need for coding. However, it seems especially true for TTRPGs, in which players usually have a voice in expanding and creating the details of the societies through the actions and backgrounds of their characters (PCs).

The question of detail, of course, applies to all levels from the nation to the village to the smallest community. Do we need the full backstory of every farmer in the village or full details on every group in the city? Probably not. Generally, we can work with just the ones that are important or notable, but, even then, can often approach them as they come up in the narrative.

Eurocentrism in Fantasy

Over the last couple of decades, Eurocentrism[11] in the various fantasy genres has become an issue that has seen growing attention in the writing and gaming industries. While there have always been some authors of non–European descent in the genres, sometimes trying non–Eurocentric works,[12] they have tended to be relatively few and possibly token-ish in effect. Of course, the industry has been very Euro-American (and male) heavy for a long time, and that has tended toward very Eurocentric models of settings and fictional societies across the board.

It is understandably difficult for white authors and worldbuilders to approach non–Eurocentric themes and society building as the potential for problems is constant, regardless of the amount of research and care involved. Even so, a few have managed it successfully, including Max Gladstone and Robert Jackson Bennett. Conversely, many have fumbled in their attempts and resorted to reinforcing stereotypes rather than building authentic non–Eurocentric societies. There is a balance between attempting to write from unfamiliar perspectives and the accidental stereotyping that can be problematic. Still, part of the fantasy genres is doing exactly the former and asking the audience to follow. Additionally, the line between cultural appreciation and cultural appropriation can be a thin one, especially when intellectual property and money are involved.

Fortunately, the tide seems to be shifting toward bringing more diverse voices and roots into the genres in all media. Over the last twenty years especially, we have seen an influx of new and old authors receiving attention for their non–Eurocentric fantasies, bringing a host of different cultural backgrounds and fictional societies to life. Among these are N.K. Jemisin, Ausma Zehanat Khan, Roshani Chokshi, Jennifer Cervantes, Yoon Ha Lee, Kwame Mbalia, Graci Kim, Rebecca Roanhorse, Sarwat

Chadda, S.A. Chakraborty, Tomi Adeyemi, Nnedi Okorafor, Zen Cho, and Fonda Lee.

Some of these, and other, authors and worldbuilders will be referenced as examples alongside more Euro-focused builders throughout the following book, to bring a more diverse selection of sample F/UF/PNR societies to the discussion.

Goals of This Book

There are four major goals behind the creation of this book.

The most self-serving comes first. I wanted to collect and put all of my thoughts, research, and ideas on the creation of fictional societies in one place. The idea is to have all these disparate sources in one place that is easily reviewed and returned to, rather than looking over hundreds of places, sites, and notes to find the pieces that stood out and were helpful to me.

Along similar lines, the goal of self-inspiration has been second in my mind. Over many years of writing and gaming, I have found that writing nonfiction and, necessarily, thinking about the subject matter often inspires worldbuilding ideas. Sometimes it even inspires small pieces of fiction, whether short stories or short-shorts. Other times, settings, characters, groups, scenes, or themes come to mind and start to be explored.

Third, my goal is to inspire others in their own creations by compiling my thoughts and the examples of others in one place. Many texts on worldbuilding, or even aspects of worldbuilding, that I have encountered in the past rarely provide or apply examples. Even then, they are usually very generalized examples. In the following pages, I intend to point to specific authors, games, settings, and series that evoke or exemplify each area, topic, or subtopic to provide concrete examples that others can find, read, and be inspired by, if they so choose.

Finally, the goals of this book include creating a checklist of sorts, or some key potential elements of a checklist, for creating fictional societies. Not all elements discussed necessarily need to be involved in every society build, or are even appropriate for all (ex. most UF/PNR does not involve creating entire nations, with exceptions such as Cassandra Clare's *Mortal Instruments* series or Avram Davidson's Doctor Eszterhazy or Jack Limekiller stories).

Roots of the Book

This project, and the resulting book, has its foundations in three areas. First, and foremost, it is deeply indebted to decades of reading first fantasy—epic, sword and sorcery, high, low, and dark—then UF/PNR and comedic fantasy. Some of my earliest memories involve reading fantasy as a kid. Comedic fantasy was probably introduced sometime in high school via Roger Zelazny, Terry Pratchett, and Esther Friesner. UF and PNR were mostly introduced in adulthood, with some vague memories of reading a Bordertown book (edited by Terri Windling) in high school. The second is an almost equal number of years being involved in TTRPGs, whether face-to-face (in the pre-internet days) or play-by-post from the days of America Online (AOL) into the present. Maybe a small amount from brief flirtations with video games from the first *Diablo* and the earlier iterations of *Warcraft* (back before it became an MMO) to *Everquest II*. Building worlds and societies for various RPG campaigns, both offline and online, set the early stages of this book. The third root is a long span of amateur worldbuilding for the sake of worldbuilding, and some dabbling in fiction, including a nine-month senior thesis collection of interconnected short stories with associated worldbuilding. All told, these three roots effectively formed a lifelong fascination with fictional worlds and societies, specifically how their creators go about building them "behind the curtain," as it were.

The ultimate framework of the book came from a collection of skeletal blog posts I threw together back in 2014 and 2016 while playing with a couple of worldbuilds for their own sake. For whatever reason, the creation process that time got me thinking seriously about and recording the process to some extent as it was happening. The impetus for this book came from reviewing those posts, considering them and what they implied or left unsaid, years after writing them. Most of the following pages came from taking the basic thinking and concepts in those posts, and expanding on them with additional thoughts, evolving ideas, and the increased knowledge that an extra five to seven years brought. In many ways, blogging was an excellent way to explore and organize ideas on the subject of worldbuilding and societies. There was also the bonus potential for feedback from readers and the questioning that comes from the online format. The ability to review several years of thoughts on the subject in an easily organized fashion helped as well.

Outline of Chapters

The order of the chapters in this book is inherently arbitrary. Where a creator starts in building societies depends entirely on the individual worldbuilder, or the impetus for their creation. For example, Tolkien began with languages and built societies to fit them, both of which he evolved over the course of thousands of years of fictional history. Harry Turtledove, on the other hand, often seems to begin with real-world history and ask "What if?" In various builds, I have begun with magic, myths, geography, places, and organizations at different times.

With that caveat in mind, what follows is the brief outline of chapters.

Chapter 1 discusses the basic concepts of the society and developing those core thoughts into a foundation to expand and detail.

Chapter 2 looks at approaches to history, the scale of history, and inspiration for what to include in a created history.

Chapter 3 provides information on, and examples of applications of, different types of governments used in the fantasy genres.

Chapter 4 covers the creation of religion and its insertion into a society, along with the relationship between religion and society.

Chapter 5 addresses the relationship between magic and society, and magic's impact on society as well as society's impact on magic wielders.

Chapter 6 approaches the intersection of technology and society, and their effects upon each other.

Chapter 7 looks at societal views, and methods, of teaching residents or specific subsets of a society.

Chapter 8 approaches the introduction of races (here meaning elves, dwarves, etc.) into a society and the impact of both race and society on each other.

Chapter 9 discusses the development of languages and society, both in terms of the number and types of languages in a society.

Chapter 10 covers societal views of and interactions with sex and gender, in brief.

Chapter 11 approaches various groups present in society, effectively discussing sub-cultures and sub-societies within the larger society.

Chapter 12 looks at the impact of geography on society, and potential societal changes to geography.

Chapter 13 works with important places within a society's space, from the smallest eatery to the largest palace complex.

Chapter 14 includes a (not all-inclusive) variety of things that do not fit in the previous chapters.

1

Concept

Virtually all fictional societies begin with a rough concept. Some of these basic concepts get fleshed out and developed into societies that are central to the world or storyline. Others remain somewhat half formed or vague, in background roles unless or until they prove to be necessary. For example, in Harry Turtledove's Videssos books, the culture of Videssos is fully formed, as it is the society where most of the action takes place. Yezd, Namdalen, and others are less well developed because they are not central to the story that Turtledove tells. Likewise, George R.R. Martin developed Westeros in great detail, since it is where most of the action takes place. Comparatively, the Iron Isles, Braavos, and points to the far east are often little more than a bare sketch because they are not central to the plot of *A Song of Ice and Fire* (*ASoIaF*). The same is true for Leigh Bardugo's *Shadow and Bone* trilogy, where Ravka is fully developed, but Kerch, Shu Han, Fjerda, and Novyi Zem are not.[1]

Whether central or background, any culture or society that appears in the setting should have at least a basic concept and feel outlined.

Basic Concept

At its simplest, a basic concept for a culture is a single sentence or even a fragment phrase that evokes an idea or reminds the creator of the concept. Using Bardugo as the example, we can see the basic concepts of her three developed societies as:

Ravka: Nineteenth-century Russia with magic.
Kerch: The Netherlands as an island.
Fjerda: Scandinavia with mage-hunters.

These examples are all nation size, but the same technique and approach can be applied regardless of the size of the culture.

Determining the size of the society is also an important part of the basic concept. These can range, as briefly noted in the introduction, from a school or monastic community to a village, a city, or a nation. Exactly what size we choose helps to give a sense of scope and, possibly, layers of sub-cultures for a society. Basic demographics will determine the quantity of necessary food, water, and transportation and might influence the physical features of the society's borders. For example, to remain with Bardugo, Ravka has at least six sub-societies: West Ravka, East Ravka, the Little Palace (where the grisha learn and live), religious communities, the First Army (the non-magical soldiers), and the royals/nobles of the country. Each sub-society is different and related to the other five, sometimes in competition with each other—such as the Little Palace (and Second Army) versus the First Army. As another example, Terry Pratchett's city of Ankh-Morpork (Discworld) is one society of many in his world, but it is also home to potentially innumerable sub-societies including the Watch, Unseen University, each of the Guilds, and The Shades among other neighborhoods, each with their own traditions, unspoken rules, language of jargon, style, and customs.

The size of a society can be as large or small as fits the setting and desires of the plot or creator. Of course, two people is probably the smallest a society can go, since it is effectively impossible to have a society of one being. The society can also be as complex and multi-layered as the creator desires, within reason—ex. a city size society has more room for sub-societies than a society of five people. These societies, especially the more complex and multi-layered ones, generally evolve over time, rather than being built all at once. For example, Ankh-Morpork did not start as fifty or more sub-societies. Rather, it began with Unseen University and the Watch. From that base, the sub-societies and the greater city society evolved as Pratchett wrote more and developed the setting, developing the Assassins, Beggars, and Fools guilds among others as they became necessary for new plots.

Brainstorming can be an effective means of developing the basic concept and deciding how deep to go in creating and shaping the details and direction of the society.

Brainstorming

The practice of brainstorming is not discussed much by authors, at least not in their works and only occasionally in social media. However, in their book *Points of Departure: Liavek Stories*, Patricia Wrede and Pamela Dean reflect briefly on getting together with other authors. The group discussed and brainstormed the traits they all would require in their ideal fantasy city.[2] The end result was the shared world setting of Liavek.

1. Concept

Brainstorming is a long-held technique for pre-writing in every genre of writing, whether fiction or nonfiction. It is a useful process for throwing out ideas and exploring concepts. In the case of building societies, brainstorming becomes guided in that there is a focused purpose behind it. The desire to create a society, and prior thought about the society in the form of a rough concept, provide structure for brainstorming. Likewise, determining the type of fantasy—Unrecorded History, Historical Earth, Parallel Worlds, Alternate Earth, Future Worlds, Science Fantasy, among others[3]—can help provide focus as well.

As useful as it is, brainstorming will not create a complete culture. It will, however, produce a list of potential elements and a skeleton to flesh out into a full society. In the process, some elements may be dropped and others added. Some may not fit in the final version, or may seem contradictory and be removed for ease. Others may take an exercise in creativity, ingenuity, and imagination to work into something that is both feasible and believable. For example, Wrede and Dean's reflection highlights the collective brainstorming that decided the city needed magic, coffee shops available at all hours, and easily accessible birth control, among other things.[4] These traits formed the basic groundwork for the city Liavek, which was built upon to create multiple anthologies of short stories and a few novels.

Brainstorming tends to work best with some guidance. For societies, some recommended guides are desired cultural traits, desired location, and sources of inspiration.

Desired Cultural Traits

Focusing on desired cultural traits is an excellent guide for brainstorming. In fact, it is the aspect that provided focus for Wrede, Dean, and their fellow authors in the example above. For these purposes, I think it helpful to breakdown traits into several categories: government, groups, laws, magic, people, and traditions.

Focusing on government, we brainstorm the desired type of government that we want in the society. Here, we can toss out ideas about whether we want a traditional fantasy kingdom/empire or something different. We might decide to try a newer or odd spin on the traditional. Or we might decide to try something entirely new. At some point, the brainstorming should probably include whether the government is competent (Ankh-Morpork) or incompetent (most of the Ministry of Magic, in *Harry Potter*) or somewhere in-between. We might even decide that there are multiple governments in the broader society—ex. the official government of nobles, the religious government of the priests, the semi-official government of the trade guilds, and the unofficial government of organized crime.

To focus on groups in the society, we might build the brainstorming session around a specific group or collection of groups that we want in the society. We can generate ideas about what traits the group(s) has/have and what social traits would allow them to exist and thrive (or not) to build a place in society. This is also where we might decide whether the group is open or hidden, secular or religious, legal or illegal depending on what we are trying to create and what social traits will allow, or not allow, the group to exist.

Another option is to guide the brainstorming through social laws. These laws tell us what a society values. For instance, Wrede and Dean note easy access to (legal) birth control, which implies that the society values women and their reproductive rights.[5] Often, social laws can be central or important to the plot or feel of the society. Therefore, laws can be a good starting point, for example laws about who can learn magic can be a major point for characters, the audience, and users of the society.

The role of magic in a society can also be an excellent guide for brainstorming. Here we might develop ideas about how magic works, how common it is, and what effects it has had on the society. The society might even be built around magic, creating traditions and holidays around the practice of magic or forbidding some, most, or all magic. Such brainstorming guidance could include who has access to magic as well.

The people in the society are an obvious starting point as well. In this guided brainstorm, we consider who lives in the society. Is there one species or are multiple species present? If the latter, how do they interact and share social authority? How does the society treat the sexes and genders? Is the society made up of people all from one nation/society (say a small village or insular community) or from multiple nations/societies (for instance, a major trade port)? We can ask what the people look like, what they value, how they dress, and related questions.

Tied to the people are the traditions of the society. That is, what do the people do? Some society builds begin with one or more odd traditions, whether a festival or a minor action, and build up from there. This is possibly the most esoteric and least tangible starting point in some ways. Maybe they have an odd festival or strange customs regarding eating. Perhaps they have one or more local gods or construction traditions that stand out among their neighbors.

Obviously, all six categories flow into and influence each other. Because of this interweaving, the brainstorming process can start moving around between them and others.

Desired Location

Broader, in some ways, than traits, the desired location is also a good place to guide brainstorming. The location of the culture or society can suggest or require certain traits as a necessity of geography, or have an increased likelihood of occurring due to geography. Four good categories for guiding brainstorming are geography, hidden vs. open location, trade, and the world.

Brainstorming geography can suggest or require certain societal traits. For example, while a South Pacific island and a northern frozen mountain valley are both isolated and remote, other aspects of their societies will be very different. Their customs, fashions, architecture, and food will be different at the very least. Here, it is good to produce words and phrases about the physical territory that the society occupies. This could be as broad as coastal, landlocked, or on a lake. It could be more specific like in mountains, on a steppe, in a deciduous river valley, or in a desert canyon. Or very specific, such as at the confluence of three rivers, in an isolated mountain valley, or in a river delta marsh. All of these levels and possibilities have different suggestions as to societal traits. These factors can help determine many elements of a settlement-level society including size, purpose, demographics, defenses, connections to other settlements, religion, and fantasy elements. They can also aid in decisions about commerce and currency, if the society relies on trade due to its geography.[6]

The question of a hidden versus open location is mostly a distinction for primary world societies, but could potentially be part of a secondary world build. If the society is hidden from others, we have to ask why it is hidden and how. We should also ask how it remains hidden and conceals any places that its people inhabit. How does the society differ from other societies (open ones, if hidden)? If it is an open society, how does it affect, or how is it affected by, others? What relations does it have with other societies (hidden or open)? These questions can help guide a brainstorm of general ideas and thoughts.

The presence and type of trade a creator desires also helps determine a location and society. If we want a high degree of trade, we need a location with trade routes—whether roads, rivers, train routes, sea/ocean routes, magical means of trade, or areas conducive to air travel (airports, airship docking). If we want low trade, then we need geography that will reduce the likelihood of outsiders and give some degree of autonomy for resources, such as narrow mountain passes that are closed part of the year or a remote island off the usual ship routes. Many locations will be somewhere in between. High trade will generally tend to yield more liberal cosmopolitan societies, where peoples, cultures, and ideas mingle (unless limited by law). Low trade will typically have the opposite effect, creating a more insular and conservative society that is often untrusting of outsiders.

Using the world as a starting point, the most obvious element to consider is whether the society is part of the primary or secondary world. This affects many aspects of the society. In the case of a secondary world, it could be a new, unique world or (in either case) an established world (ex. a new town society in Faerûn or the Potterverse). If the society is being inserted into an established world, then brainstorming needs to focus on how it fits into the world. That includes how it relates to pre-established nations, groups, and other societies in the world, which is also true of societies in new secondary worlds (or UF/PNR set in the primary world).

As in all things writing and worldbuilding, we can always look to various sources of inspiration for help.

Sources of Inspiration

Although not strictly necessary for building societies, many worldbuilders find inspiration helps their conception and imagination. While they do not directly copy the source, usually, they certainly use inspiration from various sources to suggest and possibly guide their society building. Such inspiration may come from many potential places, but the three most common are historical, visual, and literary (including TV and film).

History provides thousands of societies to draw inspiration from. These range from our best reconstructions of pre-historic cultures to Akkad, medieval France to 19th-century China, and beyond. Some are inspired by the fashions of an era, others by a specific historical event. An odd historical tradition may inspire a magic system or fictitious folklore. A particular figure might spawn a character, for whom the society is built in order to tell their story. In all, history is a fertile ground of inspiration that has been tilled and harvested by many writers and worldbuilders including George R.R. Martin (inspired by the War of the Roses), Harry Turtledove (inspired by virtually all of the ancient Mediterranean), and Leigh Bardugo (inspired by the history of Yale University). Recently, the use of historical inspiration has been tempered by a greater understanding of being careful with and respectful of the cultures involved, particularly non–European cultures, even if only on a visual level (e.g., avoiding cultural appropriation).

On the visual level, if we open Instagram or Pinterest, among others, we find thousands of worldbuilders, or aspiring worldbuilders. These individuals have created album after album of visual inspiration for societies, in the form of saved, "pinned," photos and pieces of related artwork. Visual inspiration is probably the most difficult to back-trace after the fact, unless the creator specifically states they used it. Most authors do not discuss visual inspiration at the ends of their books, though some do in blogs, Pinterest, and other social media. Most discuss historical and literary inspiration. One of the exceptions is Ransom Riggs, who spent a fair number of pages talking about the photos that inspired *Miss Peregrine's Home for Peculiar Children* and its sequels. Riggs even reproduces, in an afterword, some of the old photos that served as inspiration.

The final common source of inspiration is literary. Here, we will fold television and film media into the literary mantle, alongside "literary" and popular fiction and nonfiction. Often an aspiring writer or worldbuilder will read, or watch, something and think "I could do that better" and try it. Or they might adapt it to a different setting or genre. Some might read or watch something and think, "What if?"[7] This is a perfectly legitimate, indeed common, source of inspiration, so long as the core idea is altered enough in execution that it counts as inspiration not copyright infringement.

Some authors recommend thinking about a person's average day in the world or society, what kind of routine they follow at different levels of society.[8] Considering the social values and ethics may also provide some inspiration. Thinking about the society from the perspective of an outsider experiencing culture shock is also a good way to determine if there are "any defining details to your people's lives that another society may find odd or have in common."[9] C.L. Wilson adds thinking about what value the society places on life, such as having practical views of death or holding that death is better than dishonor. Wilson also suggests thinking about family structure and pair/mate bonding (for love, politics, victory, divination, genetics; temporary or for life) and children, and the raising of children, as a source of inspiration.[10]

As with most things, it is best to use inspiration to open doors and ideas, not to close or limit them. For example, it is great to use the War of the Roses to create an idea for a society, but it is not so good to slavishly adhere to the War of the Roses or its society (in which case, we are effectively writing a history, or alternate history, not necessarily a fantasy piece as such).

Basic Sketch

Once we have our brainstorming, and inspiration, results in hand, the next step is converting the random words and phrases of the brainstorm into a usable form. A good start to begin translating is to look over the brainstorm notes and create a basic sketch of the society. This sketch creates a summary of the society and allows us to form a baseline for later expansion and development.

The basic sketch is the briefest description of the society. It might be composed of one to three average sentences, maybe seventy-five (75) words or less. This is enough to remind the creator of the intended society or to provide a synopsis for someone else. Keep this sketch as bare bones as possible while still being useful. It should be the most foundational or core description of the society, that can and will be expanded with details later. As an exercise, maybe to inspire ideas, we might try creating basic sketches of real modern or historical societies, then see if someone else can guess the society without being told. The trick here is not to resort to relying on stereotyping or misrepresentation.

From the basic sketch, a good exercise is to pick out notable elements to potentially expand. This is only possible expansion and detailing, at this stage, not definite or locked in (see next section). Notable elements might be things mentioned in brief and applications of things that are implied in the brief sketch. They might be things that did not make the cut to get into the brief sketch. For example, a city-state might include strengths and weaknesses, food, shelter, and shopping as priorities, as Wolfgang Baur puts it, "think like a tourist."[11] To set up potential plots, we might add something the residents wish they did not have to deal with. For a nation, we might include ideals, values, how leaders communicate with the people, basic socio-political structure, and at least one internal and external conflict.[12] This gives an important sense of what the society most values. The notable elements will form the beginnings of a working paragraph or two on the society. This paragraph can serve as a quick reference for the creator and a possible short reference for others. Alternately, it might take the form of a brief sketch plus bullet points, depending on the intended use. Ultimately, though, the small paragraph forms a list of details or areas to detail, if we decide they are important enough to expand.

Determining Details

Working off the sketch, see what can be expanded and decide what should be expanded. Some details are going to be important to detail immediately for plot, background, or character development. Other reasons may exist as well, depending on the purpose of the worldbuild and society. There will also be elements that are not important enough to bother with instantly, and might wait until later, when they become useful or important to a given plot situation or world use. Therefore, the next step after the sketch is determining what details are necessary for the build, purpose, and/or plot. There is an old saying among writers and worldbuilders that comes down to "Do 100 percent of the worldbuilding, but only show 10 percent (or less)." A modified version might be "Do not necessarily do 100 percent of the worldbuilding at once; do the 10 percent that is immediately required and the rest as time or necessity arises."

The purpose of the worldbuild is also important here. Monte Cook has a useful division of reasons here. Cook notes that for a novelist, "worldbuilding [is] a backdrop for their stories … what ends up on the page is only just enough for the reader to understand and appreciate the story."[13] Comparatively, worldbuilding for RPGs, whether tabletop or video game, needs to be huge with a lot potentially happening, setting up the details and adventure hooks, as well as the flavor and underpinnings of the setting. In both cases, however, all worldbuilders have the option and ability to build the world as they go, potentially with the collaboration of players, in the case of TTRPG gamemasters (GMs).[14] M.R. Johnson notes that it is rare "for us to hear too much about clothing styles, family life, employment, dialects, class, architecture, migration, literature, music … yet these are integral to the lived experiences of everyone within that world."[15] But, the reason we do not hear much about these subjects is that they are not necessarily important for the story that is being told.

Michael Stackpole adds that successful worldbuilding, from concept to "finished" state, means "following through with all the logical consequences of any decisions you make."[16] As he explains, enhanced senses or telepathy change a society and its values in many ways. As does "taking a concept which is generally considered noble and rendering it valueless, or … evil and turning it into a virtue," both "quickly, craft details for a society that becomes a puzzle for [the] audience."[17] That puzzle makes the society interesting to and engaging for the audience.

To that end, I suggest three broad categories of details: Important Immediately, Important Later, and Not Necessary.

Important Immediately

This category should only include the most important of details. These are details that are necessary to have figured out in order for the story or world to move forward and fulfill its purpose. The question of primary versus secondary world falls here, as it is a necessity for character creation and society creation. Hidden versus open society is also here for the same reason.

As an example, let us walk through figuring out the necessary details for a magic school, as a society:

1. Detailed information about the school—including basic appearance/atmosphere, rules, how students are taught.
2. How prospective students are chosen for the school and get to the school.
3. How the presence of magic affects the school's society (compared to mundane schools).
4. Student, faculty, and staff interactions, both within and between each group—including cliques and faculty/staff factions.
5. How technology interacts with the school and magic.
6. What, if any, government involvement occurs at the school.
7. People of note in the school society, along with any hierarchy, ranks, or titles that might exist.

These seven are details that are likely to become necessary very early in any narratives involving the society. They will be referenced in character backgrounds and are likely to be focal points of plots and the society's setting. Character interaction—both with other characters and with the society—will also be shaped by these details.

Important Later

While some aspects of the society may need to be developed immediately, others can wait a little while. These are elements of the society that may appear at some time, or will probably appear, but are not urgent. They are things that can be detailed as necessary to the plot or as the world is developed.

Continuing with the magic school example, the following probably fall into this category:

1. Relations between the magical and non-magical communities.
2. Magical society beyond the school.
3. Government of the magical society beyond the school.
4. Societal careers, currency, and fashions (if it's a school that requires uniforms).
5. Society and technology or magic and society beyond the school.
6. Social groups and other organizations beyond the school context.
7. Possibly school clubs, minor cliques, and related in-school groups.

These are things that will likely be woven into the society and narrative over time. They might become necessary for the plot in the near future, but they are not necessary right out of the gate. The creator can take their time and develop these aspects slowly. It is worth noting here that Hogwarts, Ankh-Morpork, Waterdeep, Dragaera, and other well-known fictional societies developed, grew, evolved, and became detailed over time. They were not created in full, glorious detail all at once; they were built over years or decades *while*, not before, people wrote their stories.

Not Necessary

The third category covers what are generally minor elements that may never be used in a narrative or world. These can be created or detailed as necessary, or even not at all.

Continuing the magic school example, the following may be part of this category:

1. The village near the school (which may be noted early, but not detailed).
2. Any societies of aquatic beings in the school's lake.
3. Alternate ways to get to the school.
4. A full history of the school's society and community.
5. Other schools in the community and the school's relations with them.

Some of these aspects may be planned for or have their roots planted early, but the detailing may be held off until they are needed by the plot or development of the setting. Some may never come up; others may be altered in between the initial conception and the time when the builder decides to develop them.

The important thing to remember in all cases is to do the worldbuild, especially building societies, but not to get so bogged down in the building phase that the narrative or application phase never happens. The exception, of course, is the case of worldbuilding simply for the fun of it, or for the sake of worldbuilding.

The preceding pages have presented a modified version of the "standard" pre-writing process, applied to creating societies. They are more a recommendation or suggestion to help get started, rather than being a requirement to follow exactly. Every writer and worldbuilder has their own process, since every individual is different, and what works for one may simply stymie another. For example, Trent Hergenrader set up a system of four structures and fourteen substructures from governance to economics, social relations to cultural influences that he uses to build worlds.[18] Monte Cook, renown TTRPG designer, tends to divide methods into Inside-Out (small to large) or Outside-In (large to small).[19] Kevin J. Anderson, for a third approach, favors his PERSIA or GCPESRIAH system.[20] The important part is to take time, think, consider, and be willing to tweak, modify, prune, and make conscious decisions at the early stage that provide the foundation for the rest of the creative process. An individual's choices regarding details will determine the usefulness and order of the following chapters, but for general purposes I have decided to begin somewhat arbitrarily with history.

2

History

Saying so may seem obvious, but history is an important aspect of a society and its development. As some have argued, history "provides meaning to geography and place."[1] We have been aware of the power of history since the earliest civilizations, that produced written accounts of their own histories from mythic founding to their present day, often to suit socio-political ideals of the society. This fact is something that professional historians recognize and explore through the use of counterfactuals—exploring and extrapolating socio-historical change by altering one historical event—popular versions of which form the alternate history and historical fantasy genres.

Over the millennia that we have written history, many possible approaches to both recording and studying history have been developed. The so-called Great Man approach focuses on kings and conflicts, predominantly, with occasional forays into other "notable" people (typically male). This approach is an old one that came out of the 19th century and has been considered outdated for much of the 20th and beyond, and was rightly criticized during the 19th century. Others see history as a Chain of Progress, continually moving forward throughout history toward some ideal civilization or ideal humanity. Traditionally, Chinese historians adhered to a variation on the Cyclic Approach, which sees patterns and cycles of rising and falling societies. Or, rather, sees cycles of rising, decadence, and falling within a given society. These methods create a "historiography that is neat and clear, and brooks little ambiguity" much like many fantasy authors who "tell us what the world is ... using the traditional tools of history retelling."[2] Social History is one of the more modern approaches, focusing on all levels of society and acknowledging both progression and regression, conflicts and other events. Branches of Social History seek to study technologies, scientific development, social trends (such as fashion and hair styling), and gender throughout history. As Johnson notes, the "greatest benefit of social history is ... putting people ... back into the telling of history or the description of a world."[3] On the side of worldbuilding and fiction, J.R.R. Tolkien built a history that was largely focused on conflicts, great people (mostly men, of various species), and migrations, held together by his developing languages. Any of these approaches are potentially viable for creating the history of a fictional society.

Beyond the approach to history that we wish to take, at least three other major decisions should be made before building the society's history. The questions of primary or secondary world, hidden or open society, and producing an overview or in-depth history are of great importance to creating any society's history. The first two should be decided during the basic idea stage of society building, but the third is unique to this element. Regardless of the decisions, the focus should remain on the society in question, while being aware that societies do not exist in a vacuum. There is always something around them, so some rough idea of the world and other neighboring societies and social histories helps. The trick is balance—focusing on the society in question, while being peripherally aware of the others around it.[4]

Primary or Secondary World

In some ways, working with the primary world as the setting is somewhat less involved. Creating histories for primary world societies is similar to the development of alternate history settings, where the presence of the supernatural or paranormal is the change. Likewise, the idea of a hidden history or secret history is, in its own way, a variation on alternate history as well. So, the primary world society history can be a straight alternate history, as in Ilona Andrews's *Hidden Legacy* series, in which magic is publicly known and its presence alters history after the mid-19th century. Much more common is the secret history, in which the supernatural society exists alongside the normal society that the audience is familiar with. This is the set up for Allyson James's *Stormwalker*, Jim Butcher's *Dresden Files*, Lisa Shearin's *SPI Files*, and Charlaine Harris's *Southern Vampire Mysteries* series among many others. In fact, this is more or less the standard of the UF/PNR genres. An unusual case for UF/PNR is future history, in which the society and narrative are set in the near to somewhat distant future with history between our own and then filled in. This is used by Andrews in the *Kate Daniels* series and spinoffs, Nalini Singh's *Psy/Changeling* series, and Devon Monk's *House Immortal* series. In each case, building a history for a primary world society is most often a matter of adapting and extending real-world history, or adding layers to known history, using our own history as a foundation.

By comparison, secondary world societies are more involved. In those cases, the society's history is built from scratch. There is more investment of time and more development for these histories. They also cover a longer span of time, usually. While a primary world history might start with the 19th century (Andrews) or "thirty years ago," when magic was introduced to the world, a secondary world history often goes back to the origins of the society many centuries back, or even the beginning of the world. Effectively every secondary world fantasy society and author is an example here, from Fritz Leiber and J.R.R. Tolkien to Mercedes Lackey, Steven Brust, Tanith Lee, and Jody Lynn Nye to Max Gladstone, N.K. Jemisin, Tomi Adeyemi, and Brandon Sanderson. These histories tend to be mostly open magical societies, because of the nature of the genres, but may be hidden or include hidden elements or layers depending on the setting and narrative.

Hidden or Open History

The terms seem self-explanatory, but in brief: open history will be known to the general public or at least easily learned by anyone; hidden history will be concealed from the general public or difficult to learn (often requiring special effort, resources, or plot to discover, sometimes in fragments). Hidden histories inherently create a basic layered history (see the end of this chapter), while open histories may be a single history (Andrews's *Hidden Legacy* or Singh's *Psy/Changeling*) or a layered effect if the supernatural part of the history is open to some but not necessarily all. Both hidden and open can exist in the same society—for example in Harris's *Southern Vampire Mysteries*, there is normal history, an open vampire history (after they went public), a hidden vampire history (not revealed to humans), and the hidden histories of werebeasts, fae, and witches (who have not come out in the open when the series starts).

Primary world societies tend to have hidden supernatural histories, as those are the most popular. However, there are also open history ones depending on the setting. Hidden histories include Andrews's *Innkeeper Chronicles*, J.K. Rowling's *Harry Potter*, Rick Riordan's *Percy Jackson*, Jim Butcher's *Dresden Files*, and Leigh Bardugo's *Ninth House*. In each of those cases, magical or supernatural history (or both) is kept hidden from the normal human public for various reasons. Open histories include Singh's *Psy/Changeling*, Andrews's *Kate Daniels*, Andrews's *Hidden Legacy*, and Terri Windling's *Bordertown/land* series.[5] In these cases, people know at least some of the history of magic and/or the supernatural in the society, though maybe not all of it. Much of what they may not know is potentially accessible, although some may remain hidden or in the hands of a few.

In secondary worlds, the social histories are usually open ones. Some parts may be hidden, especially if the open history is false or incomplete. In the latter case, in Middle Earth, the histories of Rohan and Gondor are fairly well known between songs and tales told among humans. Conversely, the history of Lothlórien is largely unknown by Men, because the Elves shut themselves off from outsiders in a previous age. Gail Z. Martin's *Chronicles of the Necromancer* also features an open history that has a forgotten, or deliberately erased, layer. The same is true for C.J. Cherryh's *Fortress* series. While the development is, perhaps, more involved, the secondary world open history may also be somewhat easier in that there is often only one history to create. However, the creator may determine what parts are well known, what parts are easily known, and what parts are hidden, lost, or otherwise forgotten.

Depth and Overviews

The level of detail provided in the history of societies varies widely within the genres. As Wolfgang Baur notes, "[T]here's a minimum amount of history required for a setting for it to make sense."[6] That said, sometimes the interesting history is in the odd details. For instance, Tolkien and Frank Herbert (*Dune*, a science fantasy) created highly complex and detailed histories, based on their notes and prequels. This was a result or necessity of the scope and nature of the stories they decided to tell. Conversely, Rowling (*Harry Potter*) and Neil Gaiman (in *Neverwhere*) seem to start with only a sketchy history and fill in details as needed for the story.

One factor in the decision, of course, is the length of the piece. Tolkien and Herbert wrote long works in which the histories of their respective societies were central to the plots of the narratives. On the other hand, Gaiman's *Neverwhere* did not need as extensive a societal history, as it was a relatively short, standalone tale set in the Underside. Moreover, Gaiman's society was made up of the people who fell through the cracks of our society, and their descendants. For the most part, they were not shown as recording much in terms of history, versus an oral history passed among various factions.

Sometimes the question of how much detail to include is determined by how the society and setting are created. Gaiman, Herbert, Rowling, and Tolkien were largely working alone, building their societies and narratives in relative seclusion.[7] In other cases—such as Krynn (Dragonlance), Toril/Faerûn (Forgotten Realms), Azeroth (Warcraft), and Tamriel (Elder Scrolls)—the societies are built by teams of people, either individually working on different aspects or together by committee. With more people involved, it becomes easier to build a more detailed societal history, as either parts of the history or other parts of the society building can be delegated to others.

On a related note, how much of the society's history the audience needs can determine whether the history needs to be detailed or simply sketched out. For most video games and TTRPGs, a lot of the history may be sketched at first, then detailed later as different parts of the society or setting are used in the game narrative. On the other hand, for novels and related media, the parts of the history that are plot relevant are often detailed, while other parts may be sketched for future development as needed, depending on where the plotline ends up going.

Incorporating History

Once the history is outlined and developed, how do we incorporate it into a narrative?

Methods vary, but a general school of thought says to show only 10 percent or less of the created history (and worldbuild in general), despite having 100 percent of it built. Keep in mind that "most people will only know the history that's relevant to them"[8] and "won't know all the details, and what [they do know] might not be accurate."[9] For example, not many Americans can name the Presidents from 1850 to 1857, or many Vice Presidents from any decade, because that information is not relevant to their daily lives. A few common methods of weaving in history follow:

The use, discussion, and application of laws and cultural traditions can be an effective means of showing history. Most cultural traditions and many laws have their basis in the society's history. For instance, Rowling brings history in this way through references to the various goblin rebellions against wizards and the Ministry of Magic's wand use laws. Frank Herbert does similar when he references anti–Artificial Intelligence (AI) laws in the empire that are based in the Butlerian Jihad—which led to the overthrow of machine intelligences and a blanket ban on anything from calculators to full-blown AIs. Related to laws and cultural traditions are species relations, particularly inter-species relations. These are often also based on the history between the species—for example, Rowling's wizard versus non-human relationships from goblins to vampires to werewolves as well as the many vampire versus werewolf movies and novels (such as the *Underworld* franchise).

A more common means of transmitting history is the use of songs and stories within the narrative. This is, of course, also a method that was used historically to transmit history in our own world. Tolkien is, perhaps, the most obvious example and presents the heaviest usage. His songs and poetry recited by elves, hobbits, Rangers, and dwarves present snippets of the prior ages of Middle Earth throughout both *The Hobbit* and *The Lord of the Rings* (*LotR*). This follows in the footsteps of Homer, Virgil, and the *Beowulf*-poet, among many others.

If the society or setting includes formal or "traditional" schooling, then the combination of classes and school books are also options for showing the society's history. Rowling is the key example here, between the History of Magic class with Professor Binns and Hermione's frequent citing of *Hogwarts: A History*. As with anything, moderation is important with this method, as most audiences wish to read or play the narrative for entertainment, rather than to read a history textbook.

Finally, family and social relations, including the appearance of groups and subcultures, can be a means of showing the society's history. Family history can trace lineages and their effect on the social history, or vice versa, as in George R.R. Martin's *ASoIaF*. In that case, the history of the Seven Kingdoms is the history of its major families and their relationships. Likewise, the appearance of groups and subcultures can be used to evoke the society's history and past. To refer back to GRRM, the return of the Faith Militant under Cersei's regency recalls the reasons that it was banned in the first place. Similarly, in Bardugo's Grishaverse, the rise of Ravka's religious militants evokes fear on the part of the royalty, who try to remove the subculture.

There are, of course, many other possible methods, the above is not the limit of options. However, they are probably the most common or easiest to use seamlessly.

Fantasy and Historical Realism

An issue that oddly creeps up in discussions of history and the fantasy genre is "historical realism." Such discussions, or the evoking of the idea, seems to be largely limited to the online world. Overall, the concept of historical realism in relation to fantasy does not seem to be applicable, but there may be some reasons for it to come up—typically the roots of the modern genre, Eurocentrism, and amateur "armchair" historians often working off outdated materials. The concept is especially strange given that the history aspect of secondary world fantasy slides from the hyper-realistic to non-realistic, across the classics (ex. Tolkien, Michael Moorcock, Fritz Leiber, C.L. Moore) through the modern (ex. GRRM, Jemisin, Patrick Rothfuss).

Roots of the Genre

On one level, an insistence on historical realism in the genre may come out of the oldest roots of the genre—the medieval romances.[10]

However, the medieval romances lacked "historical realism," as did Thomas Malory's later Arthurian stories and Shakespeare's historically set plays. The romances had "realism" in terms of reflecting some ideals of the time in which they were written, but they did not have perfect realism in terms of the reality of life, action, or history. The romances were never intended to be accurate in those terms. They were intended to present ideas to strive for and to entertain, but not to be "true to life" in that respect. Some, particularly the Arthurian romances and the *Brut Chronicle*, were also effectively propaganda.

Even the mainstay imagery of the secondary world fantasy—the knight in shining armor, among others—is not "historical." It is also not present in the fantasy classics, such as Tolkien, Leiber, Robert E. Howard, and C.L. Moore. Still, they are closely associated with epic fantasy and high fantasy, but owe more to much later (18th and 19th century) artwork than to actual medieval or Renaissance reality.

So, if calls for historical realism are not part of the genre's roots, or early parts of the genre, why is historical realism an issue?

Reasons

Calls for historical realism became loudest in the late-20th and early-21st centuries. They mostly appear to be evoked in order to justify rampant sexism, racism, or anti-LGBT bigotry in a given work. This suggests that the cause is a backlash to the rise of diverse authorship, characters, and themes. Such calls seem to say that if women were limited in history, they should be subjugated in fantasy. Likewise, they often claim that, if people of color (POC) were not present in medieval Europe (even though they were present), then they have no place in fantasy. Calls for such "historical realism" tend to be more fan than authorial in nature. Exceptions, of course, exist, among the so-called Sad/Rabid Puppies, though even GRRM used the call to justify some problematic aspects and criticisms of *Game of Thrones/ASoIaF*.

Ultimately, virtually all such calls for supposed historical realism are based in ignorance, whether accidental or deliberate/willful. The latter occurs when individuals limit themselves to outdated sources. Sometimes, simple ignorance is to blame. Other times, "historical realism" is an excuse to justify bigotry and "keep the genre for white guys" (though it has never been "just for white guys"). Others deliberately refer to pre-"post-modern" historians and ignore the last six or more decades of historical research. Said research shows that the roles of LGBT individuals, POC, non–Christians, and women in history, even limited to European history, have been much broader and more varied than was previously acknowledged.

Does Historical Realism Have a Place?

So, does historical realism have a place in the fantasy genre, and its subgenres?

This is a complicated question due to the range of subgenres in fantasy.

In secondary world fantasies, there is absolutely no place for historical realism. Any discussions of the history of a secondary world (whether the world or a single society) should never refer to Earth's history, only to the secondary world's history, much of which the readers do not and will not necessarily ever know. Real-world history has no bearing on the secondary world's history, or only has as much bearing as the creator wishes or allows it to. Therefore, the question of historical realism in secondary fantasy is moot.

Real-world history's bearing on primary world fantasy is more complex and depends on the type of fantasy. In historical fantasy, yes, historical realism has some degree of validity. However, historical fantasy is inherently alternate history that causes social, political, and technological changes. In UF/PNR, historical realism has a place to some degree. But, as with historical fantasy, UF/PNR inherently involves alternate history, with the introduction of supernatural elements, so socio-political changes are likely, too. Susanna Clarke's *Jonathan Strange and Mr. Norrell* is more affected by actual history and magic has less effect on the setting/society. Andrews's *Hidden Legacy*, though, has magic producing a major impact on post–19th-century history to the point of completely altering society and history. Harris's *Southern Vampire Mysteries* series has more real-world history influence, because the presence of magic and the paranormal has no notable impact on society before the mid–1990s and the setting itself is in a state of evolving society, as other paranormal beings (were-creatures, witches, fae) reveal themselves.

Real as Inspiration

Where real-world history comes into fantasy is in providing inspiration. And it should be exactly that: inspirational, *not* limiting. Many events, societies, and people in history inspire fictional societies and histories. Here, it helps to emphasize that such figures are inspiring, not a source of recreating or lifting exactly from real-world history. The inspiration in this case is to adapt and tweak to fit a given setting, society, and situation (e.g., with the presence of magic and non-humans).

A few socially altering events from real history might spawn ideas, such as:

The plague in Europe yielded massive socio-economic-religious change in the mid–14th century. Likewise, the major families of the Italian Renaissance can form a model for a society of war, intrigue, and politics. Even the European sumptuary laws, created to differentiate social classes (impoverished nobles from rich merchants) by their clothing and food, can spawn ideas.

Maybe the secondary world society has its own Reformation, whereby many sects of the core faith schism and break off, leading to socio-political upheaval. Or the primary world magical society needs to deal with the Black Death and decide whether to hide and watch others suffer and die or to reveal themselves and try to help (or somewhere in between).

Myths and Legends

When we think about a society's history, its myths[11] and legends[12] are also important to consider. The myths and legends that a society holds are part of its cultural history and heritage. They may address the creation of the world (via sex, death/dismemberment, as a by product of something else), the end of the world, judgement, the afterlife, a fall from paradise, and the basic forces of the world (potentially including nature, time, entropy, fate, divination, prophecy).[13] They form a sort of pre-history for the society and roots of both culture and social mores. These myths and legends also tell us how the society perceives itself, or wishes to be perceived by others.

Myths and legends may be used to explain cultural practices, often based on the old stories. Debate may occur about whether the practice followed the story or the story followed the practice. For example, ancient Greece had a tradition of hospitality toward any traveler, because of (or reinforced by) myths of the gods walking, disguised, among mortals, therefore any traveler could be a god in disguise.

Cultural origins are also often steeped in myth and legend. These are usually based in how the society wants to be seen by others. For instance, Rome had two major founding stories—(1) Romulus and Remus and (2) Aeneas. The first story shows Rome as the descendant of survivors and wolves, that work as a pack, reinforcing Roman society and military tactics. The Aeneas story ties Rome to Troy and to the goddess Venus (Aeneas's ancestor), creating a divine lineage for the city and, eventually, empire. Comparatively, the English *Brut Chronicle* ties the founding of Britain to a brother of Aeneas, thereby tying medieval England to the Roman Empire and to Troy as successor to both.

Holidays may be formed from myths and legends and practiced to reinforce the stories. Practically all major religious holidays began as myths and legends, from Easter to the Winter Solstice. At the very least, myths and legends may form around the society's beliefs about the holiday, even if they are incorrect—for instance, the belief that Christopher Columbus "discovered" the Americas and was the only person of his day to think the Earth was round (both demonstrably false, but still fairly widely believed in the U.S.).

Myths and legends may also surround the foundation of sub-cultures and groups within the society. This is especially the case in secondary world fantasies, but also applicable to some UF/PNR. In the former case, there are the legendary foundations of the Harpers (Forgotten Realms) and Knights of Solamnia (Dragonlance). In the latter, some UF/PNR writers have played with legends surrounding the foundations of the Knights Templar, the hashishin, the ninja, and the thugee—all relatively to very secret societies that kept their pasts hidden to one degree or another from outsiders.

Finally, adventure and plot hooks often begin with legends. Stories about the old ruins outside of town or the ancient forest that no one goes near draw adventurers and heroes from around the nation or world. Tolkien employed legends about Mirkwood (Rohan) and Lothlórien (dwarves and Gondor), while Michael Moorcock used legends throughout the *Elric* series and Howard regularly used them in the *Conan* series.

Pre-History

Myths and legends of a society inherently speak to and of the past. Particularly for secondary world fantasies, they are almost invariably of a forgotten or pre-historic past. In common usage, the term myth may refer to recorded historical events, as we speak of an event or person being "mythologized," but here the use will refer specifically to stories involving divinities and near-divinities.

The pre-history of a society necessarily includes the foundation story of the society and what led to its founding. The founding of Rome in the story of Aeneas is a good example, as it follows upon the Trojan War, includes Aeneas's travels fleeing the remains of Troy, and the actual creation of the settlement that became Rome. Likewise, GRRM's tales of the foundation of the Seven Kingdoms and the Iron Throne out of the ruins of Valyria falls into this category. As does Rowling's legendary foundation of Hogwarts, with the story of the four founding wizards and witches that set the basis for the four houses and the Heir of Slytherin legend. Generally, these stories are impossible to confirm, but are likely not entirely real as founding stories, at least in real-world cases. Archaeology and the historical record sometimes confirm the basis of the legends, but more often contradict the tales. Regardless, societies tend to adhere to the legendary tales. In secondary world societies, the legends and myths may indeed be completely true, or they may be propaganda created to make the society look better.

These myths and legends help the society to shape its own self-image and the image it wants outsiders to see. Projecting these images can be an attempt to keep the society safe or to improve the standing of a society among its neighbors. They can also be a means of legitimizing a governing body. An example of the last case is the body of legends built by England's Tudor kings and queens, that they deposed a ruthless tyrant who murdered his nephews (historically, it turns out King Richard III was generally well thought of and liked by his contemporaries and very probably did not murder his nephews). A fictitious example is the legend that Gondor was first among the lands of Men because it was founded by the Dúnedain, exiles of Númenor (e.g., the "best of men"), a legend that seems to be true for the world. Sometimes the legends can be used to attempt a degree of unity within the culture, as in the tale of the founding of Hogwarts, with the four founders trying to unify the wizards and witches of the British Isles, even though they internally divided the students again with houses.

Regardless of the purpose, the pre-history of myths and legends most often comes from later in the culture's history. The legends are created by storytellers, clergy, and leaders rather than being discovered (as in modern archaeology or paleontology). Once created, the legends and myths are disseminated by cultural apparatus such as temples and schools, purposely, rather than organically growing and spreading, though both avenues are possible.

Roots and Social Mores

The legends and myths of a society reflect the social mores and values of the society. They also often set the roots of the society, even if they are not entirely accurate roots. This role of myth and legend in history building is especially true in the fantasy genres, in terms of the social roots or founding of the society. We see them in the myths of Krynn (Dragonlance), Max Gladstone's *Craft Sequence*, Jemisin's *Inheritance Trilogy*, G.R.R. Martin's *ASoIaF*, and Kevin Hearne's *Seven Kennings*. They are found throughout the fantasy genres, back to the earliest inspiration for the genre. This is likely an outgrowth of the legends and medieval romances (and non–European equivalents) that form the foundation of modern fantasy. In Europe, both legends and medieval romance regularly reference Greco-Roman mythology and/or have their own roots in

Celtic and Nordic mythology. It is important here to keep in mind that the "truth" of a situation may not be truth, or an original reason may be different from a later rationalization or later reason that takes over when an "original" no longer applies or is no longer useful.[14] Likewise, multiple "true" myths and legends may occur simultaneously, as in the case of Egyptian mythology in which the sun was simultaneously both Ra's barge sailing across the sky and a giant ball of dung being rolled across the sky by Khepri.

What is less common to see, if it is seen at all in fiction, is the use of myth and legend to reflect or create social mores and traditions. One reason is that it is rather more difficult to show or to create in some regards, especially since many people in modern society are unaware of, or do not care about, the origins of various traditions that they continue to practice. However, a few historical examples can be brought out here. The aforementioned Greek acts of hospitality are a good one, as they were built out of (or were supported by) myths of the gods visiting mortals. During the medieval era, the concept of chivalry as expressed in the Arthurian legends became an ideal to aspire to, even if it was not generally followed in practical terms. Conversely, the legends of Robin Hood set up a more practical set of ideals—loyalty to the rightful Crown, generosity, charity, standing up for the wrongfully oppressed—in which the outlaws are shown to be more chivalrous and more upstanding than the nobles, who are generally shown as corrupt, ultra-wealthy, and amoral at best.

The use of myth and legend can be a powerful means of showing the ideals of a society without necessarily spelling them out. In a narrative, they can appear as mini-myths and legends—often in a foreword or a little pre-chapter vignette—or as songs, plays, or other references throughout the narrative itself—as done by Tolkien and, to a lesser degree, Steven Brust (Dragaera).

What to Include

What to include is probably the biggest question at any level of worldbuilding, society or otherwise, and every aspect. If there is too much included, then the worldbuilding gets bogged down and the creator never gets to the story or other intended use. Too little, and the world or society does not engage the audience. To add to the issue, when we look at real-world societies, there are decades, centuries, millennia of recorded, detailed history that is impossible to reproduce.[15] With all the possibilities and all the potential data, it is best to choose what matters most for the society and its intended purpose. At first, stick to the big elements, until the little details matter for the narrative. Using Keith Baker's history questions may prove useful here: Why do we fight (large scale and personal)? How did lost civilizations fall? Who/What are the legends? and How does history affect you?[16]

The type of history (see the introduction of this chapter) also helps decide what to include. The Great Man, Cyclic, Chain of Progress, and Social History methods all suggest or require a certain focus and approach to the inclusion of events. For example, the Great Man method sees societal history as a series of isolated, great moments while Social History sees society as a whole via trends and events related to and influencing each other.

Founding and Rise of Society

A good starting place for historical events is the founding and rise of the society. This could be the actual historical founding of the society or its legendary founding. In any fantasy genre, both types of founding could be the same thing and in all cases they can coexist.

Some questions may help to guide a creator's thoughts here and give some structure to consider the earliest days of the society:

- How did the society come to exist?
- What triumphs and setbacks did it have?
- Has it changed governments? If so, how and when?
- What larger entities/societies has it been part of or contacted?
- Has anyone famous come from the society?
- Why was the society founded?

To answer these questions, we might turn to real-world history for inspiration. For example, with regard to the last question, we can look at the city of Venice. Venetian society was created by escaped slaves, who fled the city of Rome. They settled in what is now modern Venice because the land was marshy, difficult to enter, and easy to defend. On another example, modern Australia was founded as a penal colony, forced upon the people who were already living there, so most of the early colonists were criminals (or "criminals") of various sorts. For a fictional example, Naomi Novik's magic school, Scholomance, was created by a coalition of powerful magic communities to be a place to keep magic kids safe until they could protect themselves. Due to unforeseen issues (setbacks), the culture that developed in Scholomance became very dystopian.

The founding and rise of the society may connect the characters. Descendants of the founders may still be proud of that lineage, or arrogant about it, even if they themselves have done little to nothing since. There could be a divine, royal, or culture hero founding story. There could simply be a confluence of trade routes that organically formed a market, then town, then city. Or perhaps there is a town that grew around a fort, school, palace, or temple. Each choice here changes the view and character of the society.

Between the Rise and Fall

Between the founding of a society and its end, a lot happens. But, what happens and what should be included? The answer depends partly on what type of history is being recorded. It also depends on the type and size of the society as well as what type of world—primary or secondary—the society is in. Some sample categories include Conflicts and Treaties, Disasters, Divine Intervention, First Contact, Inventions, Notable People/Places, Reigns and Changes in Government, and the Rise of Groups in society. Other things to consider include assaults and invasions, extinctions and depletions (of resources), expansions, and predictions, omens, or prophecies.[17]

Conflicts can include wars, rebellions, socio-political struggles, and economic conflict. For instance, the mage guild and the temples may engage in socio-political conflict over political influence of the head of state or the drovers guild refuses to move goods until their demands are met (economic conflict). The follow-up is the treaties or other agreements that end conflicts or result from conflicts. These set the society's borders, open up plot lines, and develop the setting and society. They could also create problems or limit the responses of characters to problems, so as not to violate treaties.

Disasters could be natural (floods, volcanoes, droughts), disease (pandemic, plague), magic, or a mix. In the case of magic disasters, they could be the result of magic leaving the world (Brust's Dragaera, Andrews's *Kate Daniels*), magic reappearing (*Kate Daniels*), magical misfires (Dragaera), or the side effects of magical conflict (Scott Lynch's "A Year and a Day in Old Theradane"). The mix occurs especially in the Forgotten Realms' spellplague, a magical plague that is the incidental creation of divine action. Disasters create turmoil, chaos, and death. But, they also lead to major social and economic change. For example, the Black Death resulted in a huge loss of life, but it created apocalypse cults, incredible social mobility, and significant economic and religious change, setting the stage for the Reformation and Renaissance.

The use of divine intervention in a society's history requires the presence of active, real gods. The divinities may create an otherwise natural disaster. The disaster might be the gods leaving the world, or being cut off from it. The intervention could be a war among the gods that draws in mortals. Whatever the intervention may be, it always reshapes society (Krynn, Gladstone's *Craft Sequence*) or reflects the society (Athens and the competition between Athena and Poseidon to be the city's patron god). Divine intervention is best used sparingly, both due to the power level involved and the fact that its impact in the narrative diminishes the more it is used.

First contact is often overlooked in the fantasy genres, but can be an excellent method of social change. Contact between cultures, and species, could be peaceful, violent, commercial, or hundreds of other ways. The results of such contact could be war, trade, innovation, plague, alliances, isolationism, or a host of others, singularly or all at once. Whether the contact was purposeful—one side going out looking for others—or accidental—stumbling on another culture—can be an important factor for the character of the event itself. Regardless, first contact should lead to some kind of societal change. Because it is a bigger theme in science fiction, and has occurred many times in real-world history, those could be good places to mine for inspiration.

Inventions are another place where magic and technology can fundamentally alter a society. They introduce the potential to affect society on a surface or much deeper level. Most inventions will also lead to the introduction of new legislation or other means of attempting to control, suppress, or regulate the new thing. From history, the invention of movable type profoundly affected European society by, along with other innovations, making printed materials cheaper, to the point that it is partially credited as paving the way for the Reformation. Although not invented during the narrative, the creation of time turners had to have set the wizarding world on its figurative head in the Potterverse. At the very least, the Ministry of Magic seized physical control of all time turners and enacted strict legislation regulating their use, due to the inherent dangers of messing around with time. One that a plot was built around is the invention of jurda parem in Bardugo's Grishaverse. The drug that boosts a grisha's[18] powers, while addicting and burning out the user, presents a significant military advantage for any government that possesses the secret to its creation.

In addition to inventions, many people appear in history for good or ill, from generals to rulers, artists to scientists, actors to prelates, writers to teachers. Notably good or bad ones may deserve attention and potential development in a fictional history. Likewise, important socio-cultural places could deserve some degree of discussion or at least mention, also for good or ill. For example, a discussion of British history would be seriously lacking without mention of Hastings. Similarly, New York's history would be incomplete without some mention of Grand Central Station, and its effects on the city. One might even mention places associated with a specific famous person, such as Graceland, as cultural artifacts.

Alongside famous people, the reigns of rulers can be useful to know, at least key ones. They can be used to name eras—such as the Victorian, Tudor, and Edwardian eras or the Ming Dynasty, Mughal India, or Tokugawa Japan. From the era, they can also be used to name fashion, architectural styles, furniture trends, and other societal elements. It can also be good to note whether the ruler was hereditary, elected, came to power through conquest, murder, or other such means. Depending on level of detail, noting the ruler's cause of death, popularity, and/or notable acts (if any) in brief could be helpful. In a similar vein, any changes in government style should be noted in the history of a society. Nations often change governments, or shift them, over time. For example, Rome began as a kingdom, became a republic, and ended as an empire. Likewise, Britain began as a monarchy, became a constitutional theocratic monarchy (when King Henry VIII named himself the head of the state church), then a theocratic constitutional monarchy-empire, then, after World War II, back to a theocratic constitutional monarchy (the ruler is both head of state and head of the state church) on paper while being a democratic republic in practice (the Prime Minister and legislature effectively hold all the governmental power with a figurehead royal).

A final area to cover is the rise of groups within the society. As social, political, and ethnic groups gain numbers, equality, and/or power in a society, the society will, logically, be altered in various ways. In our own history, we can look at the rise of Catholicism in Ireland, the rise and decline of unions in the U.S. (increased prosperity, safety, and wages as they rose, reductions in all three as they declined), or the suffrage movements in the U.S. and UK that sought to secure voting rights for women. In fantasy settings, a clear example is G.R.R. Martin's use of the militant clergy and faith militant. With their new rise under Cersei Lannister's regency, the groups represent a removal of the control of state sanctioned violence from the crown and King's Landing watch, in favor of placing state sanctioned violence under the control of (largely untrained) civilians under the command of the church.

Decline and Fall

The fantasy genres, especially the secondary world settings, are filled with fallen, lost, or crumbling civilizations. The lost city/civilization is as much as staple of the genre as elves and dwarves. So, how and why do civilizations decline and fall?

Civilizations have collapsed and died out. We have evidence of this all over what was once called Mesopotamia (now Iraq, parts of Iran, Turkey, Syria, and Kuwait). Particularly in fantasy settings, there are many ways that a civilization may be completely wiped out. There could be a particularly virulent plague. The gods could become angered and wipe out the culture (ex. Krynn, where the gods dropped a mountain on the nation of Istar, turning it into a sea). A conflict between or involving powerful magicians or magical forces could destroy it (ex. Dragaera and Adron's Disaster, although that destroyed the capital and changed the society). To entirely destroy a culture, the cause would have to be almost instant and incredibly widespread, otherwise the culture changes and adapts while vestiges of the original society remain.

However, in our own history, civilizations tend to change, split, rename, or combine. In the last 3000 years or so, the total number of civilizations that have completely died is very small, maybe even zero. Cultures rarely have a clear start and end date. We have no historical record of anything like the dramatic end of (the fictitious) Atlantis (one night). That does not mean that such endings cannot happen in fantasy or UF (usually through a disaster), but civilizations falling that way become old fast. Instead, most change or dwindle with a whimper. For example, modern Italy, Germany, and China formed out of earlier versions of their civilizations—city-states, an "empire" of states, and an empire respectively. Other examples form from conquest (the creation of the Anglo-Saxon and Norman states in Britain, the Mongol invasions) then dwindle (Britain and the Mongol Empire) or change (today, the British and Mongol empires are much smaller and are democratic republics).

Oral vs. Recorded History

In most societies, our understanding of history is most often a mix of oral traditions and recorded information. We see this mix particularly in looking at places. For instance, the Tower of London, the Winchester Mystery House, or Kilmainham Jail (Dublin, Ireland). Visitors to all these places are told legends that have circulated orally for decades, or centuries, before the written record (or that were told parallel to the written record), alongside verifiable data and artifact history of the place.

One of the potential jobs of the creator is to determine the ratio of oral to written history. Oral legends and rumors are good as a basis of investigation and plot. Written history is useful for building the society and for narrative plot. In both cases, they can inspire or involve research on the part of characters seeking to piece together important information for the narrative. Both types of history may have accuracy issues, especially with translation between languages. Oral traditions may include additions, deletions, and alterations introduced by different tellers to "create a better story." Likewise, the written record may include miscopied information, poor writing and reading conditions, poor penmanship to decipher, obscure languages, and the copyist's familiarity with the information (that can introduce "corrections"). Some written history recorders also alter the history they write for the same reasons as oral history tellers.

In a pre-industrial society, or a pre-widespread literacy one, written history is typically the history of the learned, scholarly, and/or clerical elite. Usually these are the upper class and the highly, possibly magically, educated. They are the ones typically able to write and read, or to pay others to write for them. As such, the subject matter tends to be limited to things of interest to this audience. Also, such histories may be altered as propaganda—for example, Sir Thomas More wrote a history of England focused on the kings. More cast King Richard III in a poor light, in part because More had been commissioned by King Henry VII (who deposed Richard III) and did not wish to anger his patron.

On the other hand, the oral tradition is typically the history of everyone else, especially the lowest socio-economic classes, including serfs and slaves. These are the people in society who have little to no means of writing recorded history. So, they keep their history through songs, word of mouth, and stories passed from one generation to the next. This includes real people being morphed into cultural heroes, and possibly into deities, over the course of centuries or millennia. The oral histories are not necessarily verifiable, though sometimes they fit documentary, archaeological, or genetic evidence.

Layered History

The concept of a layered history is the idea that multiple levels of understanding or information about history exist. This is arguably true in our world, as the level of understanding that is taught in primary school is rather different from that taught in graduate school. Part of that effect, though, is that "[t]he flow of 'history' and its impact on the present are ... messy and contested."[19] However, layered history is effectively intrinsic to UF/PNR, whether the society has a hidden magic or open magic setting. Regardless of hidden or open, UF has a surface layer of history: the real world or "mundane" history—that is, the audience's own history. Most, if not all, also have a paranormal history, the history of non-humans and magic. This could be the history presented in Rowling's History of Magic class or Harris's vampire (and other being) history, that is not known to normal humans. It could be Andrews's history of Roland (*Kate Daniels*) that is known to only a few people in the world. HBO's *True Blood* took Harris's double layered history a step further by adding another layer of vampiric history known only to a select group of vampires—the "vampire bible" and Billith plotline. In theory, it is possible to have an infinite number of layers to history. Practically speaking, though, three to five layers seems a useful maximum, if only for the creator to keep them straight.

Known and Hidden Layers

A known, public, normal history and a hidden supernatural history is the baseline for most UF/PNR, especially those with a hidden magic setup. This is the standard presented in most of Neil Gaiman's body of work, Rowling's Potterverse, Rick Riordan's Jacksonverse (and Riordan Presents imprint), Bardugo's *Ninth House*, Novik's *Scholomance*, Andrews's *Innkeeper Chronicles*, and Harris's *Southern Vampire Mysteries*. The supernatural community is aware of its own history and possibly that of normal humans, but humanity is largely or entirely unaware of supernatural history. In many cases, even known history may be somewhat limited as "characters are generally almost completely ignorant of their 'true' history or the nature of the world" because "many important matters are vague and uncertain" since they take place far away and do not immediately impact the character's life.[20]

Hidden versus known histories can also be applicable to secondary world fantasies. Often the narrative in those cases will be driven by or revolve around the hidden history, whether discovering or revealing it. Variations can range from global to personal in this regard. This is the situation with Garth Nix's *Sabriel* (cultural history), Leigh Bardugo's Grishaverse (notably the trilogy starting with *Shadow & Bone*; personal and cultural history), and Steven Brust's Vlad Taltos (personal that ties into cultural legend). In each case, much of the cultural history is hidden from the general public, especially the protagonist. The plots may be heavily influenced by finding that hidden history (Nix, Bardugo) or the revelations may be entirely personal and teased out occasionally as side plots (Brust).

In some cases, many layers can be created. A good example is the *World of Darkness* RPG system. In this setting, the creators present one layer: normal, everyday history. The second layer is the basic history members of each paranormal species know about their own kind (e.g., werewolves, vampires, mages, fae). There is often a third, deeper, layer of history regarding the species that is not generally known outside of the oldest and most influential among the people. Arguably a fourth layer exists in the form of the histories of other beings—the assumption is that the average young vampire does not really know about the existence of werewolves or mages, and vice versa, in most cases, at least when they start the game.

Role of Layered History

For a secondary world, layered history adds depth to the society. It creates and implies the presence of things people in the society do not know or were not meant to know. As briefly noted above, it creates hidden information that could drive plots and influence the direction of events and evolution in the society. Sometimes, this information is there for characters to find, investigate, and piece together. Layered histories also create a more complex backstory for the society and characters. Case in point, imagine *LotR* without the back-history of *The Hobbit* that is unknown to most in the world. Or *The Hobbit* without the history presented in *The Silmarillion*, a history that is effectively unknown to any but the elves, Istari, Sauron, and a handful of the Men of Gondor (including the Rangers).

In primary world fantasies (UF/PNR), supernatural history is almost always inherently layered. Often it parallels normal history, but sometimes involves being concealed until supernatural beings come out into the open (Charlaine Harris) or represents a lost ancient history (Ilona Andrews's *Kate Daniels*). In these cases, the hidden history sets up an alternate or parallel history that is unfamiliar to the audience or revises/rewrites the baseline history they are familiar with. This draws the audience into the setting and society, sparking their interest. Hidden histories in the UF/PNR genres also produce information that influences events behind the scenes. Hints can be left for the audience to discover, explore, imagine, and hunt for, which leads the audience to active engagement with the society and narrative arc. Finally, a layered history can set up a backstory for characters and a hidden society. This provides a foundation for character lives and societal events that come before the beginning of the narrative, creating a sense of depth and age for the fictional society.

3

Governments

Any time a society forms, the question of governance appears. Every time people come together in a group—whether as a settlement, a school, or something else—the need to organize the society and create and enforce the societal rules becomes an issue. The question is not "does it happen" but when and how does it happen, with what result. If no system of governance or rules is set in place, the society inevitably descends into anarchy and dissolves. This is true regardless of the size or type of society. Nations have legislative, executive, judicial, and bureaucratic structures in place, as do national subdivisions such as states, provinces, counties, and duchies. Cities have the same issues, and generally the same responses. Schools appoint principals, headmasters, chancellors, or presidents alongside the faculty and, potentially, other administrators—ex. deans, provosts. Guilds, historically, had guildmasters, administrators, and master craftsmen who enforced the guild rules. Monastic communities typically have an abbot/abbess or other leading figure, often with bureaucratic subordinates who see to the daily functions of the community and serve as front line enforcers of the community's rules. In the fantasy genres, we see direct application in that governments appear throughout every society in fantasy, UF, and PNR worlds.

Clichés in the Genre

The fantasy genres tend to focus heavily on a very small number of government types. The fantasy genre, itself, leans toward three common government types: the monarchy, the empire, and the dictatorship. These are used so often that they have become clichés of the genre. Likewise, in the UF/PNR genres, the clichés are dictatorships, some sort of meritocracy, or monarchies. These typically manifest as vampire clans/covens (dictator, meritocracy by age/power), werewolf tribes/packs (dictator), magician or witch councils, chantries, or covens (meritocracy based on age, skill, or power), or the fae courts (monarchy). They have been used so often that audiences automatically associate different species with certain types of governance. It is difficult to get audiences to think about non-hierarchical/dictatorial vampiric societies, or werewolves without dictatorial-hierarchy packs founded in bad science.[1] Many audiences also seem to assume that empires and kingdoms, with the occasional theocratic state, are all that is possible, or should be, in the secondary world fantasy genre.

Expanding Beyond Clichés

Mixing things up and going beyond the clichés is a good way to make a world or story stand out. Moving outside the cliché makes the world more memorable for the audience and may grab the audience's attention as something new and different. In UF, J.K. Rowling presented a hidden magic society with a democratic republic in the Ministry of Magic. On the other end, Jonathan Stroud creates an open magic magocracy (variant on meritocracy) with *The Bartimaeus Trilogy*, in which magicians govern England through Parliament. Secondary world fantasies are not left out, as Katherine Kurtz's *Deryni* shows elements of a magocracy while Thay in *The Forgotten Realms* is a pure magocratic state. In the realm of "flintlock fantasies," Brian McClellan, Django Wexler, Adrian Tchaikovsky, and Scott Lynch all produce different types of republics in secondary worlds. *Dragonlance's* Solamnia is set up as a sort of military junta (an order of knights governs the land) with elements of theocracy (one branch of the knights is trained as priests) and bits of oligarchy (most of the knights come from noble families). *The Forgotten Realms'* Lords of Waterdeep present a complex and interesting governing body, in that the lords form a council that is largely hidden from the public eye. While it is unclear how the lords are chosen, they come from all social, economic, and other levels of the city and, in theory, any species and sex/gender.

Social Class

Connected to government (and economics), in the form of power and control of society, is the concept of social class. More often than not, governments are directly or effectively controlled by people who make up an upper class, through wealth, birth, possession of magic, or some other means. The TTRPG industry has many resources regarding "traditional" (meaning monarchic) social classes and status levels, including titles of nobility.[2] A variety of writers, particularly those in the historical fiction genre, have also collected resources and gathered real-world titles.[3] Sometimes the question is addressed indirectly, such as Kevin J. Anderson's question: "What do people do for a living?"[4] Anderson further develops the idea with questions about what society considers to be valuable and societal treatment of children, the poor, the elderly, and the sick.[5] These questions can lead us to thinking about patriarchal versus matriarchal societies, strictly hierarchical (ex. caste-based), or completely egalitarian societies as well. Any question of social status and social hierarchy in a society, or, alternately, asking where power is located, will affect characters who inhabit the world at all levels.

Types of Government

Throughout our own history, there have been many types of government, although most are arguably variants of a core set. The exact number of types depends heavily on how we define "types." They can be divided by structure: anarchy versus federation. They could be divided by the source of authority: autocracy versus democracy. They could be organized by ideology: monarchy versus republic. They could be organized by size and scope: city-state versus national. Or there are a host of other ways to divide types. In some ways, there are arguably an infinite number of possible types of government, if each variation is treated as a separate type. But there is a core group that variants are based on. This is rather like storytelling and plots, in that there exists a small core with many variations. For the purposes of this chapter, several of the more common types and variations will be defined and discussed, but the collection will be by no means complete.

Monarchy

Monarchies are easily the most common form of government in the fantasy genre. They carry over into the UF/PNR subgenres through use of fae/elf courts (Jim Butcher, Holly Black) among others. In simple form, a monarchy is a government in which the head of state is a monarch (king, queen). The role may be symbolic (no real power), constitutional (limited power), or absolute (effectively unlimited power). The post of king/queen may be hereditary or through right of conquest, or even election. It may last for life or abdication. In unusual cases, a monarch may reign for a fixed length of time. Monarchies often involve rival claimants to the throne, in fiction (and in real history). The chain of succession is also a common plot point. Many monarchies are tied to a feudal socio-economic system, especially in pre-modern societies. Often UF monarchies, such as fae courts, also use a sort of feudal system of noble ranks to indicate the socio-political hierarchy. However, UF and PNR versions rarely tie rank or titles to land, though there are exceptions.

Most secondary world fantasies, especially before 1990, are examples of monarchies. This includes Gondor (J.R.R. Tolkien), Narnia (C.S. Lewis), the *Deryni*-series (Kurtz), Valdemar (Mercedes Lackey), Westeros (George R.R. Martin), and the lands in *Stardust* (Neil Gaiman). Some examples exist in urban fantasy, notably in the *Dresden Files* (Jim Butcher) and Holly Black's *The Modern Faerie Tales*.[6]

Empire

After the kingdom (monarchy), the empire is probably the second most common government type in the fantasy genre. Sometimes, or often, the term may be misused in the genre. It is also often used for an empire in decline, perhaps reverting back to a kingdom. Empires are defined as a sovereign state made up of many territories and peoples under a single ruler's authority. Empires can form from direct conquest (ex. Alexander the Great's empire), coercion/indirect power, or a mix of the two (the Roman Empire). Emperors may be hereditary (British, Roman, Chinese), elected (Holy Roman Empire), chosen through the conquest of a new dynasty (Chinese), or a mix (the Mongol Empire, mixing all three). Some are administered solely by a bureaucracy, while others maintain some degree of feudal organization.

Although the empire is much more common in the fantasy genre's secondary worlds, it can become an element of post-apocalyptic UF/PNR. For example, the character Roland once had an empire and attempts to rebuild his empire in Ilona Andrews's *Kate Daniels* series. Michael Moorcock's Dark Empire of Granbretan is a more difficult one to place in that it is an alternate history/future Great Britain, part of his *Eternal Champion* multiverse. Secondary fantasy examples include the Seanchan Empire (Robert Jordan), The Empire (Christopher Paolini), the Final Empire (Brandon Sanderson, *Mistborn*), the Melnibonéan Empire (Moorcock, *Elric*), Nilfgaard (Andrzej Sapkowski, *The Witcher*), and Discworld's Agatean, Klatchian, Tezuman, and Unholy/Dark Empires (Terry Pratchett).

Republic

The republic is rather less common in the fantasy genres than the kingdom or empire. But, examples can be found. Republics are defined as a government in which the country is considered public, not the property of the ruler(s). Positions of power are attained through elections and leaders are therefore expected to represent the body of citizens. They can be direct democracies, oligarchic (ex. Renaissance Venice and Genoa), or democratic republics/representative democracies (ex. the U.S.). Because they, historically, came into being fairly late in real-world history, at least in common form, they tend to be associated with a variety of socio-economic systems.

Examples in secondary fantasy worlds are relatively scarce, notably the Free Cities (George R.R. Martin, *ASoIaF*) and the Andoran Republic (*Pathfinder* RPG). They tend to be the standard non-magical government for UF/PNR, sometimes mirrored by a hidden magic society, as in Rowling's *Harry Potter* series with the Ministry of Magic. They are much more common in steampunk fantasies or "flintlock fantasy," such as the works of Brian McClellan (*The Powder Mage*), Django Wexler (*Burningblade & Silvereye*), Adrian Tchaikovsky (*Shadows of the Apt*), and Scott Lynch (*Gentleman Bastard*).

Theocracy

At one time, theocracies seemed to be more common than republics in the fantasy genre, perhaps they still are. Theocracies are defined as rule by the religious elite. Religious institutions are part of state institutions. The head of the church or temple is, often, also the head of state, or the head of state is controlled by the highest ranking prelate of the religion. The head prelate and/or head of state could wield actual power or be figureheads for others, depending on how the government is constructed and the history of the society.

Examples abound in secondary world fantasies including Omnia (Discworld), Chyrellos (David Eddings, *The Elenium*), most drow cities (Forgotten Realms), the Fjordell Empire (Brandon Sanderson, *Elantris*), Norvos and Qohor (*ASoIaF*), Thrane (Eberron), and Pan Tang (Moorcock, *Elric*). They are less common in direct form in UF/PNR, but certainly possible, especially in post-apocalypse variations on the genre. For instance, Ilona Andrews's Roland constantly walks a fine line between keeping his territory an empire and becoming a theocracy with the god at its head (*Kate Daniels*). Conversely, Roland's ancestral opponent, Moloch, has become a god and rules over his territory in the purest form of theocratic state (*Blood Heir*, Andrews).

Federation

Federations are typically more common in science fiction than fantasy, for the most part (including *that* federation), but they are arguably more common in UF/PNR. Federations are defined as a union of partially self-governing states or regions under a central government. Usually, a federation is constitutional in nature, and the constitution cannot be unilaterally changed by either party. In other words, both the states/regions and the central government need to agree to change the constitution. Individual regions may or may not retain control of their own internal affairs.

The most direct examples are the Seven Kingdoms in the *Talislanta* RPG and the Federation of Magic in the *Rifts* RPG. The International Confederation of Wizards in the Potterverse might fall under a federation, but it is difficult to tell since readers do not see much of it in the books (or movies). Arguably, post–Shift Atlanta in Andrews's *Kate Daniels* series eventually becomes a sort of federation, in that a central authority is technically able to exert power and control over the city's various self-governing factions, if they so desire, but refrains from doing so.

Uncommon Types of Government

The previous government types are among the most common ones found in the fantasy genres. Those that follow are significantly more unusual and, therefore, less common.

Anocracy

An anocracy is a government in which power is placed in the hands of elite groups that are constantly competing with each other, rather than power being given to public institutions. Anocracies are usually situated midway between autocracies and democracies. As a government type, anocracy is very unusual, but may be a transition state that moves toward autocratic rule (power in the hands of one person) or democratic (power in the hands of the populace). In anocracies, often an aristocracy or collection of nobles, likely families or clans, hold power, but there could be other competing groups.

The self-titled Holy Anocracy in Ilona Andrews's *Innkeeper Chronicles*, a society of interstellar alien vampires, is perhaps the most clear example in fiction (in this case, science fantasy).

Corporate State

The corporate state is defined as rule by corporations. In such governments, both the economic and political systems are controlled by companies. As a government, the corporate state is much more common in science fiction, particularly the cyberpunk genre, but also such works as *The Space Merchants* (C.M. Kornbluth and Frederik Pohl), *Snow Crash*

3. Governments

(Neal Stephenson), and *Dune* (Frank Herbert; with noble titles coming from holding shares in CHOAM).

There are some examples in the fantasy genres, though. For secondary world fantasy, the Minothad Guilds of Mystara (D&D) are a good example. The Dragonmarked Houses of Eberron (D&D) are a more debatable example, as they do not form a nation/government as such, but do wield influence. The corporate state is the default in the cyberpunk-fantasy that is the *Shadowrun* RPG.

Kleptocracy

Kleptocracies are defined as rule by thieves. Often, the officials and ruling class seek personal wealth at the expense of the populace, in real-world applications of the term. In secondary world fantasies, and possibly UF/PNR, a kleptocratic state could literally have thieves, or organized crime, running the government.

In theory, nearly any classic fantasy "City of Thieves" would be a perfect example of this form of government. Arguably, Kerch (especially the capital city, Ketterdam) in Leigh Bardugo's Grishaverse is an example, with elements of the corporate state and plutocracy incorporated, too, in that the merchant families run the government to their own profit.

Magocracy

A variation on the meritocracy, the magocracy is a government by the wielders of magic. The role of non-magicians in such a society varies widely, of course. Often a magocratic state will take a form similar to a theocratic one. Within this category, I would not count societies in which magicians make up the entirety of the society. For instance, The Magisterium (Holly Black and Cassandra Clare) would not count, because the entire society is made up of magicians; therefore the governing body is, too.

In UF/PNR, Jonathan Stroud's alternate England in the *Bartimaeus Trilogy* certainly demonstrates a magocracy. As does Rowling's Ministry of Magic, since the Ministry exerts its authority over non-magicians including centaurs, goblins, and house elves, none of whom are represented in the governing bodies. In secondary fantasies, Anne Bishop's *Black Jewels*, Patricia Wrede's *Mairelon the Magician*, and the land of High Cromlech in China Miéville's works all represent at least one magocratic state.

Meritocracy

A meritocracy is defined as a society governed by those who are either knowledgeable in a given area or merit rule due to their abilities or contributions to society. In the fantasy genres, this "given area" or their abilities could both be magic, see magocracy above. Arguably, meritocracies are fairly common in the genres, through our lens—we often see competent, skilled leaders in the genres—but, generally speaking, in the genres, the leaders were brought in to power for reasons other than merit.

Arguably, the best example in secondary world fantasy is Ankh-Morpork (Discworld), with Lord Vetinari, whom few, if any, could claim is lacking in merit and skill.

Plutocracy

A plutocratic state is one in which the wealthy run the government. Alternately, it may be that the government is indebted to or dependent upon the desires of the rich. Usually, plutocratic elements are combined with other forms of government—the wealthy loan money to the monarch for favors and influence, the wealthy donate heavily to election campaigns for favors and influence. Practically every standard fantasy monarchy, or other state where the nobles and guilds represent the wealthy, falls into this category.

Real-world examples include Carthage, the Dutch Republic, and some of the Renaissance Italian states (such as Florence, Genoa, and Venice).

Hybrid Governments

Unfortunately, very few governments are simple, straightforward examples in determining their type. Most, particularly real world, examples are hybrids of two or more types of government, especially since the type may describe different traits. To use the real world as an example, we can look at the United Kingdom. On the books, the UK is a constitutional monarchy, since the reigning monarch is the head of state but is limited in their power and authority by the laws and legislature of the nation. Technically, though, the UK is also a theocracy since the monarch is also the, ceremonial, head of the Church of England, and the sitting monarch has been since King Henry VIII founded the Church. However, the UK is governed like a democratic republic as the House of Commons is elected by the people to legislate as a representative democracy, alongside the hereditary House of Lords.

Purpose and Role of Government

Political scientists and historians have been debating the purpose of government as a whole for centuries, possibly even as long as governments have existed. I will not attempt to find a definitive answer here, since that is beyond the scope of this book. Instead, time is better spent looking at the historic reasons that specific governments exist, rather than government as a thing. Part of the importance here is that the reason a specific government exists can determine the type of government that is formed. It can also inform the changes that the government undergoes and variations that occur within that type over time, depending on the environment. Nothing is created or exists within a vacuum, so it is good to be aware of the environment in which a government forms and outside influences that affect its evolution.

To that end, specific governments form for a host of reasons. Some are created to provide order in a chaotic society. Others are created to protect the residents of a given area (city, town, country) from each other. Some form to provide safety and security for the residents of a given area in relation to outsiders or the environment. A few are created to undo or combat the excesses of a given socio-economic class. Many form because of outside forces, typically potential threats, or for the benefit of those who live within the government. On a related purpose, most exist to maintain relations between the dominant society and any neighboring societies.[7]

Knowing why a government formed helps us determine what type of government is created and its goals. This information can also influence how the government sees itself and how it changes over time.

Sometimes, a government is created organically as the society coalesces. As people begin living and working together, some mechanism comes into place for organizing their labor and enforcing social rules. The organization of labor is, perhaps, the important part, to ensure that the society's needs are being met. Often, this sort of creation involves one or more people stepping forward to lead. In early forms, we often see despotisms of various sorts, whether theocratic or proto-monarchic, come out of this organic creation. Sometimes, a council-like meritocracy, often based on age, evolves out of this situation.

Social institutions—religious, military, magical, business—may form or shape a government to protect their interests. More self-aware institutions may acknowledge that they shape the government that allows the institutions to exist, as they all need safety, stability, and infrastructure to thrive. These may result in theocratic, military junta, magocratic, or corporate states respectively, if the institutions place themselves in power. Other times, the institutions prefer to be the powers behind the throne— as has often been the case with religious institutions in our own history, such as the (particularly medieval and early modern) Archbishops of Canterbury in England or Cardinal Richelieu in 17th-century France.

Governments may form to combat real or imagined external threats.

For instance, a confederation may be built on mutual defense treaties due to the threat of invasion from a neighbor (ex. NATO). The perceived threat may not be military, as a confederation might be founded on mutual trade agreements, to keep out foreign merchants from a given area (ex. the Hanseatic League). Sometimes, these governments fade or dissolve once the threat is removed. Other times, they find a new threat or simple inertia keeps them in existence after the potential threat is removed.

In some cases, governments could be imposed by a foreign power, whether the foreigners were asked to install the government or not. A good real historical example here is the Roman client states, nations on the border of the Roman Republic/Empire who asked Rome to come in and help maintain order. Eventually, the Romans had enough "peacekeepers" in the territory and enough control over the ruler that they effectively controlled the government (and often fully took over, too). This has a variation in the history and practice of colonization, in which the colonial governments are set in place and supported by the colonizing society.

Some governments exist because of one person's or entity's desire to expand their rule. The desire for power or control, often disguised beneath talk of unity or peace, drove several imperial powers in our history, and more than a few fictional leaders. For example, the empires of Rome, China, and Alexander fall into this category, at different points. As does the so-called Darkling's attempt to control Ravka in Bardugo's Grishaverse. This is, of course, a dangerous source of government, since it relies heavily on the existence of the founder. If there are no heirs, or no clear line of succession, then the government or society collapses. Or, if the ruler is effectively immortal, the society is likely to stagnate and fall to, or be bypassed by, outside forces.

On a related note, a government could exist due to a desire to break from the colonizer or despotic ruler. Often such governments are reactionary, initially at least. They may settle down over time. The U.S., post–Revolution, is an obvious example that began with the Articles of Confederation before settling into the Constitution. As is post–Revolutionary France, with the reactionary Reign of Terror, that eventually settled into a more stable governing structure.

Development

Regardless of the initial purpose, all governments develop and change over time. Rarely, if ever, are governments static. They exist in more or less continual change, especially the longer the society exists. On a smaller scale, even organizational societies see shifts in government. For instance, the shift in higher education's (in the U.S. at least) campus presidents, who were once faculty who led for a term, then became faculty again, but are now career administrators with CEO-level salaries. Or an abbey's shift from a single head to a council of leaders.

On the national level, there are many examples of government development. A few will be addressed here. First, ancient Rome began as a kingdom, overthrew the kings to become a republic, and then reorganized after Julius Caesar's death into an empire. The U.S. is another good example. While the country has remained a democratic republic for its entire history, with some imperial elements, changes have occurred in who can vote (adding women and POC, and reducing the age requirement). There have also been changes in the levels of oligarchy and corporatocratic tendencies in different eras. The nation of Solamnia, from the *Dragonlance* series, was originally founded due to a revolt against the king of Ergoth, but became a military oligarchy as the Knights of Solamnia took control and were mostly members of the nobility. Solamnia also carries some theocratic tones, as the Knights were devoted to the gods, and Sword Knights were partially priests.

Who Participates

The role of government may also control who participates in governing, whether to prevent threats to governmental power or to prevent threats to the people. This can also include the question of succession or the path to attaining power, in the case of hereditary (or even elected) executive and legislative branches.[8] Depending on a variety of factors—including history, bigotry, and fears—one or more groups could be barred from involvement in governing. Some major groups in the fantasy genres include magicians, non-dominant species, and the undead. There could be legitimate reasons for this exclusion. If magicians are capable of mind-altering or charm magic, they may be barred from government to prevent them from magically coercing voters or government officials. If some species have extensive lifespans, they may be banned from government for fear that they will be in office effectively forever—ex. a long-lived elf may rule for centuries or millennia leading to societal stagnation. If the undead feed on the living, there could be legitimate reasons for keeping them out of the governing bodies of the society.

History could be a factor in barring or including different groups in government. For example, if a society was freed from a tyrannical vampiric rule, they may bar vampires from serving in government as a reaction. Likewise, a history of devastating magical wars could lead to a society banning magicians from serving in government in order to keep them out of power. There could also be illegitimate historical reasons for barring participation, as happened with POC and women in American history.

Basic bigotry could be at work, as in the case of American history. Taken to the fantasy genres, people who do not understand magic are likely to fear it, and therefore bar magicians from governing. In a human-dominant society with other species being marginalized, negative stereotypes may prevent those species from being in the government. Such societies mirror events in real-world history that are often used to address, discuss, and analyze real-world history and bigotry, for better or worse.

Often bans on participation are phrased as efforts to protect the dominant populace. Only rarely are they phrased as banning or targeting the blocked community. They might even be phrased as protecting the targeted group, in a more or less patronizing or paternalistic tone. This is especially the case in the primary world forms of the genre. For example, Myke Cole's *Control Point* involves a United States in which magicians are barred from elected office, and those with certain powers are hunted down for execution, to protect "normal" humans. In another case, Rowling's Ministry of Magic takes a paternalistic tone with regard to other species, from goblins to house elves, and an often patronizing view of muggles (non-magic wielders), neither of which are able to participate in the Ministry's legislating or law enforcement processes to protect muggles and take care of other species.

Hidden versus Open Government

Most governing bodies are open and known to those they govern, probably because it is easier in fiction and normal in our own world. However, some governments might be hidden to one degree or another from their society, or may mix both open and hidden elements. There are many reasons for any of the three in a given society. The idea of a hidden or open government goes beyond the hidden or openly known society. That is, the government may be hidden from its own society or other societies, or open to its society while hidden from others.

Hidden Government

Much less common than open governments, hidden governments are entirely possible. If we work with a hidden government, it is important to ask why the government is hidden, to what degree is it hidden, and how is it hidden. Possibly the most common reason for the government to be hidden is to protect its members. The society may be such that members of the governing body are vulnerable to assassination, kidnapping, or related threats. Alternately, they may be hidden to protect them from lobbying and bribery. Some may be hidden in order to secretly pull the strings of society, for beneficial or nefarious purposes. They could also be hidden due to public opinion of both the members and those they govern (ex. the vampire leadership in the *True Blood* and *Southern Vampire Mysteries* series).

Perhaps the most common degree of hiding is that the government's existence is known, but the exact membership is hidden. This is the case of the Lords of Waterdeep in the Forgotten Realms setting. The Lords are known to exist, but keep their identities secret, except one. Presumably they are hidden to protect themselves from the Zhentarim and other foreign powers seeking to take over or destabilize the region. Another good example comes from *Babylon 5*, to briefly dip into science fiction. The Minbari Grey Council is known to exist and govern the Minbari, but the membership is by and large secret. This secrecy protects the identities of members and prevents foreign, and possibly internal, action against them.

A government could be fully secret, but that is usually the realm of the conspiracy thriller genre with shadow governments and extranational organizations secretly controlling governments. Usually, the government's existence is known to those it governs, though the members remain secret.

In most cases of hidden governments, concealing clothing may be used to mask the identities of the members—as in the Lords of Waterdeep and the Grey Council. Although not a government as such, the Council of Tides in the *Six of Crows* duology (Bardugo, Grishaverse) follow a similar technique, using their control over water and mist to enhance their concealment. Alternately, the names of those involved may be considered highly classified information present in minimal records and known only to a very few. The latter is the case of some aspects of the Texas Assembly and Innkeepers discussed below in the "Both" section.

Open Government

Open governments are the most common form of governance in society. This is true both in the real world and in fiction. That said, they may not be entirely "open" to "normal" society (see "Both" below), but are at least open and known to their own society. There is not a whole lot to say about an open government, partly because they are the default state for governments. That said, for examples, we see Lord Vetinari (Ankh-Morpork, Discworld), The Lord Regent and Senate of Palanthas (Dragonlance), the Stewards of Gondor (Middle Earth), the Iron Throne and Small Council (Westeros), and the Innkeeper Assembly (*Innkeeper Chronicles*, Andrews).

Both

Some governments freely mix elements of open and hidden traits. Often they are open in existence to their society, sometimes to outsiders, while keeping other parts secret, entirely or to outsiders. This is a common trope in UF/PNR and related subgenres. The Authority in *True Blood* and the vampire hierarchy in *The Southern Vampire Mysteries* (Charlaine Harris) both fall into this category, as both are open to vampires, but are effectively hidden from humans. The Innkeeper Assembly (*Innkeeper Chronicles*, Andrews) is open to its society, but keeps the identities of the ad-hal (its enforcers) secret from all, or most. Likewise, the Texas Assembly (*Hidden Legacy*, Andrews) works openly to govern magicians, but keeps the identity of the Warden and his deputy (both enforcers) secret, unless the Warden/deputy choose to reveal themselves. In both of the last two cases, the identities are hidden to protect the enforcers in their roles and those close to or related to them from retribution. The secrecy also allows them to investigate and observe without revealing their true purpose and potentially scaring off criminals in their communities.

Laws and Enforcement

The primary purpose of government is to create and enforce laws, or rules. This, of course, begs the question: what is the purpose of laws? There are many reasons for laws to exist, theories that have been debated for millennia, from preventing crime to outlining acceptable punishment for transgression, protecting people to preserving the existence of society. Laws may be spoken or unspoken. In the latter case, there may be elements of travel etiquette, many of which involve not drawing attention and not violating laws across societies.[9] There are also many ways to create and enforce laws and rules. The last two—creation and enforcement—are, arguably, key elements of society as they form the rules that a society sets for its own existence and membership. They are also the rules that one agrees to abide by in order to receive the benefits of living in a given society.

Who Creates Laws

The important element here is the origin of a society's laws. The source of legislation depends heavily on the type of society, the size of the society, and the type of government. This source also reflects how the society expects itself to work and what it values. In a monarchy or despotism, the laws tend to be decrees of the head of state, with the exception of constitutional monarchies that still require ratification by the king/queen. In democracies and republics, laws are generally created by a vote of an elected legislative body. In a theocracy, the laws are made by decree of the highest ranking clergyperson (e.g., high priest, pope, patriarch, imam).

Examples of rule/lawmaking bodies exist throughout the fantasy genres. In Westeros, the laws are made by the Small Council and the King, with the King having final approval. At Hogwarts, the rules are made by the Headmaster's decree, possibly with advisement from the faculty and staff (or by the Ministry's appointee during Umbridge's brief tenure). Many of Krynn's wizards (Dragonlance) are governed by the Conclave of Wizards—three, five, or seven wizards from each of the three orders—who decree the laws for all wizards on the continent of Ansalon. In Rohan, the King of Rohan issues decrees to produce laws. For UF/PNR, the Texas Assembly (*Hidden Legacy*) votes on laws and rules that affect the Houses and magicians in Texas. At Camp Half-Blood (Rick Riordan), technically Dionysus and Chiron make the rules, but cabin heads seem to have some input. Conversely, New Rome (Riordan; Roman demigods) has a senate that votes on new laws and regulations.

Who Enforces Laws

Laws are ineffective and useless unless society has a mechanism in place to enforce them. The form of enforcement varies as much as the governments do and almost as much as the societies themselves. An enforcement arm of government could be highly organized, divided from legislating, and systematic. It could be disorganized and open to personal interpretation. Or it could be somewhere in between. For example, there could be separate police and judges in a system that has set rules of behavior and processes. At the other end, there could be a feudal system in which each noble is both police and judge, as well as executioner, working off their own interpretation of the law. Criminal punishment may begin with an assumption of innocence or an assumption of guilt, which fundamentally changes how any court proceedings work (the former puts the onus of proof on the prosecution, the latter on the defense).[10] Trials, if any, may be conducted via words and arguments, or could include trial by combat or ordeal.[11]

To refer to some of the examples from the previous section, in Westeros the lords and knights serve as police and judges, with occasional appeals to higher nobles. The church operates with its own judges and policing for internal matters. At Hogwarts, the rules are enforced by the teachers, staff, and prefects, who police and judge each case individually (and have been known to interpret the rules to their own liking). In Tolkien's Rohan, the lords and king police and judge wrongdoing, presumably with the king as the final judge. In the *Hidden Legacy* world, the Texas Assembly names a warden (who might deputize one or more proteges) to police and execute Assembly law within the state of Texas. Either the warden or the Assembly may act as judge, depending on the situation.

Notable Laws

When a fictional society is created, laws can be divided into universal laws (ex. against violence) and culture specific laws. It is safe to assume that basic, universal social laws are in place, such as those against assault, murder, and theft. These seem to be core rules in every society, at least within our own history, and appear necessary for a society to function. If one or more are not present, then that is worth noting. Unusual punishments for violations of such laws would be noteworthy as well.

Overall, it seems better to focus on unusual laws within the society, or ones that affect the plot, in the case of worldbuilding for storytelling. These might be laws affecting the practice of or presence of religion (or that the temples/church have their own laws and are not beholden to secular law). They could be laws about magic use, instruction, and practice. These will probably exist in virtually every fantasy setting. A city, place, or nation may have laws about weapons and armor, including who can own, use, train with, or carry (concealed or openly) what. Most societies will have such laws, if only to minimize threats from adventurers.[12] Perhaps assassination or theft, within a certain limit, is legal in the society (ex. Ankh-Morpork). There may even be laws affecting humans only (if they are not the dominant species; ex. Steven Brust's Dragaera) or other species, if humans are dominant. Other strange laws may also exist, such as "Anyone wearing red in the sight of the emperor is imprisoned for one month."[13]

The rules can even vary from time to time as the society evolves. For instance, the rules at Hogwarts were very minimal beyond those, often year specific, ones discussed by Dumbledore at the start of term feast. But, in *Half-Blood Prince*, Umbridge created scores of rules, at least, most of which became notable plot points. Finally, in *Deathly Hallows*, the Death Eater led Ministry issued numerous anti–Muggleborn laws that affected both the school society and the broader wizarding society.

4

Religion

For better or worse, religions are a component of virtually all societies and have been since their earliest days. They have also been a significant part of the fantasy genres, likely due to the genres' roots in myth, legend, and medieval romances. For instance, Tolkien used religion more or less subtly, depending on whether we look at *The Hobbit*/*Lord of the Rings* (more subtle) or *The Silmarillion* (less subtle). Tolkien's predecessors (ex. E.R. Eddison and Robert E. Howard) and contemporaries (ex. Clark Ashton Smith, Fritz Leiber, and C.S. Lewis) in the genres used religion in more subtle (Leiber, often) and overt (Howard, Lewis) ways. The presence of religion is so pervasive that it is found in nearly all secondary world fantasies and in many UF/PNR worlds including the works of Cassandra Clare, Ilona Andrews, Rick Riordan, and Faith Hunter. Thanks, in large part, to D&D, a "loose pantheon" of deities associated with "various aspects of existence" is common in the fantasy genre, as opposed to a "tight pantheon" or a single religion or mystery cults (though these certainly crop up in adventures).[1] The inclusion of religion, especially in secondary fantasy, seems to be a virtual requirement, but is not. An exception is Travis Baldree's *Legends & Lattes* that ignores religions (though they may exist in the world, they are not visible in the narrative). However, if any religion is included in a society, certain choices should be made early in the development.

How Many?

The most important choice is to determine the number of faiths in the world/society. This affects the influence and role of faith in a given society as well as the number and, potentially, type of deity or deities. Many fictional societies have a single faith—ex. Middle Earth, Narnia, arguably the Forgotten Realms—making for a relatively simple build, even if a pantheon is involved. Other societies have two or more faiths that exist in the same space—ex. Krynn (Dragonlance; *The Chronicles* present two),

Westeros, Sanctuary (*Thieves' World*), Liavek, and post-Shift Atlanta (Andrews). The latter creates interactions and potential conflicts between faiths and the cultures that spawn them. It also creates some difficulty and complexity in the building of the world/society as interactions between the faiths, the faithful, and the deities become important and need to be developed. Obviously, more religions means there is more to build and formulate. However, more religions also gives a great deal of room to play with ideas, add conflict, and add depth to the world and society. To some degree, multiple religions adds a level of suspension of disbelief as well due to the multitude of religions existing in our own world,[2] including sects of religions as separate faiths. Religions might be monotheistic, dualist, polytheistic, animist, or species specific.[3] They could be totemist, shamanic, atheistic, agnostic, Maltheist, or involve ancestor worship. Polytheists may worship family gods, court gods, opposing gods, freeform pantheons, and satellite pantheons spawned by a core pantheon.[4] They could be popular religions, folk religions, or organized.[5] It is important to note that even within a pantheon, individuals may choose to follow a single deity as their patron, while worshipping all the other gods in a potentially more casual way.[6]

How Much Detail?

Perhaps the next most important choice is the level of detail to use in developing the religion(s) in the society. That is, should the religion(s) be sketched out in broad terms or created in great detail, or somewhere in between?

At the very least, a name and list of deities (or deity) with areas of influence associated with the individual is good. Maybe brief bullet points regarding the clergy or social influence, if those are or might be important for their use. This brief sketch is probably enough if the religions are not important for play or storylines in the society, at least at the point of creation.

If the religion is going to be important or may be central to a plotline, then more detail is probably necessary. This could be detail in the form of developing one or two deities in a pantheon (ex. Rikiki in Liavek, who is central to several story plots). Development could take the form of detailing the clergy (ex. the Red Priests in Westeros). It could be detailing the nature of divinity (ex. the gods of Dragaera). Detail could also be outlining the relationships between the deities of a pantheon (ex. Dragonlance).

Regardless, the level of detail depends heavily on the role of the religion in the world, society, and/or story. If the role of the religion(s) or god(s) is central, then more detail is needed (ex. The Forgotten Realms'

Avatar trilogy). If the role is mere background, or secondary, then less detail is required (ex. *The Lord of the Rings*).

Using Real Religions

In the urban fantasy and paranormal romance genres, it is entirely possible to use real religions, in fact both genres are likely to do so for verisimilitude, if religions are used at all. This is particularly helpful because every religion in our world has its own magical traditions. They also all have legends/myths of beings from golems to centaurs, angels to demons. Some UF/PNR authors who have mined real religions include Rick Riordan (ancient Greek, Roman, Norse, and Egyptian, as well as Islam), Cassandra Clare (Christianity), and Ilona Andrews (*Kate Daniels*—Christianity, Islam, Judaism, Norse, Slavic, Greek, Wiccan, and others). To a lesser degree, secondary fantasy worlds have had some use of real religions, notably in C.S. Lewis's Narnia—a metaphorical Christianity that becomes more heavy handed in *The Last Battle*.

In secondary world fantasy, real religions are more commonly used as inspiration rather than directly inserted into the world/society. This is, in many ways, probably a safer method to use, but it is still important to use reliable, credible research and more or less accurate representations, with conscious changes to fit the world. For instance, Tolkien's Middle Earth involves Christian allegory as the Istari (Wizards) are essentially angels and Sauron is a stand in for the fallen angel Lucifer. In a different vein, Ausma Zehanat Khan uses a fictionalized Islam in *The Khorasan Archives*. Taking inspiration from real religions is certainly easier than trying to force a real religion into a secondary world. When real faiths have been brought into secondary worlds in the past, they have typically taken the form of portal fantasies[7] (ex. Lewis or GURPS's Yrth setting). In that way, the secondary world is connected to Earth (primary world) with an assumed inter-weaving and influence to one degree or another.

Deities

A key requirement of almost all religions is the presence of one or more deities, depending.[8] In the fantasy genres, the tendency is toward pantheistic religions, but monotheistic are a close second. For example, Kevin Hearne's *The Seven Kennings*, Martin's *ASoIaF*, Andrews's *Kate Daniels*, Brust's Dragaera, Bardugo's Grishaverse, and the Forgotten Realms are all good examples of settings with pantheistic religions.

Monotheism is a component of Bardugo's Grishaverse, Martin's *ASoIaF*, Clare's *Mortal Instruments*, Harris's *Southern Vampire Mysteries*, and Andrews's *Kate Daniels*. Regardless of how many there are, if deities exist in the society and world, then they need to be created, named, and, potentially, developed. Development could include their origins, number, archetypes, symbols, relationships, avatars, demigods, and servants (messengers, temple guardians).[9] There may even be rankings of deities, such as greater, lesser, demigods, and vestiges (former deities),[10] or elder, younger, or primordial and so on.

Purpose and Role of Deities

If deities exist in the world/society, we need to ask why. Why are they? What role or purpose do they serve in the world? Do they set the world in motion? Do they lead to plots? Do they disappear into the background? Do they protect the world?

The purpose or role of deities takes us back to, or needs to be built on, the nature of divinity in the world. At the root is the question: do deities actually exist, or are they non-beings? If they do not exist, then we need to determine what purpose they serve. They may serve as incorporeal ideals. Perhaps they are ephemeral enforcers of societal rules and mores created by the clergy. Maybe they are simply characters in morality tales or creation myths with no other substance. It is also possible that the people and the clergy are unsure whether the deities exist or not. Their existence may be the subject of debate, philosophical or otherwise.

If the deities are indeed real within the fictitious world and society, then other questions arise. For instance, do they predate creation or were they created by something/one else? For what purpose did they come into being? They may exist to embody or create things (ex. the gods of ancient Greece), to protect the world/creation from an outside threat (ex. the gods of Dragaera), or they may exist to study "lesser" beings. They could also be deities, but not as we understand the term. For example, the deities of Steven Brust's Dragaera exist to protect the world (a task they took upon themselves after freeing themselves from servitude to the Jenoine). Their nature is that they are formerly mortal beings of great skill and power who are able to exist in multiple places at once but are not beholden to an external force (e.g., they are gods, but not as we generally understand and use the term). Alternately, deities could be powerful spirits, aliens, shape-shifters, or even immortal magicians (the last being the case in Bardugo's Grishaverse).

As part of purpose, what deities exist and how they came into being is important. Many real-world cultures have origin stories for the deities—ex.

Greco-Roman gods, born of titans, children of the first twelve gods, or mortals raised to godhood; Norse gods, both the Vanir and the Aesir (once warring clans of gods) seem to have been born of an earlier generation, the origins of which are unclear. Comparatively, some Chinese deities appear to be inherent to the world, while others seem to have been granted divine status for their great deeds or accomplishments. The former is the setup used by Tolkien and Ed Greenwood (The Forgotten Realms), as a single over-god is seen creating the pantheon of "lesser" divinities that in turn create mortal beings. These over-gods seem to take little involvement in the world they created, leaving meddling with mortals to their children.

Activity

The level of divine activity in the world, whether the deities are involved in the world or leave it to its own devices, affects the character of both the world and its societies. A world in which deities are directly active with some degree of regularity, whether through physical manifestations in the world, avatars, or regular spiritual appearances (audio-visual or in dreams) is going to have a rather different character than one in which the deities act only through their clergy. And both will be very different from a world in which the gods play no active role at all. Usually, there are three common options: Active (Direct), Active (Indirect), and Inactive. There can, of course, be variations and variable degrees of all three. Some settings move between two or more, for example in Narnia, Aslan[11] is active both directly (*The Lion, The Witch, and The Wardrobe*) and indirectly (most of the other books, where he acts through the Pevensies and others).

If the deities are directly active in the world, they often move openly, sometimes in disguise (as the Greek gods and Odin were said to do), in the world and societies becoming involved in the history and events of the societies. There are, therefore, no doubts about the existence of the gods, though they may choose to appear to only some members of society or to everyone, depending on the nature of divinity, any divine rules, and individual personalities. This often yields world-shaking events. Therefore, direct activity among the gods should be chosen carefully, as it can easily cause the society and world to be difficult to control, unless the gods are limited or bound in some way. Good examples of directly active deities include Brust's Dragaera (in which a few gods take direct action, albeit only in extreme cases), *The Forgotten Realms* (at least in the *Avatar Trilogy*, in which the gods are cast out of the godhome and sent to live among mortals), and Max Gladstone's *Craft Sequence* (in which the gods take up residence in different cities, sort of).

Settings in which the deities take indirect action are much more common. In these cases, the gods may take an active role in the world, but hide their actions behind chance, fortune, and the actions of mortals. Their influence is kept hidden, so their existence itself is potentially questionable. Even so, their clergy will often make claims of direct divine involvement, in order to secure their positions and influence (from a cynical perspective) or to maintain the glory of their god. Some good examples here include Tolkien's Middle Earth, Weis and Hickman's *Dragonlance* (in which the gods are, possibly, unable to act directly against each other, but can through mortal agents), Rick Riordan's body of work (in which the gods act through their half-human children or other heroes), and Bardugo's Grishaverse (in which the Ravkan saints largely seem to be acting indirectly, usually). In the Discworld, the gods appear in the narrative, but never to mortals in the world, although they are seen acting through games and unwitting agents, except in the case of Om (*Small Gods*).

Inactive deities do not get involved in the affairs of the world or society. They leave the world and mortals to their own devices. Because they are inactive, the question of whether the gods actually exist is open and debatable, with no clear divine action anywhere in the world or society, only the word of the clergy, to go by. Such settings are less common, among secondary world fantasies (though common in UF/PNR), but some clear examples exist: Kevin Hearne's *The Seven Kennings* appears to have inactive deities, beyond the tests by which individuals are granted "magic," assuming the gods are indeed choosing who succeeds and who fails, and Bardugo's Grishaverse in the form of Ghezen (in Kerch), the saints (in Ravka), and Djel (in Fjerda), none of whom are definitively active in the world.

Myths

Inextricable from religion, myths account for the creation of the world, the creation or early days of the deities, the foundations of society, and even socio-cultural practices. These stories often begin as oral tales passed from religious figures or societal elders to other members of the society. They may have begun as tales of heroic or important people who did great things in the earliest days of the society, or the prior society that the current one evolved from. Myths may be basically the same throughout a region that the religion encompasses, but are likely to have local and regional variations, even within the same nation or culture. These variations may be introduced by traveling storytellers including the local ancestors, by different priorities in a given region, or even consciously on the part of local clergy to better position their temple/church or to support a local patron deity.

Most, but not all, religions include some kind of creation myth, often there will be more than one creation story. In the case of multiples, they may compete or be complementary, or they may compete yet both be considered true at the same time. Multiple versions may occur due to changing times or an evolving society. They could also come from the adoption or conquest of or by other cultures or trade and other forms of contact. For example, the ancient Greeks adopted Persian gods and Rome adopted the gods of every society they conquered. Sometimes, creation myths stack upon or build upon each other, especially if the deities involved destroy and remake the world once or more, as happens in ancient Greek myths and the Abrahamic creation myths. Most secondary world fantasies include this sort of myth, whether in Middle-Earth (*The Silmarillion*), the Grishaverse ("the making at the heart of the world"), *The Forgotten Realms*, *Dragonlance*, Lewis's Narnia (*The Magician's Nephew*), or the Elder Scrolls/Skyrim world (creation of Mundus).

Myths may also cover the early days of the gods. This is often used to establish relationships between deities (ex. ancient Greek myth with divine lineages) or to set in motion world conflicts (ex. Egyptian mythology, that also sets relationships; Norse mythology, that sets up the Vanir, Aesir, and Jotun with their relationships and conflicts). Such myths also exist in secondary fantasy worlds, such as Middle-Earth (*The Silmarillion*) and Krynn (*Dragonlance*; ex. the story of the Greygem).

A society's religious myths also involve the creation or founding of the society itself. This divine creation is used to provide divine right or provenance to the society and its rulers. Leaders are often anointed in temples or chapels to reinforce this divine right, as in England (Westminster Abbey), Mesopotamia, and Egypt, or, for a secondary world, the Grishaverse's Ravka and Fjerda. Primary world examples of divine foundation include Rome (via Romulus and Remus or through the Trojan prince Aeneas, descendant of Aphrodite), Athens (through a myth about the competition between Athena and Poseidon to be patron god of the city), and China (via the divine first emperor).

Myths may also create or support various socio-cultural practices. The stories tell why the practice was adopted or why it continues to be performed. For example, ancient Greece had stories of gods traveling the countryside in human form. Those who took them in and provided hospitality were rewarded (Baucis and Philemon) while those who broke the rules of hospitality and the gods were punished (Lycaon). These myths gave the reason for cultural hospitality practices, because one never knew if the poor traveler they met was really a poor traveler or a god in disguise.

Spheres of Influence

A deity's sphere of influence is basically the area(s) or thing(s) associated with the deity, such as the god of death. Depending on the world, society, and faith, there could be a single area per deity or each deity may be responsible for multiple areas of life. For example, Demeter was the goddess of agriculture but Athena was the goddess of wisdom, war, peace, and crafts (such as weaving and spinning). There may also be areas that are represented by multiple deities, ex. Athena was responsible for honorable war while Ares was the god of violence and the brutality of war. In the cases where a deity has multiple spheres of influence, they could occur due to absorbing other, often minor, deities. For instance, Athena became the goddess of war, absorbing Pallas's area, after accidentally killing Pallas. In any case, if multiple areas are present under a single deity, the combination should be logical to the society in question. A good example is Inanna (Mesopotamia), who was a goddess of love, beauty, sex, war, justice, political power, and fertility. She was also, probably, a hybrid of a few different regional deities.

For a list of sample spheres of influence, see Appendix A.

Clergy

Once deities are determined, they need worshippers. That introduces the question of whether there is a specific class of people who lead worship services and speak with other mortals on behalf of the gods, e.g., clergy. If a religion is organized, there is going to be some form of clergy whether they are called priests, ministers, clerics, druids (although this one is culture specific), hieromonks (priest-monks), or any other title. In some settings (such as D&D), the clergy might include paladins.[12] In some cases, deities who cover multiple spheres of influence may have specialized clergy who could be at odds over the "true" worship of the deity.[13] Monks and related religious orders are also possible, but typically exist outside the hierarchy of clergy, so will be discussed later. The organization and hierarchies of the clergy are part of the next section. Here, the focus is on who can join the ranks, how they join and train (recruitment), and what they look like (vestments) and do (duties, rituals, magic).[14]

Who Is Allowed?

In most cases, the presence of deities means the presence of clergy. We see this throughout the fantasy genres from the TSR/WotC worlds

4. Religion

to Katherine Kurtz's *Deryni*, Martin's Westeros to Bardugo's Grishaverse, and shared world settings such as *Thieves' World* and *Liavek*. In some rare cases, there are either no clergy, or only occasional clergy (part-time). For instance, Hearne's *The Seven Kennings* has visible clergy in few nations (Hathrir has the only definitive clergy in the first two books). In Brust's Dragaera, there are no priests as such among the Dragaerans, although the Issola occasionally fill a similar function in that part of their duty is to know of the gods, while the Easterners have many priests.

So, if gods, or at least religion, exist(s) and clergy exist, who is allowed to join the ranks of the clergy? Every religion, possibly every sect, is going to be different. The requirements for joining are affected by the deity, the religious organization, and the society involved. Some may only allow one sex or gender or have separate roles for each sex or gender. Some may accept only one species as clergy—say an elven god may only allow elven clergy. Some may require magical talent or ability. Others may require social status. Still others may seek specific character traits aligned with the deity, at least ostensibly. Depending on the society, clerical positions could be elected or appointed positions that one holds for a set length of time (as in ancient Rome) or hereditary, rather than a divine calling. Further, entry into the ranks of the clergy may be limited to only those the deity specifically chooses through visions, signs, or powers (granted, in theory, by the deity). Of course, if the existence of the gods is debatable, there may also be those who claim that they have received visions, visitations, and powers, usually with inactive or non-existent gods as active deities are not likely to approve unless they are distracted.

How Can I Join?

Once we know who can join the clergy, this begs the question of how they join. Most religions have some sort of process to transition from laity to clergy, often involving a transition ritual.[15] Methods of joining range from being born into the proper class/caste, being elected/appointed, experiencing visions, education, and undertaking a quest.

Possibly the simplest methods of becoming clergy are being born into a clerical class/caste, for hereditary clergy, or being elected/appointed, for societies in which clergy roles are civic roles. In the latter case, religious and secular life are often not divided from each other in any clear way. Both methods are still likely to have an investment ceremony, whether public or private, in which the role and rights of the clergy are granted to the person. Hereditary clergy also often have an educational component, but one that begins very young and possibly within the family. In hereditary cases, the investment ceremony may also be a coming-of-age ceremony, as the individual becomes both a cleric and an adult.

A common method in different parts of history was the experience of visions, signs, powers, or other symbols of divine favor. Such factors were/are not necessarily limited to official clergy, though, and the difficult part is proving the claim. Proof is especially problematic if the individual preaches in opposition to an established and entrenched religious hierarchy. Most religious organizations will look askance at or dismiss, at best, or repudiate and seek to destroy, at worst, anyone outside the hierarchy who claims a direct conduit to the divine if their words contradict the organization. Those who claim to receive visions and support the organization tend to be absorbed, possibly to control them. A potential real-world example is Tibetan Buddhism, in which the Dalai Lama is determined through a process in which the candidate chooses the correct possessions of the former Dalai Lama (e.g., a past life), as a sign that they may be the reincarnated Dalai Lama. There may or may not be an investment ritual in these cases. The existence of a ritual depends on the religion, the organization, the society, and whether the claims are proven or accepted by the religious authorities.

Easily the most common method of joining the clergy is being educated at the feet of the current clergy. The length of education can be as short or long as the organization desires. In some cases, education may take mere weeks, in other cases decades. For practical purposes, months to years seems most common. That said, different layers of the religious hierarchy may require more or fewer years of training, depending on the rites, rituals, theology, and required knowledge among the religious organization and faith. In modern terms, many Christian ministers and priests hold an undergraduate degree (bachelors), often in theology or religious studies, some hold a graduate degree in the same field or a Doctor of Divinity degree. Some sects require or recommend training in non-theological areas—for example, the current Catholic Pope, Francis, studied the humanities (specifically philosophy, literature, and psychology) as a Jesuit novice. Typically, the education method will culminate with an investment ceremony, often public to show the community and share or celebrate the new ordination.

Some religions may require that the initiate/novice undergo a quest to become a full member of the clergy. This could be a physical quest—ex. to retrieve something, make a pilgrimage to a holy site—a service quest—ex. to help the impoverished, to transport a sacred text to a new shrine—or a spiritual one—ex. a vision quest. Regardless of the type of quest, the result is generally either a physical one (a sign of completion, perhaps a mark such as a third eye or an injury) or a notable change in the individual (awareness, personality shift). Depending on the deity, religion, and society, failing the quest may prove lethal. The quest itself may serve as the investment ritual, or it might be followed by one, depending on the religion and its tenets.

Education

The education of clergy varies widely based on culture, society, and religion. Some faiths have little to no formal education or training, as is often the case where the deity chooses the clergy via visions and signs or where there is no religious organization in place. Others may require decades of learning—from reading, writing, and basic math to philosophy, the sciences, and theology—from a young age. A few of the more common methods—apprenticeship, formal education, and divine learning—are discussed below as examples, but are by no means the only options available.

Training by apprenticeship is most likely to happen in a less organized religion, though it is possible as a prelude to formal education in an organized one. Sometimes, apprenticeship may be a quick alternative in a highly organized religion that needs an influx of clergy quickly, for instance if the clergy has been devastated by plague or warfare. The length of apprenticeship could range from mere months to years, depending on the faith and the need. In this method, potential clerics train under an established member of the clergy. Often they learn the rites, rituals, and ways to petition or redirect the attention of the deity. They may learn other skills such as counselling, medicine, performance, or music, depending on the role of the religion in society and the nature of the religion. Some might learn the basics of magic, if divine magic exists or if the clergy use non-divine magic. Depending on the context, the instructor, and the religion, meditation might be part of their apprenticeship as well. A good example of this method is M.H. Boroson's *Daoshi Chronicles*, in which the protagonist is taught the proper rites, rituals, and magic by her father.

A formal education for clergy is most likely with organized religions, possibly with layers from potential to novice to acolyte all the way to the top ranks of the hierarchy. In these cases, the religion may operate formal schools or have potential clergy serve in lesser roles among temple clergy. In either case, they are likely to learn the rites, rituals, cosmology, theoretical theology, the faith's hierarchy and internal social structure, and the faith's philosophy (including the nature of divinity). They might learn about other deities in a pantheon or other religions in the society to some degree, depending on the deity in question. As with apprenticeships, formally instructed clergy will also learn other skills related to the deity's specialties, if any, and the religion's role in society, or their role in the religion. They may also be instructed in magic, science (as medieval Christian monks often were), meditation, or even martial practices.

Divine tutelage only works in societies with active gods. It is also probably the rarest, because the deity chooses to train the clergy itself. Because of this, the faith will likely have a small body of clerics, but this depends on the nature of the divine and how much divine attention can be split. What is covered in training is entirely up to the deity and its whims or wishes. It is also possible that no two clerics are taught the same, depending on the deity, its whims, and its evolution, if any. Much as martial and other instructors often alter their focus and training methods over decades of teaching, so might the deity evolve, focusing on one aspect or on aggressive expansion of the faith in its youth then becoming more sedate, settled, and complacent centuries later.

Vestments

Once training is complete and the cleric is invested or ordained, how do they stand out from other worshippers? Their placement in a temple or church during services is one way, but what about beyond the site of worship? Many religions have special clothing for their clergy, at least during services or in official roles. More often than not, this takes the form of vestments. For example, Catholic priests wear black clothing and a white collar, plus more ornate robes while officiating; in many sects Buddhist monks don saffron colored or black robes; and the fictitious clergy of R'hllor (*ASoIaF*) are always clad in red. In each case, the clothing acts as a symbol not only of the cleric's separation from the normal but of their service to the deity and of the deity itself. The Red Priests wear red to represent R'hllor's fire. The clothes serve a purpose beyond simply standing out. They usually incorporate the deity's symbol(s) and reflect the deity's views or sphere of influence. For instance, a priest dedicated to Dionysius will not be clad in armor, that does not fit with the god of wine; conversely a priest dedicated to Ares would be expected to be outfitted with armor and weapons to serve on the battlefield as befits the god of war. Some divinities may go further and use more permanent marks to show their clergy. Tattooing, branding, or scarification may be part of an investment ritual, to literally mark the new cleric. In other cases, a divine mark may appear on the new cleric through mystical means, presumably placed by the deity itself.

Rituals

Once invested, what do the clergy in this religion do? Do they perform services? If so, how regularly? Do they attend births, naming ceremonies, marriages, deaths, and funerals? How? What do they do during these ceremonies? Where do services take place and how often? What holy days and festivals do they officiate at and how? Are there any cultural superstitions about members of the religion officiating at any given ceremony? For example, Ilona Andrews's *Kate Daniels* series includes priests of the Slavic gods Belobog and Chernobog (twin gods of sun/life and night/death respectively); asking the priests of Chernobog to officiate a wedding is a distinct oddity that is rarely, if ever, done due to the symbolism of the god of death officiating a wedding.

In any case, if the religion is organized, then different ranks of clergy will probably perform different ceremonies or will do so at different times. As an example, typically Catholic monks do not lead lay services or sacraments (because they are not ordained priests), the senior priest in a parish (the pastor) may take the "bigger" masses (Sunday, holidays) while junior priests perform the morning or evening services on weekdays, that are less attended, and both pastors and junior priests will hear confessions depending on who is available.

Organization

Religious organization is deeply tied to who and how people join the clergy as well as how the clergy are trained, if at all. Organization is also connected to whether the religion has consistency, and even geographic range, as well as what, if any, hierarchy exists. The organization, or lack thereof, can also determine what is considered canon, e.g., part of the faith's accepted beliefs or practices, and what is not, e.g., what is heretical or forbidden.

Organized or Not

The decision about whether the religion is organized or not determines a host of aspects of the faith and the very feel of the faith in the world/society. To that end, we will look at three broad gradations of organization: unorganized, somewhat organized, and organized.

Unorganized religions tend to be regional or smaller in spread and scope. Communications technology may alter this, to a great degree, as seen with the spread of disorganized, reconstructionist, "pagan" religions in our own world aided by increasing access to the internet. Typically each cleric has their own take on the faith and their own views, rites, and decisions about the deity and new clergy. In short, the clergy have essentially unlimited freedom, only restricted by what both the society and the deity (if one exists) will allow. Unorganized religions will have no hierarchy beyond local or regional clerics and their trainees. There is no religious authority to hold clergy accountable or to support the clergy. Unorganized religions will also typically be limited in resources and protection from "secular" authorities, if secular and religious life is separated. An exception may be found in a number of Paleolithic and related cultures, in which unorganized religious practices seem to have spread surprisingly far and clergy may have wielded a fair bit of influence and power over the non-religious authorities (through advising, supposed powers over the world, and/or anointment of leaders).

In somewhat organized religions, the clergy are largely on their own with no central authority. However, they likely have schools of thought and practice as well as mentors and notable leaders respected by many in the faith. The clergy may be largely autonomous, but also meet with each other regularly to discuss matters of faith and the religion. In these cases, it is likely that there will be some degree of standardization, possibly beholden to other clergy and followers of the faith. Often, a singular holy text may be at the core of the religion, providing a standard core for all clergy. In our own world, Islam, Judaism, and most branches of Buddhism seem to be good examples in that they have no central authority and little to no hierarchy, but do have some broadly agreed upon standard practices and texts. Different schools of clergy (imams, rabbis, abbots/monks) exist in all three as well, each with their own political, theological, or philosophical interpretations of the core beliefs and/or texts.

Most organized religions present clergy with some form of central authority—ex. a pope, ecumenical patriarch—religious/theological standards, and protection from secular authorities. There are core decisions that have been made about accepted texts and interpretations of said texts, even if debate continues. The central authority's decisions are effectively law, in most cases. Set standards include clerical attire and vestments, rites, rituals, practices, and membership. Often there is a hierarchy or layers of clergy. Catholicism is a good example, beginning with lay deacons to priests, pastors, bishops, archbishops, cardinals, and popes (with monks, abbots, and other leaders of religious orders forming a sort of side hierarchy outside the main line). The organization as a whole provides oversight of clergy, protection from outsiders, guidance, support (political, financial, spiritual), and resources. However, the organization also expects respect for its authority and usually commands and tells individual clergy where they are to be stationed and minister.

Sects

In time, organized religions, even somewhat organized ones, tend to form offshoots, or sects. Often sects form due to doctrinal differences or differing interpretations of scripture. Sometimes there are issues with succession in the hierarchy, or the idea of hierarchy itself. Other sects may form due to regional differences, perhaps focusing on different aspects of a deity, or the relationship between the deity and the people. The formation of sects generally seems to lead to a conflict. Such conflicts may be socio-political or military in nature accompanied by declarations of heresy depending on the nature of the religion and its place in society (ex. the history of Christianity's Protestant Reformation or the division between Sunni and Shiite Muslims). Other times, the sects may form and exist more or less peacefully (as in Buddhist history).

When doctrinal or textual interpretation differences cause division, the offshoot sects tend to believe marginally to greatly different things about the deity (or deities), texts, and faith.[16] The "mainstream" may continue unaltered, while offshoot sects form around it, with varying degrees of tension and conflict in the process. There could be official splits made by different councils of clergy or they could be organic splits that have their roots in individual or local worship and leaders. Sometimes the latter gain momentum and spread across the entire geographic range of the faith, often beyond the control of those who started them (ex. the Reformation in Christianity).

Questions of hierarchy and inheritance of authority can cause significant sect splits. In these cases, the rival groups disagree about who should lead the faith (ex. Sunni v. Shiite), where the seat of leadership is located (ex. the Catholic v. Coptic popes and the Greek, Russian, Ukrainian, and Eastern Orthodox ecumenical patriarchs), or even if there should be a hierarchy at all (ex. the Reformation). In secondary worlds, the question of whether primacy of authority should be held within a given temple or site—say where a deity appeared or an avatar sits—could divide a faith into sects.

Regional differences may be an organic and non-confrontational method of creating sects, especially if communications are relatively slow and the religion stretches into remote areas. These differences in practices, worship, and leaders could create different branches of the religion, as happened between Ireland and mainland Catholicism between the fall of Rome and most of the medieval era. Even the relationships between the leaders of the religion and the local rulers of secular society could impact sect formation, leading to enough changes that the sect counts as sufficiently different.[17]

As temples or churches focus on different aspects of a deity, they may divide enough to be considered sects. This could also be applied to the position or existence of other near-divine beings (ex. angels, saints). For instance, the Mesopotamian deity Ishtar was a goddess of love, desire, fertility, leadership, and war. One temple-sect may focus on her war aspect, perhaps due to its location on the border with another state with which regular conflict occurs. Another temple, perhaps closer to the center of power, focuses on her aspects of love and desire, emphasizing those traits of the goddess in their ceremonies, rites, and preaching.

Views of the relationship between deity and worshippers may be another cause for schism and sect formation. Offshoots may spin off due to discussions of how the deity relates to its people, or how it actually interacts with them if the god does exist and is active. On one hand, an organized religion may say that the clergy are needed to intercede or be a conduit between the deity and the average worshipper. Another sect may claim that the average worshipper can contact the deity directly, without the intercessor priest, that there is a direct line between the deity and worshipper. Such interactions can become more complicated, and create more sects, if there is an active deity and/or the presence of avatars (and false avatars) in the world and society.

Places

The level and type of organization may also affect the places associated with the religion. Unorganized religions typically have fewer and smaller places, perhaps more natural sites. Comparatively, somewhat to fully organized religions will typically have more and possibly larger sites, such as the Hagia Sophia, the Vatican, or the Temple Mount. Exceptions, as always, occur, such as in the case of many branches of Daoism, where most places of the faith are monastic-temples or natural places (ex. the Nine Sacred Mountains). Three of the more common—natural sites, shrines, and temples—will be discussed here.

Most religions, regardless of how organized they are, have natural places that they claim as sacred. These may include springs, wells, streams, caves, groves, hills, rocks, even entire mountains said to be associated with a specific deity, saint, prophet, or other figure of devotion. Such sites often become pilgrimage destinations for the faithful or those seeking penance for wrongdoing. The site might also be said to have certain powers—usually prophecy (ex. the Temple of Apollo at Delphi) or healing (ex. St. Brigid's Well in County Kildare, Ireland)—tied to the deity or figure. Often the clergy will build a shrine or temple on or near the site, to hold services, receive pilgrims, protect, and control access to the site. A site could be tied to a given figure as the place of their birth (Delos for Apollo), their death (a Catholic saint), a divine visitation (the Dome of the Rock), or the performance of miracles (most healing wells).

A shrine is a small place of worship. It may be maintained by a clergy person, if it is large or important enough. Alternately, a dedicated lay person or simply the local residents may be responsible for maintenance, in many cases. Shrines may have itinerant clerics who visit on a circuit of shrines, or no cleric at all. They can range in size from a small roadside altar to an alcove to a small building that a few people can attend at once. In some cases, all three may be combined. Shrines may be set up in remote areas not frequented by clergy. They might also be set up in a city neighborhood, to see to the community's needs. This is especially likely if the city has a "temple district" for large places of worship or has poor communities that do not rate their own temples or churches. Personal and family shrines may also be set up within a home, for use by the residents and guests; some such shrines might be sanctified by a cleric or not depending on the faith, society, and availability of clergy.

Temples (or churches, mosques, synagogues, meetinghouses) could range from a village temple that sees a priest once a month to the Vatican or Masjid al-Haram. Often temples are host to at least one itinerant cleric, up to hundreds or possibly thousands of clergy (mostly in administrative roles) for large organizations. The latter are likely to be central or otherwise highly important temples in the faith. Most will fall somewhere in between. The architecture and appearance will likely vary by location and local resources, but should have some typical features based on the religion and deity—ex. a deity of trade and commerce probably will not have shields and swords in its temple artwork, but will very likely have representations of currency and wealth throughout. For architecture, most, if not all, Christian churches of the medieval era were built in the shape of crosses with standardized uses for each of the four arms and the center.

Monastics

Beyond the clergy and the organization of the religion, there may be those who exist outside the hierarchy and system. These individuals exist somewhere between clergy and laity, no longer laypersons, but not ordained as clergy: monastics (monks and nuns). Not all religions will have such people (ex. Protestant Christianity), and some religions will substitute monastics, or semi-monastics, for clergy (ex. Buddhism). In other cases, both will exist side by side, but perhaps with different roles and structures (ex. Catholicism).

If monastic orders exist in a faith, they are likely to come in a variety of types: service, meditating, learning, and militant. Many monastic orders will mix two or more of these types and add others. Any monastic order's types and goals will depend on the religion they represent, the deity they follow, and the founding purpose of the order. For example, Christian monastic orders have several sets of practices called Rules (ex. Benedictine Rule) and follow certain daily schedules of activity, prayer, meditation, and work. Each order (ex. Benedictine, Franciscan, Dominican) adds its own requirements and practices to a base set of rules. To look at another faith, Zen Buddhist monks are different in outlook and practices than Tibetan monks, and both are different from other Buddhist orders/branches.

Some orders of monastics are focused on service to the community, whether that community is the monastic community, the wider religious community, or their geographic community. Often this means performing good works among others. Most also work within the monastic community, in the past this traditionally meant anything ranging from farming to woodworking, copying manuscripts to cooking.

Some orders devote themselves to meditation and seeking to attain enlightenment. In theory, this means that they spend most of their time sequestered from others and engaged in group or solo meditation. Most will also spend a certain amount of time performing the necessary work of maintaining the monastic community (e.g., raising food, cleaning, maintenance), often as a form of meditative work. This type of monastic fits the stereotypical view of Buddhist and Catholic monks that we commonly see in photos and documentaries.

Other orders may be engaged in learning and sciences, as many monks were during Europe's Middle Ages. In the case of those monks, they spent time praying and working, but part of their work involved copying, and often commenting on or expanding, scientific, philosophical, and other manuscripts, including occasionally translating Arabic and other texts into Latin or the local vernacular. Such monks studied, preserved, and advanced the sciences, as well as founding schools such as some of those that became components of Oxford and Cambridge Universities.[18]

Monastics may also be martial in nature or practices. Perhaps they use martial practices to meditate, combining mind and body. The order may have been created to protect a specific place or pilgrims, or to otherwise serve lay members of the faith through martial means. Martial monks would certainly not be out of place in service to a deity of war, but are not limited to such cases. For instance, the Shaolin monks use(d) martial arts as a form of meditation, and historically may have patrolled certain roads to keep them free of outlaws. Likewise, The Poor Fellow-Soldiers of Christ and of the Temple of Solomon (Knights Templar) and The Order of

Knights of the Hospital of Saint John of Jerusalem (Knights Hospitaller)[19] were founded as orders of knight-monks, the former to protect pilgrims traveling to Jerusalem while the latter was charged with protecting and caring for "the Holy Land" as a whole.

Lay Organizations

In addition to clerical and monastic orders, it is also possible for a religion to form official groups of non-clergy. Most of these exist to advance the religion's goals and to serve the faithful in various ways. In our own world, among the most famous such organizations are the Knights of Columbus and the Knights of Malta; both are Catholic Christian and focused on service (refugee relief) and political (opposition to same-sex marriage and abortion) activities. The Sovereign Order of Malta also exists as a sovereign entity with diplomatic relations to various countries and the UN, focused on humanitarian service. The presence of such groups depends on the deity, organization of the religion, and the role of the religion in society. Typically, they exist outside the religious hierarchy, but may or may not be officially recognized and supported by religious leaders.

Most such organizations are service focused. The lay orders of a religion often spend their time devoted to service to the faithful or anyone in general. They may specialize in certain types of service, ex. relief or medical. Some might be quasi-monastic, performing spiritual service, among other possibilities depending on the deity and the nature of the religion.

Lay organizations could also be militant in nature, such as orders of knighthood (ex. The Order of Malta, technically)[20] or non-knight, possibly untrained or barely trained, militants (*ASoIaF*'s faith militant in Westeros) devoted to spreading the faith and protecting sacred sites. Some exist to defend the faithful, or pilgrims, among other purposes. Militant lay organizations are potentially present in all cases, but especially so with war, guardian, and related deities.

Many lay groups will combine types and roles. For example, the Order of Malta performs humanitarian relief but maintains a Military Corps (in the Italian Army) and logistics (running a 28-car, 192-bed medical facility on a hospital train in Europe).

Role in Society

To return to the core of this book, we should ask what role the religion plays in our fictitious society. On a related note, we can ask how much, and what, influence the religion has in society. There are, of course, a variety of levels and layers to both questions from the presence of official state religions (the UK, Denmark) to theocratic states (the Vatican, sometimes Iran). There are societies in which clergy hold or held public office to ones where they are banned from office to societies where clergy and religions are, officially at least, banned entirely.

Popularity and Respect

The question of a religion's popularity is more than just how widespread it is. A state religion may be widespread, but deeply unpopular due to excesses or repressive actions. Meanwhile, a religion that is technically illicit may be quite popular among the populace due to performing acts of service for the public. Popularity may also vary by socio-economic class, profession, gender, sex, even species. This sort of popularity could be an indicator of influence at different levels of society. For instance, the religion at least nominally followed by the nobles may wield significant political influence, but a religion that is popular among the masses may also wield political influence, as well as social, due to sheer numbers. The legality of a religion in a given society will also influence its popularity, either directly (reducing popularity) or inversely (increasing its popularity) depending on why it is (il-)legal, and thus its influence on society.

Respect for the religion also becomes a factor of influence. If people respect a religion's positions, clergy, and actions, they are more likely to support it. This is true even if they do not practice or follow that religion.[21] Conversely, if the public has little to no respect for a religion, it loses influence (ex. Scientology). As with popularity, respect is not necessarily tied to the legality or official standing of the religion or deity. More often, respect for a religion is connected to its actions as an organization of people in society or its teachings and how closely its clergy follow its teachings. Sometimes "respect" for a religion is a matter of inertia and social pressures, as a tenth generation nominal practitioner may not feel comfortable with, or may suffer social consequences from, declaring their lack of faith/belief. Mockery and satire are potential measures of respect in this case, as they undermine respect and influence. This is one part of why some faiths attempt to end satire if they gain the political power or influence needed to do so. An exception is ancient Greece and Rome, both of which seemed to have no problem with mocking the gods, or publicly pointing out their fallibility to some degree.[22]

Role in Government

Even in a non-theocratic society, there is great potential for religious involvement in the government. As some have noted, religion and politics "vary so widely between ... worlds that no 'generic' description is possible.... [they] are very powerful [and] usually interconnected."[23] The question is how much or how little of a role does the religion have and how or why. There are a host of possibilities and relations that could exist between the religion and the government. It is also possible, especially with a state religion, that the head of state must follow, at least ostensibly or publicly, the state religion. The religious leaders could be directly involved in government or they could exert unofficial influence. Religious leaders could also officially advise the secular leadership, but often be ignored or steered as well, as in the case of Hughnon Ridcully, High Priest of Blind Io (Discworld, Ankh-Morpork).

In some societies, the clergy of a religion may have direct involvement in the government. That is, they may hold official government posts or semi-official positions in which they advise the leaders of the society. Historically, we see examples of this with Cardinal Richelieu in France, who held a number of government posts between 1616 and 1642,[24] and Cardinal Wolsey of England, who was King Henry VIII's Lord Chancellor (chief advisor; 1515–1529). Both cardinals were in positions to greatly influence, or directly control, what their respective governments did. In fiction, Westeros's High Septon (*ASoIaF*) holds no official government role, but crowns the kings and determines their legitimacy. Likewise, some of the clergy of Ravka (Grishaverse) hold official positions whereby they advise and crown the kings of the nation, thereby determining royal legitimacy.

Even if the clergy are officially banned from government positions, they can still exert influence and have an unofficial role in government. A good example here is the city of New York, in which the Catholic archbishop has historically wielded a fair amount of political influence over mayors, at least from 1965 until recently.[25] This becomes more interesting if the "ban" on clergy in government (official or not) only applies to some religions but not others or if it is self-imposed. For example, in the U.S. two Catholic priests served in Congress (none have since Pope John Paul II banned priests in secular government in 1983); all of the other ministers in Congress have been Protestants.[26] Such decisions could be tied to the religion's status in society or to the leaders of the religion and their rules. They could also be tied to how the religion wishes to be seen by others; that is, as politically neutral or uninvolved in worldly affairs.

Relationship with the Law

The relationship between a religion and a government/society also manifests as relationships between the religion and the law, or law enforcement. The key question here is whether the religion and its clergy are subject to secular law or their own system.[27] Historically, in our world, in medieval Europe, both secular and canon law existed. The Church had its own laws and courts so, in many cases, clergy and monks (and university students) could choose to have a case/lawsuit heard in ecclesiastical courts instead of secular court. Likewise, crimes that occurred on Church property fell under canon law, not secular, for trial and enforcement. Depending on the influence, relations with society, and the deity, a given religion may be independent of secular authorities and law or beholden to secular law. The decision can be very important for society and culture, including how it is applied. For instance, if a priest can only be tried by canon judges (e.g., other clergy), even if the plaintiff/victim is non-clergy, then the cleric has a decided edge in trials, as their fellow clerics are more likely to decide in their favor. Such a situation may lead to resentment among the populace when, not if, abused.

In addition to its own courts and judges, a religion may have its own law enforcement arm. This could range from the classic sword and sorcery temple guards[28] to constables patrolling every property or neighborhood the religion owns to detectives and jails run by the religious organization. At any level, religious law enforcement could, and likely will, cause conflict and plot as they clash with their secular equivalents over jurisdiction, investigation, capture, and punishment. On the other hand, such division could be a source of relief—the murderer is not *our* problem, the temple guard get to deal with it—or resentment—as one group or the other interferes with or blocks investigations. Depending on the type of religion, its history, its views of sects/heresy, and its influence, there could also be inquisitors enforcing doctrine and hunting heresy. There could even be a sort of religious secret police spying on or monitoring the faithful.

5

Magic

What is fantasy, or any of its subgenres, without some form of magic? Since magic is integral to the genres, all fantasy and UF/PNR societies have to address and deal with it somehow. Some settings, of course, have a rather low level or more subtle forms of magic, which may call for less addressing than those with greater levels of, or more blatant, magic. To some degree, societal reactions to magic or the relationship between society and magic is somewhat universal. Most societies will share core potential concerns about the use and misuse of magic. However, especially in terms of specifics, the system of magic is important to decide on as each system determines what magic can and cannot do, which will in turn raise or negate different concerns.[1] Regardless of the choices made, it is important to consider the consequences and ask logical questions about the effects. Magic in a society impacts transportation of people, cargo, and troops, as well as speed and where travel occurs. It influences warfare (power level—magic grenade vs. magic nuclear device—and whether technology is used). Magic can also potentially affect everything from medicine to communications, light sources to crime.[2] Before delving into the specifics of relations between society and magic, a few broad questions should be discussed as well as a brief discussion of different types of magic.

How Much Magic?

One of the most important questions to begin with is: how common is magic in the society? Obviously, the more common magic is, the greater the social impact it will have. Conversely, less common magic may or may not have a lesser impact, depending on the role of practitioners in society and how powerful the magic is. A lot of little magics will have at least as much impact as a small bit of powerful magics. Consider the social impact of magic in Rowling's wizarding world, with magic used for even the most mundane things like washing dishes, and in the Marvel Cinematic Universe (MCU), where a small group of magic wielders—including Stephen

Strange and Wanda Maximoff—perform world, even multiverse, altering spells.

Answers to this question can be layered, with different responses for different parts of society. Many to most UF worlds deal with a hidden magical society in which the broader "mundane" society has no magic. Meanwhile, the hidden society has close to ubiquitous magic. Good examples include any of Rick Riordan's novels, the *World of Darkness* setting, the Potterverse, Ilona Andrews's *Innkeeper* setting, and Charlaine Harris's *Southern Vampire* setting. In each case, we see two split societies, albeit two that are beginning to merge in Harris's case: one with no magic and therefore no response to it, and one saturated with magic and/or magical beings (even if some or most may be alien in origin).

In secondary world fantasies and open magic UF, the range and response runs the gamut from magic being rare and in few hands (Middle-Earth) to limited (Grishaverse, Liavek, Moorcock) to ubiquitous (*Kate Daniels*, Dragaera). Some tabletop roleplaying game worlds fall into the limited to ubiquitous range as well, but it can be harder to tell. For instance, the *Forgotten Realms* and *Dragonlance* worlds are probably between the high end of limited and low end of ubiquitous, depending on era, region, and nation or society. Both cases are difficult to determine because of the perspectives presented (exceptional people versus average people), and the differences between their use in novels versus their use in RPGs by gamemasters (GMs) and players.[3]

Ultimately, the question of how much magic exists has a significant impact on how, or if, a given society tries to control magic. In some cases, controlling magic may not be possible, or it may not prove to be worth the effort (ex. if there is very little magic).

Who Can Use It?

One element that intertwines with the question of how much magic exists is who can use magic. The more people who can use it, the more widespread magic is likely to be. Additionally, who can access and use magic affects, and may be affected by, how society addresses the issues that magic raises. If the nature of magic limits who can access it, then access affects society's reaction. On the other hand, if nature does not limit access to magic, then the society might restrict access to magic in order to control it and try to keep it out of the hands of those who oppose the society or status quo. The important question here is: Who or what controls access to magic? This helps determine the social views of magic (ex. is it only in the hands of villains, is it only a tool, have most people never actually seen it used), as well as legal restrictions.[4]

Natural limits to who can use magic could be genetic (*Harry Potter*, Tanya Huff's *The Enchantment Emporium*), gender based, or myriad other things. Regardless of the actual limit, natural restriction could create a social class of magicians, whether upper, lower, or in between. It could also create a guild-like structure within the society, possibly as a means for magicians to protect themselves from others—physically, politically, socially, or all three—or to ensure that the power is controlled and used with minimal collateral damage while learning.

Societal restrictions on who can use magic could limit access by social class (*The Black Magician* series, Dragaera to a degree) or sex (Discworld). A given society may also limit access to certain professions (ex. artisans, priests), species (ex. human, elf), or ethnicities. The society might even require that all who learn magic also engage in government service, whether for life or a set time span (ex. *Seven Kennings*, for the air, water, and earth magic practitioners). All of which are possible social reactions designed to limit access to the potentially destabilizing power that magic represents.

How Is It Learned?

Beyond simply looking at who can access magic, the question of how it is learned also affects social responses. Later in the chapter, magic education will be discussed in relative depth, with the assumption that some form of apprenticeship or other formal training is required. However, formal education is not always needed. If learning magic is most often solo or instinctive (ex. *Seven Kennings*), society may react to restrict access to magic. Alternately, the society may ostracize or embrace budding magicians. Others may require government service and provide guidance to minimize damage and self-injury. If learning magic comes in the form of extra-worldly agents (ex. deities, demons, proto-deities), the source of the tutelage will most likely determine the social response. If the gods teach magicians, then society's view of the deity will influence the societal response. If demons or other such entities are the tutors, there is likely to be some level of negative reaction from social avoidance of practitioners to outlawing magic to hunting and executing magicians.[5]

A great deal of the response to all three questions depends heavily on the type(s) and system(s) of magic involved in the society.

Types of Magic (Brief)

Due to space and other limits, this section will not cover every single type of magic in the fantasy genres, history, and mythology. Instead, the section will cover some of the more important and more common basic types of magic in general terms here.[6] The following are also the most likely ones to cause notable social effects. For these purposes, they will be divided into two categories: techniques (the form or source) and branches (the effects).

Techniques

Alchemy is the creation of magic infused elixirs, basically magical chemistry. It involves acquiring ingredients and combining them via various processes according to recipes. Notable examples include Dr. John Dee and Nicholas Flamel (history), Andrzej Sapkowski's witchers, and Kevin Hearne's *Iron Druid* (in the form of tea brewing).

Blood Magic uses blood to fuel spells, or involves the control of blood through spells and power. Notable examples include Netflix's *The Order* (fuel) and the *World of Darkness* (the Tremere clan of vampires especially). Huff's *The Enchantment Emporium* and Sapkowski's *The Witcher* also make brief mentions of uses, the latter in connection to alchemy.

Chi is the use of internal energy to produce superhuman feats of physical and martial prowess. Notable examples include Fonda Lee's *Jade City* and Jin Yong's classic *Legends of the Condor Heroes*.

Divine Magic involves the use of prayer, invocation, or other divine contact to fuel or employ magic. Typically "spells" will take the form of prayers. Notable examples include George R.R. Martin's *ASoIaF* (the Red Priests) and fantasy RPG (FRPG) clerics, whether tabletop or video game versions.

Ley Line magic uses contact with ley lines to fuel or cast spells, or for other magical purposes. Notable examples include Robert Asprin's *MythAdventures* (ley lines fuel all magic) and Andrews's *Kate Daniels* (ley lines are used for long-distance travel).

Powers as magic occurs when magic takes the form of special powers used by the practitioner. Basically, it is a fantasy form of superpowers. Notable examples include Kevin Hearne's *Seven Kennings* and Leigh Bardugo's Grishaverse.

Sex Magic involves the use of sex, desire, and/or related acts and emotions to fuel magic or cast spells. Notable examples include Huff's *The Enchantment Emporium*, Allyson James's *Stormwalker* (power), Grossman's *The Magicians*, and Michael Scott's *The Thirteen Hallows* (divination).

Sigil or Word Magic uses symbols or words to focus energy, fuel magic, or shape spells. Often this is combined with other techniques, such as blood, divine, or sex magic. Notable examples include Naomi Novik's

5. Magic

Scholomance, Jim Butcher's *Dresden Files*, Sapkowski's *The Witcher*, Rowling's *Harry Potter*, and Tolkien's Middle Earth.

Spirit Magic uses summoned spirits or ghosts to produce magical effects. Sometimes the spirit's energy is drawn to fuel spells, in other cases the spirit acts directly on behalf of the summoner. Notable examples include Jonathan Stroud's *Bartimaeus Sequence*, Shakespeare's *The Tempest*, and European history (witches, among others, were believed in some areas to summon spirits to act on their behalf).

Branches

Alteration includes spells that change or alter the subject, from hair color to full species change. Notable examples include *Harry Potter* (transfiguration), *Seven Kennings* (particularly the water and plant practitioners), and most FRPGs.

Communication includes spells that allow the exchange of information between two or more points via magic. Notable examples include *Harry Potter* (flue powder, howlers, patronuses), *Stormwalker* (shards of a magic mirror), and *Dungeons & Dragons* (various spells, including Message).

Conjuration includes any purely magical transportation of objects, beings, or people through space, for these purposes. Notable examples include *Harry Potter* (accio charm, flue powder, apparating), *Jonathan Strange & Mr. Norrell* (mirror travel), and Marvel's Doctor Strange ("sling ring").

Crafting is the creation of magical objects and devices, sometimes known as artifice or, confusingly, as enchantment. Notable examples include all FRPGS, *Dresden Files*, *Kate Daniels*, Middle Earth (especially the elves), and Rick Riordan's *Percy Jackson* series (Hephaestus kids).

Divination is magic used to foretell the future via a wide range of means from rune casting to augury. In some cases (D&D), it can also include almost any spell that produces information for the caster. Notable examples include *The Thirteen Hallows*, *ASoIaF*, *Harry Potter*, *Kate Daniels*, and most FRPGs.

Enchantment is used, in this case, to refer to any mind-affecting spells, from emotion control to charm, to mind reading to mind control. Notable examples include *Harry Potter* (legilimency, veritaserum), Andrews's *Hidden Legacy*, *The Order* (memory modification), and *The Witcher*.

Healing spells are used to cure illnesses and disease and heal wounds, potentially both physical and mental. Notable examples include FRPGs, *Kate Daniels*, *Harry Potter*, *The Witcher*, and all of Riordan's mythology-based series.

Necromancy involves spells that communicate with, control, bind, or raise the dead, or create undead beings. Notable examples include FRPGs, *Percy Jackson* (Hades/Pluto kids), *Kate Daniels* (The People), Tamsyn Muir's *Gideon the Ninth*, and *The Order*.

Impact on Society

Any time that magic is introduced to a world, it will impact society to some extent. At the very least, magic will likely cause reactions of convenience, awe, and/or fear.[7] How much of an effect depends on the type(s) of magic, how widespread magic is, and whether magic is hidden, among other factors. In its way, magic acts like technology in this situation. As technological advances impact and alter society, including access to technology, so do magic, access to magic, and advances in magic. If we substitute the latest smartphone with the latest alchemical product or magic ring effect, or swap cutting edge healing magic for experimental medical techniques, the effect is very similar, if not the same. This section will look at six focal areas: governance, laws and crime, technology, education, social class, and economy. All six are potentially, or very, complex areas that will necessarily be brief, compared to what could be discussed with them. Each could possibly be a chapter or book unto itself.

Governance

Magic is likely to have an effect on who can govern society and how society is governed. In some cases, those with the ability to use magic may control the government or be prevented from taking part in government. Magicians may be required by law to join guilds (themselves a source of political and social influence), serve in some government role, or join the military (ex. Freeform's *Motherland: Fort Salem*).[8] Unless magicians are in control, any society that knows of magic is likely to put in place some measures to prevent the use of magic from unduly influencing the governance of the society. Depending on the setting or society, there could be magical self-governance, non-magicians governing magicians, or both. Hidden magic societies (most UF) largely deal with self-governance, while open magic settings tend to necessarily work with both options.

If a magical society in hiding has a government, then we simply refer to Chapter 3 and build its government. In some cases, there may be relationships with the normal government, but not always. For the most part, we can treat the magical community as a self-contained society, at least for purposes of government, with its own governing body and laws. Some good examples include the Potterverse (Ministry of Magic), the Percy Jackson–verse (New Rome), *Dresden Files* (White Council), and *Lost Girl* (TV; Light and Dark Fae councils and leaders, The Blood King).

Open magic societies, on the other hand, have the potential to become much more complex undertakings. In some cases, they may only have non-magicians governing magicians (ex. Myke Cole's *Control Point*, some nations in Hearne's *Seven Kennings*), but many address both non-magical government and self-governing magicians. Good examples of the latter include Weis and Hickman's Dragonlance (nations and the Conclave of Wizards), *Kate Daniels* (limited national government and each city faction's leadership), *The Black Magician* series (national governments and the Guild), Discworld (the Patrician and Unseen University), and the *Hidden Legacy* series (U.S. government and state level magician Assemblies).

If the magical and non-magical governments remain apart, or parallel, then we are effectively creating a pair or collection of related governments. In both cases, we first create both or all of the governments, referring to Chapter 3. Then we add the relationship between the two (or more) governments. A variety of potential relationships exists. They could be mutually balanced (ex. Dragonlance, in which the governments largely keep to their own realm—mundane or magic). They could also pretend the other has authority, so long as neither actually tries to exert that authority (ex. Discworld—the Patrician agrees not to tax the Unseen University and the wizards agree not to start throwing fireballs). One or more governments may be dominant over the other(s), as in the case of the *Kate Daniels* series, in which a number of magical governing bodies (witches, the People) have more authority than the mundane government. Or they could be closely tied, although separate, by social relations, as in the case of *The Black Magician*, in which the magicians are almost entirely children of the nobility.

A non-magical government exerting sole authority over magical beings is where things get really complex. When there is no governing body of magical beings, but only a non-magical government, the core question is: How do non-magical authorities deal with magic wielders? In addressing this question, there are clear concerns about the safety of non-mages and the government itself that come to mind. Likewise, questions arise about the exploitation of magicians and even the very existence of society, if magicians simply decide to take over. Responses to these concerns, and whether they even arise, depend heavily on the type and spread of magic. If magic is largely impractical or rare, then there is probably less reason to be concerned.

Some governments may attempt to exploit magicians, as in *Control Point* (where certain mages are conscripted into the military) or, to a lesser extent, *Hidden Legacy* (where, again, certain mages are brought into the military, perhaps for a single specific mission). On a related note, some governments may try to control magic through mandatory government service (ex. *Seven Kennings*) or by limiting where magicians can work or how much/where they can move in the society. Other governments may even entirely ban magicians from holding public office, including noble titles or other hereditary government titles, as in *The Black Magician*, in which virtually all magicians are children of noble houses, who give up their titles and inheritances to study magic. Many governments will at least require registration of magicians, whether directly with the non-magic government or through a magical governing body, as potential weapons or "for public safety." Alternately, they might restrict access to, for instance, protection and weapons for magicians, as in Krynn (ex. Magius in *The Legend of Huma*, who notes that wizards are legally not allowed to wear armor or carry any weapon other than a staff or dagger).[9] The most repressive may ban magic entirely as their attempt to control it.

Non-magical governments could accept magical governance and work together with a magical governing body, or create one either as an independent government or an agency/branch of the non-magical government. Where this response could be problematic, e.g., could lead to tension and plotlines, is if the magical governing body is international in nature, especially if the government is paranoid or at war. Good examples include Krynn's Conclave of Wizards, *The Black Magician's* Magicians' Guild, and *The Witcher's* Brotherhood of Sorcerers. An international governing body of magicians could serve as diplomats or negotiators to end or prevent conflicts between nations. This could lead to resentment, focused on questions of loyalty, as in the case of *The Witcher's* Brotherhood. A much less common scenario is one in which the government integrates magicians into the government in official roles, or magicians serve as head of state (ex. *The Witcher* or Gail Z. Martin's *Chronicles of the Necromancer*, both of which feature magic wielding heads of state in exile). The magocracy, in which being a magician is required for entry into government positions, or the ruling class/nobility, is also an integrated option, of sorts, albeit one in which non-mages may be integrated into a mage-based government.

In cases of repressive governments, representation of magicians in government is likely to be nonexistent. The exception is if the repressive government is a magocracy (ex. Thay in *Forgotten Realms*), or there are mages secretly infiltrating the government. Most governments, though, will fall somewhere between fully egalitarian integration and complete bans on magicians, in the case of open magic societies.

Laws and Crime

If governments create laws regarding the use and practice of magic, it helps to know what those laws are and how they are enforced. In some societies, magic may be used alongside traditional, "mundane" law enforcement techniques to investigate both magical and non-magical crimes. In general, we can probably assume that magic would be subject to most laws (ex. harm, property loss). However, certain types of spells may be further regulated—sacrifice, summoning, mind control—and there may be different levels of regulation—ex. beneficial, regulated, reserved, prohibited.[10] Due to the breadth of law and crime, this section will address four key areas: the legality of magic, law enforcement, evidence and investigation, and courts.

The first element of magic and law is the question of whether magic is legal in the society. For some (ex. hidden magic), the answer is obviously yes, though there may be limits. For others (ex. open magic), the answer is less clear. At one end of the spectrum, magic may be entirely legal within the society. Although legal, magic may be regulated or hold other legal standing. It may require licensing, whether akin to firearm ownership or more like trade/professional certification or licensing depend on the society. Regardless, there is no need in this sort of society for magicians to hide their activities and they have legal protections and rights. Most UF hidden magic societies fall into this category. The majority of points along the sliding scale, however, are limited magic. In limited societies, one definition is that some magics are legal and others are illegal (ex. Cole's *Control Point*). Another definition may be that magic is legal, but some uses are legally restricted or deemed illegal. Examples include necromancy in *Kate Daniels* (highly regulated), mind reading in *The Witcher*, or time travel and truth serums in *Harry Potter*. Another variation appears in Andrews's *Hidden Legacy*, in which there are laws about inter-House warfare, to protect normal human bystanders. Whether non-magic government or self-governing, or both, limited magic societies will have codified restrictions placed on magic use. Finally, at the other end of the spectrum are societies in which the practice of magic is entirely illegal, whether officially or effectively. There could be many reasons that the society gives for bans on magic including public safety, history, and the political influence of anti-magic groups in society.

If a magical society has its own laws, or has laws imposed upon it, we have to ask how they are enforced and who enforces them. A related question is whether magic is integrated with normal law enforcement in a fully mixed society. Self-governing magical societies typically have their own enforcement arm of magicians such as the wardens of Andrews's *Hidden*

Legacy and Butcher's *Dresden Files* or *Harry Potter*'s aurors and Ministry officials. This is a typical system for organized hidden magic societies. If the magical governing body includes many or all magical beings, the enforcement arm may incorporate non-magician magical beings (ex. werebeasts, elves, goblins) or even normal humans (ex. Lisa Shearin's *SPI Files*). Societies with entirely normal governing bodies, or mixed normal and magical, are likely to form special policing forces, units, or something similar (ex. Cole's *Control Point* and Andrews's *Kate Daniels*). The job of these special units is to train to deal with magically active criminals or crimes involving magic. They may or may not include magicians on the force (who may be regular employees, freelance consultants, or closely monitored conscripts).

In a hybrid situation, the magical governing body may retain its own enforcers as well, or integrate with normal police. Such situations are also possible in hidden magic settings, using the example of *Hellboy*'s BPRD, a secret normal government agency that pulls agents from the FBI, and presumably other agencies. It is also possible that magicians may be fully integrated into normal police forces. This opens a host of questions and possibilities, including the use of scrying to find perpetrators and victims, divination to prevent crimes, and the use of magic to gather evidence (including magical evidence). Use of deadly force via magic is likely to be treated the same as other uses of deadly force. A number of questions regarding the rights of suspects with regard to magic may also appear, including whether magic (including mind affecting magic) may be used to restrain suspects or whether enchantment may be used like a lie detector or to read a suspect's mind. Most of these questions only matter if a plot or concept requires it. A paranormal police procedural or hard-boiled paranormal detective needs to consider these issues. However, a wilderness society of magicians probably does not need much detail, though any magical society will likely have limits and rules about things like mind reading.

Other limits on magic in law enforcement are also likely to involve how it is used in investigations and acquiring evidence. This raises questions about admissible evidence, privacy, and investigative methods. One obvious concern, that ties in with mind reading above, is evidence gained through magical coercion, such as charm or hallucination inducing spells. Whether such methods of acquiring evidence and confessions are accepted depends on the government. For example, if the government holds rules against self-incrimination (ex. the U.S. Constitution's Fifth Amendment) or the use of torture to get confessions, then magic is probably not allowed either. If the government is more authoritarian or less concerned with the methods just the results, then they may not care how the evidence and confessions are acquired.

Looking more directly at mind-reading magics combines the issues of privacy and admissible evidence. Many governments are likely to consider mind reading and related magics as illegal or highly restricted, probably inadmissible evidence, and invasions of privacy, especially in UF/PNR. Other governments may have little to no problem, resulting in more problematic, possibly repressive, societies. For examples, we can also look beyond the fantasy genres to how science fiction treats telepathy (ex. *Babylon 5*). A related issue is spells or other magics that provide evidence solely to the caster—including clairvoyance, clairaudience, enhanced senses—that cannot be recorded. The fact that such information cannot necessarily be confirmed, and potentially constitutes an invasion of privacy, can be problematic for the society's legal system, or could be standard procedure. In effect, such magics create a situation of the caster's word versus the suspect's, rather than one of presentable evidence.

What magics are allowed, socially and legally, for investigation and evidence is important, if the focus of the story/setting is the investigation aspect. For example, scrying may be accepted to track criminals, or spells that track an article of clothing or blood to the owner (whether victim or suspect). But, charming a suspect to get information or a confession may be illegal. A good fiction example is Brust's Dragaera, in which it is legal to use magic to trace the owner of a murder weapon (via witchcraft, which the authorities do not use), but the use of mind-reading or truth-detecting magics is highly restricted (as in the case of testifying under the Imperial Orb).

Once suspects are determined, how do the courts deal with magicians? Do magicians have their own courts (particularly in an open magic society)? How is sentencing handled? Most of these questions make the assumption that there is an open magic society. An all-magical community, or hidden magic society, might be a little easier, depending on the rules of magic. Both share the issues of restraining and, potentially, incarcerating magicians, as will be discussed at the end of the section.

In an open magic society, if we assume that magicians and non-magical humans interact, we should ask whether magicians can serve as judges, legal counsels, or jurists. The question raises a number of issues about being able to magically influence judges, opposing counsel, and juries through a wide variety of magics from enchantment to curses and beyond. If magic is common, then a society will have some protections in place, whether magic-wielding guards/detectives or anti-magic jails.[11] Some methods may be more subtle than others. In these cases, depending on the magic system, there may be court employed magicians responsible for warding the courtroom. Or the courtroom could be made of a magic-dampening material. Perhaps magicians in the courtroom are required to wear some sort of magic-dampening material or device. All such options are potentially open to being circumvented in a variety of ways from bribery and blackmail to counterfeiting devices.

Additionally, there is the problem of restraining magicians, or preventing them from using magic, while in the courtroom as plaintiff or defendant. This may become more difficult if magicians who serve in law enforcement are intended to retain their ability to use magic, e.g., a mage on trial's power is removed but a police mage's remains. In our own world, it is fairly easy to ensure that a murder suspect, once arrested, does not get a weapon into a courtroom. It is potentially much harder to ensure that a magician cannot get magic or a weapon in, depending on the magic system and its technical aspects. One example in use is Rowling's Potterverse, in which, at least in the UK, the defendant's wand is taken and some are bound in magic fetters and/or are flanked by dementors in major threat cases. Each of the three precautions individually reduces the chances of the defendant casting spells in the courtroom, all together it becomes effectively impossible.

Some open magic societies will have separate courts for normal humans and magicians. These magic courts may be official (ex. Krynn's Conclave of Sorcerers) or semi-official to unofficial (ex. *Hidden Legacy's* Assembly courts). They may also either supplement or replace mundane courts, like canon and secular courts in medieval Europe. This division takes the problems of containment and restraining magicians out of the hands of those who lack magic and puts them in the hands of those with the capability to handle both. However, it also makes the magical community self-policing, which could introduce concerns about excessive leniency in sentences and cause festering resentment of magicians in the broader community.

Sentencing is one of the greatest concerns and, depending on how magic works, potentially the most problematic one. However, means of incarcerating magicians can be built into the magic system. Some broad means may include removing access to the tools of magic (ex. wand, staff, spell components) or removing access to the energy needed to fuel spells. Two excellent examples exist in literature. First, *Harry Potter* shows Azkaban, with wandless wizards guarded by dementors, sucking joy and focus, patrolling the halls, as well as Nurmengard, briefly shown with wandless inmates and, presumably, other containment measures. The other is the Imperial Prisons of Brust's Dragaera. The Imperial Prisons include black and gold phoenix stone that cut inmates off from the Imperial Orb (preventing sorcery) and block psychic ability (preventing witchcraft and psionics).[12] In both cases, the energy, focus, or tools necessary to use magic are removed from the inmates. Other options might include spell resistant/proof materials in the building, heavily warded cells, or even the use of technological (or techno-magical) devices to prevent escape (the first and last of which are seen in *Motherland: Fort Salem*).

Technology

The effects of magic on a society's technological development depend heavily on the nature of magic in the world. If technology and magic are inimical, then technology will probably become stunted (open, high magic), completely separate (common in UF), or replaced by magical equivalents (ex. *Kate Daniels*). Separation is more common in situations where magic causes technology to become unreliable (ex. Riordan's *Kane Chronicles* or Butcher's *Dresden Files*). In other cases, technology and magic may complement each other or work together. That said, magic does not need to be more reliable than technology, nor does, as our everyday world shows, technology necessarily have to be reliable. Magic could even replace technology or make certain technologies possible, as in Yoon Ha Lee's *Dragon Pearl*, in which star travel occurs via magic infused FTL. Obviously, magic can potentially affect military, medical, and agricultural technology and methods. Magic may be an alternative technology that influences public health, daily life, and conflicts. It may also replace technology, if magic is sufficiently widespread.[13] A few areas of development—communications, light, sanitation, and security—will be discussed here, to imply, and to spawn, thoughts about others.

Magical communication—via mirrors, crystals, or other means—could replace technological communications, or appear earlier than technological development might. For example, imagine an ancient Rome with instant long-distance communication, rather than taking weeks to get a message from the British frontier to Rome. Good examples of magic replacing tech include Krynn, among the masters of the Towers of High Sorcery; Dragaera, in which psychic communication is common through the medium of the Orb; and *Stormwalker*, in which shards of a magic mirror are used akin to walkie-talkies. Additionally, magic could be combined with technology to enhance it. This could change the power source of communication, avoid service charges, or allow access to different information. A good example is Tanya Huff's *The Enchantment Emporium*, in which magically modified cell phones accrue no charges, never drop calls, and always have service (unless magically interfered with).

The presence of magic could also lead to alternate sources of light. This is a seemingly minor change, from a modern perspective. However, innumerable medieval to 19th-century writers, students, and readers would have killed to replace candles with a bright, steady light source. The effect of magical lighting would vary by how widespread it is, but our own history 14th-century Europe, in particular) shows that the presence of more artificial lighting yields increases in literacy among pre-gas/electric lighting societies. Magical lighting could come in a variety of forms depending on the magic system. It could be smokeless or non-consuming flame (torches, candles), glowing crystals, or a host of other things. The exact form is based on the magic system. There could also be significant environmental benefits, including clean energy and reduced to non-existent whaling (for lamp oil). Alternately, the use of widespread magical lighting could create a different sort of negative environmental impact (if magic produces byproducts or an energy source is drained), depending on the source of magic (and whether magical energy is finite or infinite in nature).

Magic can also be applied to greatly improve society's sanitation. In some cases, it needs to be—in the case of flying or otherwise mobile castles. This leads to obvious health benefits, even before we look into healing magics in society. As suggested, magical sanitation allows the creation of, or explains, self-contained environments like flying castles, floating cities, or even magic-based space stations. A few ways magic could be applied include water magic to purify or create water sources, fire magic to fully dispose of waste, earth magic to ease the laying of sanitation pipes, air magic to clean out pollutants, conjuration to remove waste (and send it elsewhere, which may lead to other issues), or magical constructs to clean streets.

One area of technology that magic alters, that is as old as magic itself, is the area of security. Many of the earliest uses of supposed magic in our own history and prehistory were protective in nature, whether protecting people or places. Magic could replace technological security systems, with wards, alarms, traps, and constructs. Magic can also be employed to supplement or support technological systems, as an extra layer of protection or monitoring. Obviously, magic may also be used to circumvent or disable technological security (as well as magical), as in Riordan's *Kane Chronicles*, in which simple spells are used to disable security cameras. Examples of magical security appear in virtually all fantasy, UF, and PNR. Some specific examples include the magical defenses of Camp Half-Blood and New Rome (Riordan), the titular character's apartment in *Kate Daniels*, the gates of Moria in Middle Earth, and the protections surrounding Hogwarts, the Ministry of Magic, the Quidditch World Cup stadium, and Harry-Ron-Hermione's camp (*Deathly Hallows*) in *Harry Potter*.

Education

A discussion of magic and education not only covers magical education but the impact of magic on normal education and societal integration (for open magic societies). The three key variables at the start of any such discussion are hidden versus open magic, magicians only versus mixed society, and society's response to magic.

Hidden magic societies tend to be all magician or magicians with other magical beings. For the most part, education in these societies tends to be self-taught (*Stormwalker*), apprenticeships (*Dresden Files, Iron Druid*), or formal education (*Harry Potter*, Holly Black and Cassandra Clare's *Magisterium*, Novik's *Scholomance*). Other possibilities also exist, but are less common. In most cases, these are guided methods of education. The purpose of such guidance tends to be either to protect the safety of budding magicians (or those around them) or to keep magic concealed. Since these are typically entirely magician, or magicians with magical beings, societies, magic is basically accepted and embraced by the society.

In open magic societies, education becomes more complicated. Magicians in open magic societies could learn apart from others, whether in apprenticeships or more or less formal venues, or both. This is the form used in *The Black Magician, Earthsea, Dragonlance*, and the Grishaverse. Alternately, they could be integrated into education with both magical and mundane subjects taught side by side, an uncommon to rare variation. A notable example here seems to be Yoon Ha Lee's *Dragon Pearl*, at least among the military. If society accepts magic, the decision could go either way. If society embraces magic, it could also go either way, depending on how dangerous magic is to learn. Magicians could be trained apart from others for safety, as in the *Seven Kennings* setting (solo training) and the *GURPS IOU* setting (the university is apart from the normal world, and magic is its own college).

If the society has problems with magic, it could use mandatory education to control access to magic, and what magicians learn. Apprenticeships could be used to keep magicians relatively disorganized (or a resistance to a repressive government might use this method). Those who rebel against the government might be self-taught. Formal education can be used to identify potential magicians and track and control the individual. It also formalizes what budding magicians learn. This can appear in hidden magic societies, as evidenced by Hogwarts under Dolores Umbridge's tenure as Defense Against the Dark Arts teacher (which led to self-teaching for Dumbledore's Army as a form of resistance). Such societies are, however, unlikely to integrate magical and normal education, except in very limited or unusual circumstances.

Magic in society might also affect normal education in several ways, even without integration. Magic may be used to replace or enhance technology such that new information is available. A good example is Brust's Dragaera, which is basically a Renaissance to early-18th-century Earth level of technology, but magic allows extensive knowledge of genetics, among other things. Magic, in this way, allows for information and knowledge of things that were not present in the equivalent technological time periods of our world. It is also possible that magic could create teaching tools that are unavailable in an equivalent Earth. Illusion-based "holograms" and 3D reconstructions of places, people, and animals could be used for architecture and biology. Magical goggles, or other eyewear, may be capable of microscopic, macroscopic, infrared, and ultraviolet effects, allowing a greater range of knowledge based on visible data. Of course, access to much of these potential education advances may be limited by social standing.

Social Class

There are many ways in which magic might affect social standing in a given culture. At the most basic level, the ability to use magic could determine social class (ex. *Bartimaeus Sequence*). It could also place practitioners outside the social hierarchy (ex. *The Black Magician, The Witcher*). It could require a certain social standing in order to be taught in the first place.

Particularly in magocratic societies, the ability and/or training to use magic automatically places the magician in the ruling or upper class. In this sort of society, magic is a necessary requirement for entry into the uppermost social classes. In a society where magic is demonized, having the ability may automatically make a magician into an outlaw. Most fall somewhere in between. This concept of magic determining social class applies mostly to open magic settings and societies, where magicians and non-magicians interact. Arguably, it might apply to hidden magic settings in a couple of ways. First, the hidden society may consider itself better than the normal human society and populace. Second, if other magical beings exist, being a magician may grant the individual either higher status (ex. *Harry Potter*) or lower (ex. if other beings look down on human magicians as "upstarts" or some such). Also, the ability to use magic may not require status, or even automatically elevate the magician to the upper levels of society, but may simply make becoming part of the upper class easier to achieve (ex. *Hidden Legacy*).

For the purposes of controlling magic, or other reasons such as magicians having an international organization, mages might be outside the social class systems. Setting magicians outside the system might be done to reduce the influence of magicians or to keep them out of government. For example, in *The Black Magician*, potential magicians have to give up their noble titles and family ties and influence. Likewise, sorcerers in

5. Magic

The Witcher become upper class in appearance, but seem to have no official social class as such, even if they advise kings. The Grishaverse presents another example in Ravka, where the magicians live, learn, and train apart. They even have their own army (in Ravka), with their own officers, outside the regular army's chain of command. Even from outside the social structure, magicians may, like medieval European priests and monks, possess influence through advising rulers (as in *The Black Magician* and *The Witcher*) and may have diplomatic possibilities (ex. *The Black Magician*). In these cases, their position may also make those in the social hierarchy suspicious or wary, as they may serve as advisors to heads of state with no one being sure if they have the authority to, say, deliver orders to a noble.

Economy

The presence of magic, magical objects, and magical constructs could profoundly impact an existing economy, create a sub-economy, or form an entirely separate magical economy in a given society. Four of the most likely forms of impact will be explored here: magical services, magic devices, manufacturing, and the service industry. Of course, the impact and presence of an economy is entirely up to the creator. Some hidden magic settings show no economy at all (ex. James's *Stormwalker*, Riordan's Jackson and Kane books). Others show or imply some, even tiny, degree of economy (ex. Grossman's *The Magicians* and Novik's *Scholomance*). Some have full-fledged magical economies (ex. *Harry Potter*). The same can be true of open magic UF settings, with Andrews's *Kate Daniels* perhaps being one of the biggest. Other open magic settings skirt or ignore the entire discussion, implying the possibility of a magical economy but not developing or discussing it much (ex. most FRPGs, whether tabletop or video game—with vendors buying looted magic items and selling some as well).

A magical services economy is probably the most obvious, and the one that has been used the most. It is also one that we see throughout our own history, even today (via self-proclaimed psychics and mediums). People may visit the magician for healing, curses, finding lost objects or people, and speaking with departed loved ones. They may also seek magical aid for improving or decreasing fertility or getting it to rain or stop raining. These are all familiar uses of magic, and all things that a magician could easily be paid to do. In terms of literary and game examples, we see magical services for hire in Graci Kim's *Gifted Clans* series, *Dresden Files*, Novik's *Scholomance*, Andrews's *Kate Daniels*, Brust's Dragaera, and most D&D settings (and other RPGs, both video and tabletop). The cost of such services and impact on the local economy (e.g., how easy they are to come by) varies widely and at the whim of the creator.

Depending on whether magic items can be made, how widespread magic is, and how easy magic items are to create, they can also be a significant part of a magical economy. The sale of magic items forms or impacts any society's economy. For instance, something has to happen to all the extra magic items that FRPG video game adventurers loot and sell to various shopkeepers in town. And the money that the shopkeepers pay to buy such items has to come from somewhere.[14] This could take the form of a hidden magic economy (ex. *Harry Potter* or *Scholomance*'s barter economy) or as part of an open magic society (ex. *Kate Daniels* or Discworld, in which technomantic devices become increasingly common). The amount of impact depends on the magic system and society. It could be barely a ripple or it could form the foundation of a society's income and livelihoods.

Even if magical items cannot be mass produced, magic could impact manufacturing by at least three means. Summoned creatures—such as demons, elementals, or faeries—could replace human labor, or could be paid, whether in currency or something else. Magical constructs—such as golems—could work 24/7 in various factories (as seen in Pratchett's Discworld, in particular *Feet of Clay* and the Moist von Lipwig books), likely creating anti-construct resentment as they replace human workers. There may also be means of enhancing human workers that could be used. They could be made faster, more alert, or to require less sleep (or no sleep) via magical means. Morality issues may be introduced by magically charming otherwise involuntary laborers as well (or via semi-magical drug addiction—ex. the Grishaverse with jurda parem).

Finally, magic could significantly alter the service industry. Magicians, magic items, summoned beings, and constructs could take over everything from housekeeping/cleaning (ex. *Harry Potter*, Pratchett's *Going Postal*) to carrying luggage, message/package delivery (*Going Postal*) to food service. The effects in this case are likely to be similar to the introduction of technology, in terms of human layoffs and probable resentment, then acceptance and normality. At the very least, magical cleaning methods could make the industry more efficient and less laborious, for example, although magic may make for more interesting cleaning issues as well.

Impact on Religion

The existence of magic in a society affects, or can affect, religion, even if divine magic is not present. Whether divine magic exists or not, there will or should be some effect as the two interact on a social level. Since

5. Magic

both religion and magic address the relationship between the human and something paranormal, they are likely to either become rivals or intertwined. Often, both approach the paranormal in different ways, but not exclusively so. Sometimes, they merge into one thing, as discussed below. Sometimes they are rivals, even if only on the socio-political level. Sometimes they are simply parallel to each other. In this section, two major areas will be addressed: magic's relationship with deities and magic's relationship with the clergy.

Relationship with Deities

The relationship between magic and the gods may be an important one for society and for the clergy. On some worlds or in some societies, the gods are, or are seen as, the source of magic. They may be the only source or simply one source of many. In some cases, they may be a conduit or filter for magic, depending on the nature of both gods and magic. Alternately, the gods may have nothing to do with magic of any sort, which also colors their relationship. Or the gods may have started as powerful magicians who attained godhood in some way. A few examples should demonstrate the possibilities.

In the cases of Krynn (*Dragonlance*) and Toril (*Forgotten Realms*), the gods are effectively the source of magic. For Krynn, this means the three moon gods—Solinari, Lunitari, and Nuitari—effectively control magic, until the events of the *Chronicles* trilogy when the goddess Takhisis circumvents them. In Toril, Mystra and, later, Midnight control magic through their control of and connection to the Weave. If the gods are lost or interfered with, then magic is affected as well.

Max Gladstone presents a different approach in the *Craft Sequence*. Here, the gods were a filter for magic, a conduit of sorts. Then some humans found a way around them, a means of directly tapping magical energy from the stars. This resulted in a war between the gods/clergy and magicians, one that the gods lost.

In Steven Brust's Dragaera, the gods and magic are independent. However, the gods use magic at levels far beyond that of mortals and may have used magic to become gods. Here, becoming a god is defined as being able to manifest in multiple places at once and not being subject to any other being's will, usually through mastery of multiple forms of magic.

Finally, in Pratchett's Discworld, magic and the gods are also independent. The wizards "don't believe in gods in the same way that most people don't find it necessary to believe in, say, tables. [...] either the gods are there whether you believe in them or not, or exist only as a function of belief, so either way you might as well ignore the whole business."[15]

Likewise, "[m]ost witches don't believe in gods. They know that the gods exist, of course. They even deal with them occasionally. But they don't believe in them. They know them too well. It would be like believing in the postman."[16] Both witches and wizards on Discworld hold a practical relationship with the divine. On one hand, it is a sort of "to each their own" or business relationship. On another, both witches and wizards deal with all sorts of strangeness and do not need or want to deal with gods, too. In some ways, this is similar to Unseen University's relationship with the Ankh-Morpork government (see Chapter 3).

Divine magic, of course, entirely changes the relationship. When the deity can choose not to grant or to withhold magic at will, magicians become much more amenable to the gods. Good examples here include the clerics in any *D&D* world (and, technically, any FRPG clerics), Andrews's *Kate Daniels*, and the Red Priests of *ASoIaF*.

Relationship with Clergy

In some ways, much more complex than the relationship with the gods is the relationship between magic and the clergy of any religion. The added complexity comes from the introduction of politics, influence, control, doctrine, and laws into the mix. This mostly applies to secondary fantasy societies, but may be adapted to some UF/PNR as well. Depending on the deity and its views of magic, the clergy may hold faith based views of magic that inform their actions and doctrine. Alternately, or otherwise, their views may be based more on temporal matters than on the spiritual, and may be influenced by societal views.

Friction between clergy and magicians is most likely to occur, at its root, due to the question of miracles. Most religions are built around one or more individuals who were supposed to have performed paranormal acts, or miracles. Whether the example is turning water into wine, speaking with burning bushes, inhuman feats of strength, a healing touch, or a host of others, many of these miracles, or all of them, may be potentially replicated with magic. This could lead to a questioning of faith (ex. the Grishaverse, in which the saints were shown to be powerful magicians/grisha). Obviously, this can become a serious issue for the clergy, both for their power base and their very existence, especially if the deities of the world are inactive. This is a concern that the *D&D*, and many FRPG, worlds avoid by giving the clergy and magicians different spell lists. Therefore, magicians cannot heal people and priests, generally, do not throw fireballs.

When we look at politics and influence, the clergy and magicians could be rivals for the ear of temporal or societal authorities. Or they could largely ignore each other or coexist in relative peace (ex. Discworld with High Priest Hughnon Ridcully and Archchancellor Mustrum Ridcully, brothers and respective heads of the Ankh-Morpork clergy and Unseen University). The role of the faith and the role of magic in society and government is the key to determining this sort of relationship. In the example above, in Ankh-Morpork, neither temple nor magicians have any notable governmental influence, beyond occasionally being asked to advise in their respective specialties during crises.

In some societies or religions, the clergy may try to control magic, or magicians may hide themselves among the clergy or use the temple to protect themselves. In these cases, membership in the clergy might be the only legal way to learn and practice magic. Non-temple magicians may be considered lesser in ability or status, or outlawed and hunted outright. Magicians may be given the option of joining the temple or being severely punished, or banished. Secular authorities may support such a situation as a means of controlling magic, and possibly the religious apparatus.

The doctrine created by the clergy may divide magic between miracles (temple controlled and good) and magic (not controlled and bad). This is essentially what the medieval European Christian church attempted to do.[17] Unfortunately, the line between miracle and magic becomes blurred to the point of non-existence when we look at the practical effects. The divide is really more about whether the religion controls the practitioner or not. Religious doctrine can also be a means to, or reason to, limit, restrict, or outlaw different types of magic. Doctrine may be invoked to restrict or limit who can learn magic, and where or how. As with religious control of magicians, the secular authorities may support doctrine that affects magic as an effective means of controlling magic or as a basis for restrictive secular laws.

Finally, the religion may establish internal laws about magic, as we see historically in the Old Testament and at the medieval University of Paris.[18] Depending on the religion's socio-political influence, these internal laws could be applied only internally or to the general populace of the society. They could be accepted by those outside the clergy, or a source of resentment or rebellion. The latter is especially true if the clergy control access to magic, e.g., the people are forced to go to the clergy for magical services, such as healing.

6

Technology

Just as magic affects society and social development so does technology. Unlike the effects of magic on society, we have the advantage of seeing the influence of technology in our own world. Therefore, it is easier to predict and model societal effects by looking at our own past and present. In the case of the fantasy genres, the additional element of magic complicates the effects of technological development and may create unusual interactions or products. Technology also has potential effects on, and a relationship with, religion as a specific aspect of society that may produce interesting interactions. The level of technology and its relationship with both magic and religion, among other parts of society, can set the tone for the society. In its own way, technology impacts everything from travel and construction to communication and economics, education and information storage to agriculture and government. As a base, some of the most important technologies of any world are those of transportation: moving people, goods, and information. This can be vehicular (airships, sand ships, boats, cars) or beast (horse, griffin, dragon) or pure magic.[1]

Traditional Fantasy/Urban Fantasy Divide

Traditionally, at least in English language fiction, technology has formed a divide between the fantasy and urban fantasy/PNR genres. Most "traditional" fantasy is set in pre–Industrial or, at least, pre-gunpowder secondary worlds, with some notable exceptions that are largely steam-tech. But, otherwise, these settings typically mix different eras and levels of technological development that come earlier than this apex point. Comparatively, most "traditional" UF is set in an era of development contemporary with the author/reader, with modern technology (or possibly somewhat outdated, depending on how long the work remains in print).

In the last few decades, a shift has occurred. While old "traditional" versions of both genres still exist, the rise of steampunk and Victorian

UF (among other subgenres) combined with the introduction of fantastic explosives and firearms in video games (ex. *Warcraft*), board/wargames (ex. *Warhammer*), and collectable card games (ex. *Magic: The Gathering*) has begun to close the former divide, bringing the subgenres inexorably closer. The rise in popularity of certain anime and "Western anime" series (including *Avatar: The Last Airbender* and *The Legend of Korra*) has also influenced and accelerated closing the divide. This is especially the case with settings that seem to randomly mix technological development levels, often for aesthetic purposes or plot. The divide has dwindled enough that UF is now often referred to as Modern or Contemporary Fantasy, and UF is sometimes used for, say, medieval fantasies set in urban environments. One of the results of the closing divide is settings like Janloon, capital of Kekon, in Fonda Lee's *Green Bone Saga*, a secondary fantasy world with revolvers and cars, and wuxia-style martial arts in *Godfather*-style families. Another good example is Leigh Bardugo's Grishaverse, a secondary world fantasy setting with magic, rifles, and the beginnings of industrialization (and eventually aircraft, submersibles, tanks, and ironclad ships).

Level of Technology

Determining the level of technology of a society is important for setting the tone of both the society and the overall setting. Additionally, it sets some expectations for and aspects of the society, such as fashion, transportation, and communication. Most of the decision depends on what the creator likes and thinks feels "cool" for the society, setting, or in general. In many ways, the decision goes to Steven Brust's "Cool Stuff Theory of Literature": "All literature consists of whatever the writer thinks is cool. The reader will like the book to the degree that he agrees with the writer about what's cool."[2] Since Brust, himself, likes rapiers and cloaks, that is what he put in his world, instead of full plate armor, greatswords, and advanced military hardware. This decision ultimately affected and shaped the setting and society that he built, including the need to explain why the technology developed the way it did.

There are those who enjoy high-tech magic military thrillers, and those "purists" who believe firearms have no place in fantasy. Both, plus all other points on the spectrum, have their place in the genres, fandoms, and readership. So, the level of technology is mostly guided by the whims of the creator, with the caveat that said whims be deployed in such a way as makes sense and is coherent within the created world. Ultimately, the most important element is that the choices need to make sense, and the repercussions of the tech level should be understood, at least behind the scenes. With that in mind, four broad ideas appear: blanket technology level, piecemeal tech levels, á la carte technology, and technomagic/magi-tech (a.k.a. alt-tech).

Blanket Tech Levels

Possibly the simplest technology level option is to set a global tech level. With this option, every part of the society is at the same level of technological development, regardless of the type of technology. There may still be variance by society in the setting, within reason. Some cultures may be below the global baseline, and some might be a step or two above the base, or on the edge of rising. Regardless, "No system of tech levels can perfectly describe the course of human inventiveness."[3] In this, and really all, case(s), it could help to create a sliding tech scale to make determining multiple societies easier. This is not necessary, however, just potentially helpful. Steve Jackson Games' (SJGames) GURPS presents an easy, useful scale in *GURPS Lite* 4th Edition.[4] The blanket tech level is the simplest solution because all areas of technology are set at the same point. It is, perhaps, not the most realistic, as we know technology does not necessarily advance at a steady pace across different areas, such as communications, transportation, and scientific equipment. Often, even within one area, say transportation, different modes may advance at different rates within a society—ex. trains may advance slower than cars, aircraft may advance faster than watercraft. The blanket tech level also assumes an even spread of technology and even access to technology, for simplicity's sake. This is easier, but also not necessarily realistic due to the costs and supply.

Piecemeal Tech

For piecemeal technology, every area of technology gets its own level or description rather than every type of tech being the same. In some ways, this becomes a more realistic system and allows for fine control of representing different cultures and societies. For example, one society may excel at medicine while another had a breakthrough on sea travel technologies. This form can allow for a further level of differentiation and refinement of different societies in a setting. As some have noted, "Inventions aren't perfected in an instant."[5] They go through trial and error, reverse engineering across cultures, and sometimes move backward before moving forward. Compared to a blanket level, piecemeal is more complicated as each area of technology needs to be defined for each society. This means there is more to keep track of, or to lose track of. However, piecemeal does account for a realistic spread of knowledge and access to technology throughout and across societies. Some sample areas of technology might include power (energy), communications, transportation (sea/water, land, air, other—interdimensional, space, time), armor, weapons, medicine, scientific, data storage, and manufacturing. These are not limits, just some common options to get thoughts rolling.

À la Carte Tech

In the most simple terms, à la carte tech is at the pure whims of the creator. This is the type at which Brust's "Cool Stuff" theory applies best. Basically, à la carte takes whatever the creator likes or wants and puts it in, or takes out what they do not want. This set is not 100 percent random, though. The creator still needs to consider their choices and those decisions need to make some kind of sense or have some sort of, even behind the scenes, reason for the choices. A couple of non-fantasy, or science fantasy, examples come to mind here. For instance, *Dune* decided on knife fighting, which Frank Herbert explained through the invention of personal shields that prevent energy and high-velocity projectiles from being effective weapons. *Cowboy Bebop* is another good example in which 1980s computer terminals sit alongside holo-phones and record players on FTL capable spaceships. Another consideration is that some degree of consistency is required. That is, if technology exists, it should be available to everyone, or at least those who can afford it with reasonable access (e.g., equal, roughly, that of the character using/owning it). Exceptions should be made for highly experimental and unique creations. Obviously, there will still be variation across social classes (access) or societies (development),[6] but otherwise consistency should be retained or an explanation of why it is not consistent (experiment, mad science) should be present.

Technomagic/Magitech

In any fantasy or UF society, the concept of divergent technology can come into play. Divergent, or alternate, technology, in these cases, occurs when technology and magic combine. This can create an effective boost in the level of technology, as often seen in gaslight or steampunk fantasies. In a magitech setting, magic will often boost the technology level in strange or unusual ways.[7] Good examples of magitech settings include post–Shift Atlanta (*Kate Daniels*) with its enchanted water engines for cars; SPI (Lisa Shearin) with the "magetech" mirror portal device of *The Myth Manifestation* and later *SPI Files* books; Camp Half-Blood's Festus the dragon (Rick Riordan); and D&D 5e's artificer class (either from Eberron or *Tasha's Cauldron of Everything*). The magitech setup is different from simply bespelling an item of technology (ex. putting a spell on a car or a phone). Both technology and magic, in this case, are integral to the device functioning—placing a spell on a car may give it extra functionality, but the magic can be separated and the car still functions; in post-Shift Atlanta, a car with an enchanted water engine will not work if the magic is down. Of course, unwanted side effects may also occur when magic and technology are fused. For instance, enchanted water engines allow cars to function in post-Shift Atlanta when a magic wave hits, but said engines are incredibly loud (to the point of largely preventing conversations between passengers). Additionally, magitech is not simply a case where magic replaces technology—ex. Brust's flashstones (flash-bang grenades), Allyson James's mirror communications, or the entirety of the wizarding world in *Harry Potter*.

In most cases of magitech settings, simply having tech skills or simply having magic skills is not enough to make sense of, fix, maintain, or reproduce magitech. Typically, a combination of tech and magic skills, or a team that has such a combination, is required. Magitech does allow, though, for quasi-tech and some creator hand waving in certain circumstances. Some fantastic elements may thus be added to give additional character to a society or setting. Naomi Novik's *Scholomance* series is a good example of magitech, in the school itself. Discworld may present some examples as well in technomantic products and dwarf "devices." *Gunnerkregg Court* provides a good example of divergent tech and the hybridizing of tech and magic. *Girl Genius* may also be a good example with spark science that, while couched in steampunk technobabble, seems to have elements of the magical.

Technology and Magic

Building on the previous chapter, if a society has both magic and technology then there is a need to consider the interactions between the two. Since every fantasy and UF/PNR setting has both, even if one or the other is minimal or there is magic based tech, this is a question for every society. The relationship between magic and technology has been a topic of discussion in the genre from the beginning, more or less. Most early fantasy authors decided on societies based on medieval European technology, or a strange mix of medieval and bronze age. This decision hearkened back to stories of King Arthur, Beowulf, Sigurd, and Robin Hood, stories the authors grew up on. Come the 1930s and 1940s, Fritz Leiber, Tolkien, C.S. Lewis, Jack Williamson, Edgar Rice Burroughs, L. Sprague de Camp and their contemporaries juxtaposed magic and technology in various ways. Leiber had tech as magic (*Gather, Darkness!*); Tolkien effectively set them in opposition (as the elves and magic left Middle Earth, a certain level of technology began to enter). Lewis did a portal fantasy (juxtaposing World War II England with mythic, rustic Narnia), Burroughs played with "a sufficiently advanced technology" in the Barsoom books.

The 1970s and 1980s brought urban fantasy into its own, through Terri Windling's *Borderland/town* series, Charles de Lint, Emma Bull, Glen Cook, Mercedes Lackey, and others. The interaction between technology, particularly modern tech, and magic took a host of different directions ranging from completely inimical to fully integrated, with most falling somewhere in between. The results include Bordertown, where low magic causes tech to be sporadic and unreliable; Newford (de Lint), where pixies live on the internet (*Tapping the Dream Tree*); and post–Shift Atlanta (Andrews), where modern tech and magic take turns working.

Interactions

As indicated, technology and magic have interacted in a variety of ways in the F/UF genres. Here, we will look at the genre and subgenre as different entities, rather than merged into one. Generally speaking, when we use "technology" in this case, it applies to post–Renaissance (European) technology. Ultimately, there are three basic possibilities for tech-magic interaction: they work together, they are diametrically opposed, or somewhere in between.

In the first case, technology and magic have no significant impact on each other. Technology works, magic works, neither impedes the function of the other. High technology items may even be bespelled in some cases, including enchanting a cell phone (Tanya Huff), car (Gaiman and Pratchett's *Good Omens*), or a laptop. Good examples include Tanya Huff's *Gale Women* series, Charles de Lint's Newford books, Michael Scott's *Secrets of the Immortal Nicholas Flamel* (aside from the shadowrealms), Ilona Andrews's *Innkeeper Chronicles*, Terry Pratchett's Discworld, Lisa Shearin's *SPI Files*, Allyson James's *Stormwalker*, and Leigh Bardugo's Grishaverse, to present a mix of primary and secondary settings.

In the case of high technology and magic opposing each other, technology beyond a point set by the creator and magic are inimical to each other. Either they cannot exist together or they cause each other to fail, sometimes explosively or terminally. This option is often used as a means of limiting the tech level of a society or setting. In some cases, there may be societies in the world that reject (or otherwise lack access to) magic and develop technology alongside high magic-low tech societies. Examples here include Ilona Andrews's *Kate Daniels* series (alternating magic and tech waves), Rick Riordan's *Kane Chronicles* (in which a spell cast directly on a CCTV camera causes it to fail due to the interaction), and elements of Shearin's *SPI Files* (specifically, the high magic, low tech goblin and elf homeworld). The presence of magic as inimical to technology can be an argument for halting technological development and for preventing the use of magic in some places.

The space between these extremes is fertile ground for all sorts of possibilities. There could be societies where tech and magic become sporadic and unreliable when they are together. Failure of either tech or magic could occur under certain specific conditions. They could interact normally, except in specific places for a host of reasons. Examples include Windling's Bordertown/land (Faerie is all magic, Earth is all tech, the Border is an unreliable mix of the two), Jim Butcher's *Dresden Files* (where even passive magic, such as the presence of a wizard who is not actively casting spells, makes modern technology unreliable), and J.K. Rowling's *Harry Potter* (where high concentrations of magic cause electronics to fail, e.g., at Hogwarts).

Technology and Religion

The question of technology and its religious impact, or relationship with religion, has been a complicated one in our own world. It is, potentially, even more so in a secondary fantasy society, though perhaps less so in UF/PNR (or at least not addressed as much). The presence of active deities could add extra dimensions to the relationship. Likewise, the level of influence of the religion on society impacts the relationship. The impact could be relatively benign, including technology being used to help spread the religion. On the other hand, it could be seemingly negative, as tech development may call into question the tenets of the religion.[8] Different religions in the society may also respond in very different ways. Even a single religion could have multiple, contradictory, responses at once. A religious response to tech development could even become encoded in societal language and sayings, such as "If God had meant us to _____, He'd have given us _____."

Good Relationship

Depending on the type, presence, and role of deities in the society, a given religion could either embrace or otherwise have good relations with technology. Faiths focused on crafting, smithing, and knowledge deities are likely to embrace technological development. Such faiths might even be the driving forces behind tech development. Whether they embrace technology across the board or only in their own hands is another story (see "It's Complicated" below). This relationship and situation is one we would expect to see in the *Forgotten Realms* setting with Gond, the god of craftsmen, inventors, and smiths or Krynn (*Dragonlance*) with Reoryx, the local equivalent of Gond. Although not explicitly religious as such, the children of Hephaestus and Athena in Riordan's *Percy Jackson* series could fit as well, since they are demigods and inventors of all sorts of alternate tech.

Bad Relations

Far from embracing new technologies, some faiths may perceive technological development, or the information and learning that result, as a threat. On one hand, technology could take some power, say literacy, enjoyed almost exclusively by the clergy and make it available to all. Technological development could also make it possible to disseminate "heretical" views and branches of the faith much more easily. It could give access to sacred texts to all people in the society, without the mediating hand of the clergy. It may also be true that technology of a certain stage could replicate miracles. Similarly, with new tech advances come new industries and new challenges. Some such industries could be directly or indirectly harmful to a religion, such as nature focused deities faced with the development of factories. In other cases, the information and knowledge gained through technological advances could call into question religious dogma. Some such fields include genetics, astronomy, and geology. In such cases, a flexible, embracing faith may alter and adapt its dogma and doctrine. On the other hand, an inflexible, tech rejecting faith may deny and demonize the new information and the technology that allowed it to be produced.

It's Complicated

Most societies and situations will fall somewhere between the two extremes above. That is, they fit the "it's complicated" territory. For example, Fritz Leiber's *Gather, Darkness* features priests (and their "evil" counterparts) who embrace and use advanced technology, in their own hands, but attempt to keep it from others in order to maintain their own power and place in the society. C.J. Cherryh's *Sword of Knowledge* trilogy is built around a group of scientists and engineers who create a religion (and monastic fortress) in order to preserve technology and learning against an encroaching "dark age" (sort of a shorter, fantasy version of Isaac Asimov's *Foundation* series). Looking to our own world, medieval Christianity embraced scientific technology (among monks at least) and both preserved and advanced scientific and technical knowledge, but also opposed the moveable type printing press (as a threat to the Church due to the easier spread of heresy).

Technology and Society

To say that technological development impacts, shapes, and alters society is to state the glaringly obvious.[9] In the last 40 years (since the early 1980s), our own societies have gone from personal computers being rare to carrying powerful computers in our pockets and wearing computers on our wrists. In the last 30 years, we have gone from an internet of pure text to an internet where graphics nearly outweigh text, especially if we include streaming video. Those brief spans have profoundly altered most of the societies in our world. The same should hold true, at least to some extent, with fictional societies. The rate of change and dissemination of technological advances may be slower, depending on the starting level, but present. Leigh Bardugo's Grishaverse (ironclad ships, submersibles, rockets, aircraft) and Terry Pratchett's Discworld (the clacks, trains) are excellent examples. Travel, communications, and commerce technologies are likely to be among the most obvious in their impact, but all come into play to change and direct society down different paths. Here, the focus will be on the impacts to government, social interaction, economics, and law.

Government

Perhaps the four most important areas of technology that affect governments are communications, data storage and retrieval, military, and travel. These are also the areas of technological development that governments attempt to legislate, control, restrict, and/or keep ahead of other societies in. They are, often, the ones that governments invest the most funding, research, and work hours into.

Communications technology allows communication within and beyond the society. It also introduces opportunities for trade and other commerce across internal and external borders with greater ease. With this, of course, is an exchange of ideas, cultures, and views, as well as knowledge of how other societies work and what people are like elsewhere. Open governments will likely encourage such technologies to build bridges with other cultures and create greater understanding across cultural lines. Insular and repressive governments are more likely to try to prevent, stifle, and control such technologies as threats to the stability of the regime and its power. Most will fall somewhere in between.

Data storage and retrieval technologies are huge for governments. They help to determine population trends, growth, and movement. The ability to store and easily retrieve data helps with aid programs, determining spending/resource distribution, and even elected government representation. With such technologies, a government can track licensing and court rulings much more easily (or lack of such technology can make both more difficult). More open governments will keep much of this technology open to researchers, journalists, legal practitioners (lawyers, judges), and related individuals. More repressive governments will seek to control and limit such technology. All governments will, of course, have some sort of classified data, to protect covert intelligence and military operatives and their own technological development. This is even true in secondary fantasy settings.

Military technology is obviously one area that governments throughout history have wanted to keep on top of, in relation to other societies and civilians (once a military-civilian divide occurred). This sort of development ranges from iron versus bronze to modern drones. There can, and often are, conservative elements on the government (and military) side in this branch of technology—a favoring of the old, tried, and true technology that is known to work over the untested new tech. How this works in specifics varies and depends heavily on the government type. Obviously, a more diplomacy oriented government is likely to tend toward less development here, while an expansionistic, militarist government is more likely (but not required) to be heavily focused here.

Travel technology tends to aid in communication and commerce within and beyond a society. Advances in travel tend to broaden the horizons and experiences of people in a society. In more liberal/open societies, such technologies are more likely to be encouraged, both within the bounds of the society and beyond. Comparatively, more repressive governments are likely to restrict access to, or attempt to control, such technology whether aircraft, ships, or canal boats. They are also likely to attempt to repress nomadic and semi-nomadic subcultures within the society for the same reasons.

Social

The impact of tech development on social aspects of a society are complicated. Communication technologies are the key area here. On one hand, people have argued, since the first newspapers or earlier, that there are detrimental effects, but we also see positive effects across societies. Some technological development could reduce personal, face-to-face, communication and limit the reliance on or connection to others as work becomes easier to perform alone or communication tech allows for less direct interaction. On the other side, tech development can allow for organization in society to become much easier—as seen in civil rights organizing or protests against governments. Such developments can also create connections between people across society and beyond, depending on the range of such technology and access. Technological developments can allow for a wider spread of ideas and, therefore, a wider connection to people, often with similar interests, thereby bridging cultural gaps. The development of the clacks in Pratchett's Discworld is a prime example (as it mirrors the rises of both the telegraph and the internet).

Economic

Any sort of technological development, and magitech development, has an impact on a society's economy. The level of impact depends on the specific development, the type of technology, and how widespread it is (or access to it is). Any new tech development, whether during worldbuilding or behind the scenes, creates new industries or parts of the economy. They may also minimize or remove old, outdated industries. For example, cassette tapes ended 8-tracks and CDs ended cassettes, so the music industry and manufacturing had to adapt and change or become obsolete (also true of the move to streaming technologies). The old industry may resent and attempt to derail new technologies (as seen with the modern fossil fuel versus renewable energy industries), which could spawn internal culture conflicts and plots.[10]

New technology developments could free up sections of the populace, allowing or causing a shift from rural to urban centers, or vice versa. The population thereby moves out of some industries, such as agriculture or manufacturing, and into others. Historically, our own world saw, and continues to see, this shift. A key example is the aftereffects of the Black Death in 14th-century Europe, when the population moved from villages and farms to cities and farmers took up more financially lucrative trades and crafts in the urban centers. Similarly, tech development can also entirely change an economic focus. An agricultural society could become industrial, an industrial one could become service/ideas based in its economy. Only rarely does it appear that an old economy is entirely replaced, but development could be a cause for an historical shift. Depending on how the magical arts/craft work, magitech could bring a cottage potion economy into a mass produced potion economy, for example.

Laws

In our own world, laws have been employed, historically, to limit and prevent technological development. Sometimes those "laws" are solely referred to as tradition, with the force of law (or more force than law), but are still used in attempts to stifle technological development. At the same time, laws notoriously tend to be too slow to keep up with changes in technology after a certain point (maybe the 19th century or so). This means they are often years behind tech developments or decades to centuries ahead due to ignorance of current technology. The purpose or role of laws regarding technology depends on the government, both the type and who controls it. Benevolent, open governments are likely to enact laws to protect citizens from the negative effects of technological development—including issues of pollution, privacy, and body autonomy. Repressive governments, conversely, are likely to enact laws to stifle tech development or limit access to it, to retain power—this is what happened for a time with the printing press in Europe and China. Governments controlled by guilds, or corporations, may enact laws to stifle tech development, or to keep it solely in their own hands, to retain economic power. Societies controlled by a religion or clergy interact with technology laws in myriad ways, depending on the faith's reaction to technology. Finally, if technology (beyond a certain point) and magic are inimical, laws may be enacted to protect magic and end tech development, if magic is deemed to be the preferred of the two.

7

Education

Hogwarts School of Witchcraft and Wizardry, Unseen University, Miskatonic University, and Illuminati University (IOU).

Most worlds have some sort of education involved, whether mundane, military, paranormal, or something else. These are situations and places that offer a shared experience with the reader and, for places, present an interesting site to be explored outside the regular constraints of society.

In setting up the chapters and discussion on the subject of building societies, I decided to give education its own chapter for a couple of reasons. First, education is my own professional background, therefore it is something I think about and discuss a lot. Second, with the proliferation of young adult literature, especially since 1990, education and the school story have become increasingly a part of the fantasy and urban fantasy genres. This is true at all ages from children's through the adult/collegiate level, as evidenced from LeGuin's *Earthsea* to Rowling's *Harry Potter*, Black and Clare's *Magisterium* to the *Vampire Diaries* spin-off *Legacies*, or Grossman's *The Magicians* to elements of Harkness's *A Discovery of Witches* and Olivie Blake's *The Atlas Six*.

This chapter will not go into pedagogical theory and such, as this is not the place for those discussions. Additionally, others have been exploring fictional depictions of pedagogy, especially with *Harry Potter*.[1] Instead, the chapter is divided between general and specialized education with subtopics covering the how, what, and who questions in relatively broad strokes. The questions of where and when will be left partially on the sidelines for the time being.

How Society Teaches

As noted, this section will not get into pedagogy or education theory. There is no reason for such things to appear in most fictional works, at least not consciously or directly. In some cases, they might, if the classroom is part of the focus or takes a significant role in the narrative (as it occasionally does in *Harry Potter, Magisterium,* and *The Magicians*). Sometimes the pedagogy does give insights into the character of the instructor, as we see in Rowling's work. Instead of focusing there, this section will broadly focus on two major classes of "how" society teaches its members: informal and formal teaching. Informal teaching has a variety of sub-possibilities and techniques, while formal teaching's variety of techniques are often based on a specific type of study. Both are used in societies for different purposes and types of information. In this way, they work together to create and affect society and shape those who live within the culture. These effects and methods help to make the culture distinct from others around it.

Informal Education

For simplicity's sake, this section focuses on three major informal methods of education: stories, self-teaching, and family. Each of the three has an important role in most societies and comes with its pros and cons. They also have specific uses for which they work, and others for which they are, perhaps, not the best approach.

Stories—including folklore, legends, and myths—of all sorts have been employed throughout real-world history to convey social norms and values. Stories also appear in some fiction, often in excerpted form, for the same purpose and to add depth to the created world. Individual types of stories tend to have their own purposes and uses. For instance, folklore and fairy tales most often express acceptable behaviors and punish divergent behavior, according to social views. We see this in the 17th-century tendency to add explicit morals to the end of older stories (ex. Charles Perrault's versions of fairy tales, that end with a variation on "The moral of the story is …," a construct lacking in earlier versions). In a similar vein, cultural legends and myths build the culture's view of itself. They reinforce what the society wants to be known for or how it wishes to be seen by others, regardless of the reality of its actions or situation. These stories perpetuate and pass on traditions and social practices. They even keep languages alive in some cases, as translations always lose something, however little, so passing the stories on in the original is often best. Many authors tap into this essential element of societies to breathe life into their fictional cultures, from Tolkien's inclusion of songs and stories (usually from elves, Aragorn, or the occasional hobbit) to Terry Pratchett's introductions to several *Discworld* books (ex. "quoting" quasi-religious stories about the dwarf "not-a-god" Tak). Most cultural teaching via stories is unconscious, in that the listener/reader picks up the lesson on a subconscious level and the teaching is not necessarily done with intent. Most who transmit such stories simply think they are telling amusing stories, or carrying on a tradition their parents or grandparents had with them as children.

Conversely, self-teaching requires conscious effort on the part of the learner. Self-teaching ranges from trial and error to watching YouTube videos. Obviously, this is easier for some fields and subjects than for others. For example, changing out a light switch via watching YouTube videos is pretty easy, but many self-taught alchemists in history ended up killing themselves by inhaling or ingesting toxic materials (such as mercury, in both liquid and gaseous forms). Self-teaching is never the only method of education in a society. At the very least, it tends to be paired with or grounded in societal stories and family teaching. Even more often, self-teaching builds out of some form of formal education. As a method, self-teaching is limited by access to materials—instructional texts, videos, raw materials if necessary—and ability to understand instructional materials, if any. The ability to learn from, or survive, mistakes and adapt to failures (e.g., trial and error) is also key, as is the ability to accurately identify and correct the cause(s) of failure. If attempted at random, self-teaching can cause a great degree of frustration or misinformation. If approached in a scientific manner, it can be an effective method of learning at least the basics of many things. Self-teaching does often seem to be at its most effective in relatively simple or beginning level situations.

The third major element of informal education is that passed on by families. Like stories, family-based education tends to be unconscious in that the teachers do not necessarily consciously think about teaching and the "student" learns on a subconscious level. Families educate in a variety of ways from passing on cultural stories to family history. They pass on a certain level of ethics, examples of personal relations, outlooks on the world, and the parents' values (both stated/claimed and actual—what they say versus what they do). Family-based learning can also include certain skills like cooking, home maintenance/cleaning, possibly basic carpentry, plumbing, gardening, landscaping, car maintenance, and whatever other skills others in the household possess, or choose to pass on. More often than not, this type of education occurs through observed behavior and overheard conversations, though assisting parents or older siblings can also be a factor. Availability of information—via books, television, radio, access to the internet—may also be a factor. The conscious level of family-based education tends to be piecemeal, for instance a parent is unlikely to teach their child everything about electrical work, but does teach the child how to change out a bad light switch, possibly explaining each step as the child observes or hands over tools.

Formal Education

In most cases, formal education is primarily outside the home and conducted by experts or otherwise skilled professionals. Formal education also tends to be more specialized, structured, and in-depth than informal education. For these purposes, formal education will be divided into three key varieties: apprenticeship, school, and tutoring.

Apprenticeships are one of, if not the, oldest forms of formal education. They evolved over time from what was probably an informal practice to a highly formal, sometimes complex, practice involving contracts to eventually being little more than a job rank. In the pre-modern era, a potential student, usually a child, entered service with a master of a craft or trade. A financial transaction with the parents, in which the parent paid the crafts/tradesman to take on an apprentice, might be involved in some cases. The student then worked for the master in return for room, board, and instruction in the trade/craft. Eventually, the trade/craft guild system and related groups formed and formalized the ranks of apprentice, journeyman, and master, among others. They also formalized and attempted to standardize the requirements and duties for ranks, the apprentice-master relationship, and the contracts of apprenticeship. The apprenticeship process taught the craft, trade, or skill as well as basic business practices, guild society and politics (if a guild was involved), an introduction to trade secrets (and magic or rituals, if such things existed in the trade), and possibly reading and writing. The practice has been adapted in many works of fiction for the instruction of magic, as seen in E.B. White's *The Once and Future King*, LeGuin's *Earthsea*, John Flanagan's *The Ranger's Apprentice*, and Asprin's *Myth Adventures*.

Schools arrived somewhat later than apprenticeships in many cultures. They bring the masters of a diverse body of knowledge together in one place, or may be a single instructor who gathers students to their home or a public place (ex. the Greek agora). The school typically has a greater number of students per instructor than apprenticeship. They also allow for a wider dissemination of information and greater variety of information in one place. In most cases, schools tend to focus on non-craft/trade subjects. In our own history, the focus tended to be on languages, history, philosophy, literature, natural history (science), medicine, law (canon and secular), and theology. Today, school instruction has expanded to virtually anything. A physical school could be a single building or a place composed of several related buildings, such as a schoolhouse or a modern university campus. Alternately, it could be spread across a wide variety of rooms in several unrelated buildings, as in the medieval universities.[2] Instruction methods vary from lectures to discussion to practicum or a mix of multiple methods. In some ways, the formal school seems a natural growth from the guild standardization of apprentice requirements as school curriculum, but covering a broader range of learning. Schools are common in the fantasy and UF genres, from Hogwarts School of Witchcraft and Wizardry to Unseen University, The Citadel (Westeros) to Scholomance (both legend and Novik).

Today, tutoring tends to refer to extra help for a student, presented in combination with teachers. Historically, however, a tutor would be the sole teacher working with one student, or perhaps multiple children in the same household. Historically, private tutors were common among nobles and the wealthier craftsmen and merchants. Today, private tutoring is still present with child actors and some others. Subjects taught via tutoring depend heavily on who hired the tutor—the medieval and Renaissance wealthy often hired tutors to teach their daughters languages, music, and reading whereas modern tutors are often hired to teach child actors a full range of subjects or to help any student with one or two specific areas in which they struggle. Examples of private tutors are fairly slim in modern F/UF, but are perhaps present in Sapkowski's *The Witcher* among others.

What Society Teaches

Depending on the focus of the world or narrative, knowing what society teaches can be as important as how society teaches. What is taught could be addressed in broad strokes: the Orders of High Sorcery in Krynn do not teach certain magics or in the *SPI Files* world most magicians are not taught "dark magic." On another hand, this could be more specific—such as in *Harry Potter* where classes occur as part of the narrative and the curriculum is occasionally discussed. What level of detail is needed depends on the focus—for Krynn and SPI the learning component is not a focus, but education is a major element of *Harry Potter* and all other school based settings and stories. What methods a given society uses often depend on what is being taught and the society. For these purposes, the section will look at five areas: social mores, religious education, trades and crafts, scholarship, and magic.

Social Mores/Values

All societies inherently teach social values and mores. This is part of what makes a society a society, and is also true of subcultures. Typically instruction in social values is done in an unconscious or subconscious fashion, but it can certainly be overt. Usually, instruction in social mores/

values appears in assumptions made by the society and the lessons found in folklore or other stories told by members of the culture. It could include depictions of heroic figures—both who is depicted and how or why they are depicted. Such lessons likely include basic things that allow society to function—ex. theft is bad, killing your neighbor is bad. The lessons can also be less positive or outright negative—ex. nationalism, classism, racism, sexism, and other bigotry, often in the form of exceptionalism. Lessons in social values may also come from family education as parents and extended family consciously teach and unconsciously demonstrate behavior that reflects the values they learned from family and society. A good example here is the character Ron Weasley, who verbally repeats societal values in his reactions to both the revelation that Remus Lupin is a werewolf and Hermione's creation of SPEW.[3] Instruction in social values can also be found in formal education, particularly schools. The schools' chosen curriculum, from both subjects to actual course content, can reinforce social values, including biases in the instruction itself (ex. teachers who consciously or unconsciously favor male students in science classes and dismiss female students). This can also be seen, perhaps, to a lesser degree in apprenticeships and tutoring. The latter are more like family instruction, but also may include subcultural values—ex. a guild may have its own values or private tutoring may reveal gender biases/values based on the subjects taught.

Religious Education

In most societies, people also tend to learn about the culture's dominant religion(s), even if there is no official state or single societal religion. At the very least, members will see the prevalence and location of religious iconography; locations, size, and prevalence of places of worship; and other public displays of religious affiliation (and possibly belief). Folklore and stories are a key informal method here. For example, most people in the Americas know the Christian stories about Christmas and Easter, even if they do not practice that faith, because the stories have saturated the societies of the continents. Such stories may spread and teach religious beliefs via transmitting the full story. More likely, they get passed on through references (the Good Samaritan, appearing in the name of various non-profit groups) and common sayings ("For Pete's sake!," referring to Saint Peter), or, in the modern world, through memes. Families are the other major informal transmitter of religious education. Parents tend to teach their children about their own faith, or lack thereof, and tend to expect conformity to that faith. Private tutoring may also include religious instruction, even if only the basics passed on to the laity. This could occur directly or indirectly (through art, music, literature, and philosophy). The exact method in tutoring depends on the tutor, a tutor who is a member of the clergy may be more overt than a lay tutor.

Apprenticeships are only likely to teach about religious subjects if the society is pantheistic or has saints/angels. If the trade or craft has a patron god, saint, or angel, then masters are likely to teach their apprentices the proper rites used by the trade/craft to acknowledge or worship said divinity (or semi-divinity). These rites are probably going to be different from the formal rites performed by clergy of the deity or faith, adapted to the trade's workspace. Schools are similarly variable. Some faiths may have formal schools to teach potential clergy, at least in theology though possibly in history, philosophy, languages, and other areas. If a given faith controls education, then they might control all schools, or they may have religiously oriented schools (ex. Catholic schools, in our world). Even secular schools may offer religious instruction, on a scholarly level, for lay persons—ex. modern Religious Studies or Comparative Religions majors at the university level, or the Doctor of Divinity degree.

Trades and Crafts

Societies that achieve a certain point of size and technological development always develop specialists in certain areas. Virtually all eventually have a need for brickmakers, smiths (of various sorts), carpenters, stonemasons, and related professionals. Eventually, they may broaden out to include scribes, bookbinders, printers, weavers, and hundreds of other trades and crafts. In our own world, historically, the trades tended to be taught through apprenticeships, to the point that the guild-apprenticeship language of rankings still holds to some extent today in Euro-American societies. Apprenticeships in trades may be more or less formal, could be hereditary, or could be overseen or even assigned by guilds. This all depends on the size, location, and views of the society, and the presence or strength of guilds. Modern societies, as with our real ones, may use formal schooling to teach trades and crafts. Trade schools exist for this reason, alongside some college level programs at community colleges. Even non-trade college level courses may involve trade/craft training—ex. art departments often include pottery, metalworking, weaving, welding, and jewelry making while theater departments may teach carpentry (set construction) and tailoring (costume making). In some cases, types of magic, such as alchemy, may also be considered a trade. They may not even be considered a magic as such—ex. Discworld's alchemists, conjurors, and thaumaturgists—leading to trade-style methods of instruction. Self-teaching through trial and error is not uncommon in some trades, along with video

7. Education   119

instruction (e.g., YouTube) in more modern practices. Family instruction is also possible, potentially even likely, causing hereditary apprenticeship instruction or a self-taught parent teaching their child.

Scholarship

Societies that move beyond a subsistence level see a degree of specialization into trades. Most also see the evolution of scholars, people who pursue intellectual activities in a variety of fields and subject those fields to intense study, thereby increasing the collective knowledge of the society. There may be many possible names for those people in various societies, from scholars to maesters (Westeros). In some societies, scholarship is an apprenticeship based education. The potential scholar (sage, wiseperson) works and studies under a single individual with the intent of assisting them and eventually inheriting their position in society. This could also be related to private tutoring as the mentor/master may fulfill both types of roles. In some cases, the role of scholar could be inherited by a family line, thereby adding family education as part of tutoring and apprenticeship. This is not uncommon in caste-based social structures. For the last informal method, despite some people's claims, self-taught scholars are rare enough to be statistical anomalies.

Formal schools tend to be the source of most scholars and scholarship, at least in our own world's history. This is true regardless of culture or society, once a society reaches a point at which it can support such an institution. These students follow the practice of research and study in classrooms, libraries, and laboratories under the guidance of experts in various subjects. Ideally, the experts also conduct their own research and push the boundaries of current knowledge while instructing future generations to extend those boundaries even further.

Magic

Since working magic exists in F/UF settings, societies will adapt methods to teach it. Often societal means of teaching magic exist to protect the other members of society from mishaps, to protect the student from mishaps, to control magic, to limit access to magic, and/or to protect the secrets of magic. It may help us to think of magic as a weapon or as a potentially dangerous profession or field of study (like explosives or nuclear engineering). Self-taught magic could be possible, depending on the nature of magic. Likewise, self-taught magic could be exceedingly dangerous, again depending on the nature of magic. In our own history most magicians were self-taught, as are many practitioners in Hearne's *Seven*

Kennings, to generally good ends. Conversely, Novik's Scholomance shows semi-self-taught magic that must be approached carefully or things can go horribly wrong, with deadly consequences.

Magic instruction via apprenticeships is common in literature and could be family based. This method provides the guidance and instruction of a master to keep the student safe. Examples include Arthurian legend, *Myth Adventures*, Scott's *The Secrets of the Immortal Nicholas Flamel*, and Stroud's *Bartimaeus Sequence*. Apprenticeships provide relative safety and a possibility for a degree of standardization in practices. This could tie in with tutoring, though the tutor/master may not be mortal. The instructor could be demonic (ex. history, Stroud) or otherwise otherworldly as in a spirt or quasi-divine entity (ex. Netflix's *Wu Assassin* or *Dungeons & Dragons*' warlock class).

Formal schools of magic have been an idea since at least the Renaissance with the Scholomance, a legendary school of dark magic supposed to be run by Lucifer itself. The concept appeared off and on for centuries, then hit a sort of apex in the mid–1990s with *Harry Potter* and those influenced by it. Key examples include LeGuin's *Earthsea*, Pratchett's Unseen University, Rowling's Hogwarts, Ilona Andrews's post–Shift Atlanta, Novik's Scholomance, Asprin's *Myth Adventures*, and S.A. Chakraborty's Citadel (*The World of Daevabad*). Schools take many forms, sometimes tied to a period of apprenticeship before or after formal schooling. Usually the school creates a relatively safe environment to learn the basics of magic, protecting the populace and students while also limiting access and controlling both what is taught and how fast it is taught (ostensibly for safety of the students).

Who Has Access to Education

Once we have established how and what our fictional society teaches, we should look at who has access to education. Depending on how in depth we wish to get, this could be quite simple or very complex. The society's approach to education and what areas we look at are important factors. Likewise, the what and how can create different levels of education access, as we see in our own history—e.g., nearly everyone has access to stories, family, and self-teaching, fewer have access to tutoring, and access to apprenticeships and school are limited beyond a certain point.

The last opens up the question of access to different types of education. In most societies, everyone hears folklore, fairy tales, and cultural legends. They are difficult to miss, as they appear in music, advertising, political documents, and art. Most, nearly all, have access to family based education, whether birth, adopted, or surrogate families. And many to most have at least some access to self-teaching. As indicated, apprenticeships tend to be limited, by the master seeing traits they look for or the ability of the parent to pay/contract the master. In a modern setting, apprenticeships may be limited by school programs or by socio-economic class. Traditionally, school access has also been limited by economic class—or access to certain levels of schooling, or quality schools, has been. This could be through financial requirements or connection to social-religious institutions. Likewise, tutoring is often only accessible to those who can afford it, though in modern settings it might be available through schools or public libraries.

Access could also be limited based on what is being taught. Most people in society have access to learning about social mores and values, through stories, entertainment, and the people around them. However, access to religious, scholarly, trade, martial, and magic education are often limited. Sometimes this is done consciously, other times unconsciously, or systemically, by society or by those who control education. For example, several branches of Christianity limit religious instruction, beyond a certain point, to males only, while others teach women as well but do not allow instruction based on sexual orientation. Access to literacy, for example, was also often limited, in large part because "literacy governs history, science, knowledge, accounting, debts, records, land claims, justice, and the law," creating a great deal of power for those who control it.[4] Who has access to education has a profound effect on the spread of knowledge and information. Restrictions, or openness, can be used to control information and knowledge for nefarious or altruistic purposes. That is, it can be used to retain power or to protect society, sometimes both at the same time. Access can be used to control social mobility or to control certain segments of the population (based on race, species, ethnicity, gender, sex, class, or faith, for instance). Typically, societies that restrict access tend to be seen as less positive societies, for modern audiences. They may not be seen as wholly bad or "evil," but generally as problematic, which could be the point, and the beginning of a narrative's plot.

Everyone (in Theory)

The most inclusive option in education is that all education of all types is available to all people in society. As we can see from our own world, more often than not, perhaps always, this is an ideal rather than a reality. That does not mean that such a system is impossible in a fictional society, though, even if it is potentially utopic. On one level, fully inclusive education access seems like a perfect ideal. In fact, it has been a key element in some works of utopian fiction. However, utopias, as we know, cannot exist even in fiction, the very name says so.[5] In theory, a society allowing, or making possible, access to any level of education to any person would be a great leveling force in society and encourage advancements and social progress. In theory, it would eliminate overlooked and lost genius and innovation that are untapped due to limits on education based on gender, race, or finances.

Completely open access to education does not, however, mean that everyone in society gravitates toward formal schooling and scholarship (or religious education or magic), as some might think. Rather, it simply means that all options exist and are available. The individual may choose a trade apprenticeship, a religious apprenticeship, magic tutoring, or any other option (or no option) that they desire. This choice will, ideally, be made without social or family pressures, though those will likely exist.

On a potentially negative side, this also means that dangerous education could be easily accessed by those who will abuse it. Imagine here, the sociopath with access to a solid education in magic (several villains fit here) or a similar situation. This has the makings of a good, if fairly typical, antagonist story—ex. Rowling's Tom Riddle or Bardugo's Darkling. In this way, the universal access to education can be the source or vehicle of a narrative's plot, and the undoing of the utopia that it creates.

Very Limited

At the far extreme from access for all, access to education could be extremely limited, beyond social mores, stories, and family. Even self-teaching can be restricted, or made more difficult, due to access to materials. All types of formal education—apprenticeships, tutoring, schools—could potentially be restricted by any factors from social class to sex, race to faith, orientation to citizenship status. In extreme cases, all levels and types of education may be limited to a single, very narrow category—ex. upper class, male humans of the state religion who are full citizens.

Plenty of examples of societies with very restrictive education limits exist, both in our own history and in the F/UF genres. Sometimes the restrictions are based not on education as a whole but by what is taught or how it is taught. For example, medieval Europe's schools were only open to male Christians, as the Church operated all universities. Most such students were technically clergy, albeit lay or secular clergy,[6] an odd category, in most cases (many "secular clergy" were children of wealthy merchants or tradesmen who continued in the family business). For various reasons, in Pratchett's Discworld, Unseen University is only open to men (for education in wizardry), while the apprenticeship-self teaching hybrid method used by witches is only available to women (with one notable exception of a female wizard in *Equal Rites*). Steven Brust's Dragaera setting only mentions schools in passing and rarely, but magic instruction (sorcery, wizardry, necromancy) is only open to the noble houses (not peasants). Of course, the noble houses are all the Dragaeran houses except one (the Teckla), but it does also exclude virtually all Easterners (humans), except those able to buy themselves titles in House Jhereg (known as the source of the empire's organized crime). Chakraborty's *The City of Brass* limits magic instruction by race (djinn versus part-djinn) and social class (the ruling tribe of djinn gets more advanced access than the other tribes in the city have access to, deliberately). U.S. history is also a long example of restricting access to education based on race (denying access to PoC), sex (denying access to women), and faith (limiting non–Christian access).

Limits to access can be more or less restrictive. On one level, all access to all education could be limited to one group of people. Alternately, each type of material, or subject matter (ex. magic, religion), could be limited to a specific group. Or access to specific types of education (school, apprenticeships) could be limited to a specific group, giving that group an edge in other areas of society or as a feature of a restrictive caste society (ex. only members of the religious caste can get religious training, only those of the bottom most caste can get apprenticeships in plumbing). Whatever the restriction or limits, though, it tends to be socio-economic-political-religious minorities who have their access to education restricted or forbidden outright, not those in the majorities.[7]

Somewhat Limited

Falling somewhere between everyone and extremely limited, the "somewhat limited" category covers the majority of the spectrum of access to education. Rather than one class, sex, race, gender, faith, or whatnot having sole access, some to most have access depending on where the society falls on the spectrum. This is where the ideal of unrestricted often falls in practice due to societal pressures, biases, economics, and a host of other factors. The somewhat limited level often means that access to education is not guaranteed, but may or will require more work for some than others. This could be at specific levels of education, or for specific types or areas, or in all areas. Connections, contacts, and wealth within a family, among other factors, may play a part in access to education. Additionally, government programs may exist to assist potential students, whether in the form of preparation programs or financial grants, loans, scholarships, or placement and regulation. As with the extreme ends of the spectrum, access could vary by what is taught or by the method of instruction. For instance, schooling may be more available than tutors or a trade education may be more accessible than a magic education. Playing with these restrictions on access can be a way to limit the impact of things like magic, technology, or religion on a society. Conversely, limited access can also give practitioners of magic/technology or clergy additional mystique (as in the case of blacksmiths, historically) or greater influence and power in society.

Creating a School

Most education methods discussed above require only minimal preparation. A formal school, however, needs something more, even if it only exists off-stage as it were. To that end, this section has a few major elements that are useful for creating a school—whether mundane, magical, or something else.

First, we should know what the place looks like. Is there one building or many? What do the buildings look like? What is housed in each building? What are the grounds like? Are there any special rooms, ex. Hogwarts's Room of Requirement or Unseen University's Library? What is the visual and emotional feel of the school? The description is a key to the overall feel of the place and sets the tone, from Hogwarts's castle in Scotland to the Tower of Wayreth surrounded by its moving forest (*Dragonlance*), Unseen University (an urban, walled, university) to Brakebills University in NYC (a hidden, urban, modern, university).

Another important factor is the school curriculum. On one level, this is what the school teaches (ex. magic, mundane subjects, martial arts). On another, it is how the school teaches (ex. formal classes as in Hogwarts, individual or group mentorships as in the Magisterium, or a hybrid of the two). Curriculum can also include how long it typically takes for students to graduate (ex. Hogwarts takes seven years). It also includes whether there are any required subject areas, and/or for how long (ex. it takes five years to graduate, but History is only required for two years). This gives a basic understanding of what graduates go through and a baseline of experience and knowledge for educated members of the society.

A faculty and staff hierarchy can also be an important factor, especially if the narrative is set in the school itself. In these cases, knowing if the faculty are divided into groups (ex. departments) or ranked (ex. junior, senior; assistant professor, associate professor) can be important. Likewise, knowing who is in charge of the school's daily operations, including maintenance, can be useful. This is mostly the staff from caretakers to librarians, as well as who they report to. Finally, it involves who oversees the school. On a simple level: is the head of the school a headmaster, chancellor, president, ArchDean, high magister, or something else? Do they have an assistant? Is a group in charge instead of an individual? How does one become head of the school (ex. appointed, elected, volunteered)? Is there oversight of the school from outside, if so who (ex. a board of trustees)? What powers does the oversight individual/group have (ex. can name the school head, but cannot set curriculum)?

Perhaps of greatest importance is the question of what requirements, if any, exist for someone to become a student, staff member, or faculty at the institution? Do students need to apply (The Citadel) or are they automatically enrolled (Hogwarts) or "head hunted" (Brakebills)? What age do they have to be as students? Are there any species, gender, or skill requirements (ex. human, 11 years of age, talent for magic)? The same is true for faculty and staff, with the addition of asking what process a hopeful staff/teacher needs to go through and what background they need. For example, at Hogwarts, the Headmaster seems to simply appoint whoever s/he wants as faculty either based on interviews (Trelawney) or just because (Lupin, Slughorn, Moody).

If a narrative is set at the institution, it is also important to know what rules the school has. That is, what sort of things are forbidden at the school? Are students allowed to have pets, be armed, live on campus, live off campus, or have vehicles (either all the time or under certain circumstances)? Is there contraband, and if so is there a student black-market? How are the rules enforced and who does the enforcing (ex. faculty and staff, a campus security team)? Finally, what punishments can be handed out by the enforcers and/or the school?

Last, and possibly of least (or greatest) importance, is the school history. This is more important if the school is a major part of the world/narrative, less so if it is not. Assuming it is important, then we ask what has gone on at the school? When was is founded? How many leaders has it had? Was it involved in any major historical events? Was it built all at once or over several decades/centuries? Has its role changed over time? Has it expanded over time? Are there any rumors, legends, or other stories about the place?

8

Species

The issue, or question, of race and/or species rises repeatedly throughout the fantasy genres and it does so in multiple layers of questions: whether to use humans and ethnicities only or to include other beings, how to define those beings and their cultures, among others. For some, perhaps many, writers, the issue of ethnicities or species can be problematic. On one hand, there are issues of race and ethnicity in the real world that cannot help but come to the minds of the audience and creator. These concerns influence how we deal with race in fiction, even among different species like elves, dwarves, and orcs. Additionally, the problem of biological determinism rears its head, especially in games, both video and TTRPG, although many are taking steps recently to make this less common, or to remove it entirely (as seems to be the plan in the next iteration of *D&D*). Other issues can arise when the creator and/or audience see the merging of real-world race issues and the fictional world's, with non-human beings standing in for real-world peoples. For example, J.K. Rowling, consciously or otherwise, uses her goblins to introduce and discuss, obliquely, anti–Semitism and her house elves to, however ineptly, discuss colonial-era slavery. Both are, arguably, good in theory and helpful to discuss the topics, but also potentially problematic, as noted by some,[1] as they effectively dehumanize the victims, literally—e.g., Jews become inhuman goblins and Africans become inhuman house elves, rather than being humans.

This chapter will discuss problems and potential pitfalls of including species, make a case for including multiple species, and present guidance for including multiple species in a worldbuild. But, first, it will define the terminology and briefly discuss some degrees of one species versus many.

Defining Race and Species[2]

The question of defining the term "race" comes down to two major levels, for the purposes of worldbuilding: defining the term "race" itself and finding the dividing line between creatures/beasts and "species" in a world populated by elves, dragons, gryphons, and orcs.

The first part is relatively easy, as easy as defining any term that is used across a variety of fields of study, plus common usage, can be. The *Cambridge English Dictionary* defines race as "one of the main groups to which people are often considered to belong, based on physical characteristics that they are perceived to share such as skin color, eye shape, etc." (ex. Black, White) and "a group of people who share the same language, history, characteristics, etc."[3] (ex. British, French). The former is more in line with common usage, while the latter seems more a definition of ethnicity.[4] Comparatively, the American Anthropological Association implicitly rejects the term noting that "any attempt to establish lines of division among biological populations [are] both arbitrary and subjective."[5] Meanwhile, sociology says that "race is a human classification system that is socially constructed to distinguish between groups of people who share phenotypical characteristics."[6] Based on these different directions, the first definition from Cambridge or the idea of species seems most applicable in the case of the fantasy genres. It seems obvious from most uses of elves, orcs, vampires, were-creatures, and the like that their differences from humanity are not social constructs and that the biological divisions are objective. Interbreeding (half-elves, etc.) cause some biological questions—whether half-elves/orcs are sterile like mules or many other hybrid animals or whether they can reproduce—but the presence of magic can address such problems.

The second part of the question is less easy, in fact it is quite difficult. People have been asking where the dividing line between human and beast is since at least ancient Greece, possibly even into the prehistoric era. There have, therefore, been numerous attempts to answer the question. The presence of intellect was posited, then the capacity for reason, but both were demonstrated to be present in other animal species. The presence of a soul was posited by Christian thinkers but is unprovable and other faiths believe in animal souls and spirits. The concept of werebeasts, beings able to take human and animal forms, further problematizes the question. There may be no good place to set a dividing line. Intelligence has its issues—dolphins, whales, and apes have displayed intelligence; also, what standard of intelligence do we use? Likewise, self-awareness has issues (apes, cats), sentience (the ability to experience feelings) does not work, the creation of societies is problematic (ants, bees, lions, elephants), communication is definitely out (all animal species), and selflessness does not work (dolphins, cats, and elephants have shown it; and many humans seemingly lack this capacity). That said, I do not think that saying pegasi are beasts and elves are a sentient/sapient species is arbitrary, but also cannot exactly say why without finding flaws in the argument. Most creators have this issue, some more openly than others. For example, Rowling writes of werewolves as people, but includes them in a book of beasts; her centaurs and merfolk demand to be classed as beasts, not people, to be unassociated with humans; and no one questions the place of goblins and house elves as "people" or "species" (except, of course, Death Eaters and their sympathizers). Ultimately, each creator needs to find the divide for themselves and determine where they are happy (or least unhappy) placing it.

One vs. Multiple

The decision to have humans only, or otherwise only one species, versus multiple species is a potentially daunting one with a variety of possible choices: one species, a few species, or "all the species."

Having only one species, whether human or elf or something else, is the easiest in many ways. There is only one species to create in terms of appearance and abilities (if any). There may possibly be only one culture (see Problems below) as well, or it will be easier to adapt to multiple cultures. Having only one species makes it easier to show the people in depth and with variety, thereby avoiding most of the potential pitfalls discussed below. However, if the species is non-human, there is a tendency to fall into the "one species, one society" trap discussed below. This is true even in Earth-based UF/PNR—ex. *Blade* and *Underworld*, in which all vampires all around the world have the same culture and social structure.

Having a few species (say two to seven) presents more difficulty in having to develop many types of beings. It also means more possible cultures (unless they are integrated into a sort of "main" culture in a setting, but even then a subculture is likely). This level is probably the most common, though. It allows the creator to play with different figures from myth, legend, and the genres while exploring some other routes for societies and histories. Good examples include *The Lord of the Rings*, *Shannara* (Terry Brooks), *The Southern Vampire Mysteries* (Charlaine Harris), *Psy/Changeling* (Nalini Singh), and *Sabina Kane* (Jaye Wells).

The everything including the kitchen sink method, or "All the Species," makes avoiding stereotyping and tokenism more difficult, but can be rewarding. It opens up all sorts of possibilities for fun and exploration with thousands of years of myth, legend, and folklore alongside over a century of fantasy to mine and play with. Unfortunately, the more species there are, the more likely the creator is to fall into one or more of the pitfalls discussed below. It also means many or most species will be relegated to the background, as in George Lucas's famous cantina scene in

Star Wars: A New Hope. Good examples include *Discworld* (Terry Pratchett), *Kate Daniels* (Ilona Andrews), *D&D* worlds (ex. *The Forgotten Realms, Dragonlance, Spelljammer, Greyhawk*), and most FRPG worlds, whether video game or tabletop.

Problems of Species

Although, or perhaps because, non-human species are a staple of the F/UF/PNR genres, they come with a number of potential problems. These issues have not necessarily been recognized as problems until relatively recently, though there have been writers and other creators who have been attempting to resist each problem since at least the 1980s to some degree. Some of the potential problems and pitfalls have become so endemic that resistance took the form of humans-only secondary worlds and urban fantasy. Others ignored the issues entirely, as if pretending they did not exist would make them go away or would deny that they ever existed. Both directions, and others, continue across various authors and creators today in the fantasy genres. They form the subject of a significant amount of debate in blogs, message boards, conference/convention sessions, and other venues. For the purposes of this chapter and section, the three potential issues that will be addressed are social uniformity, biological determinism, and tokenism.

Social Uniformity

Often, adding other species beyond humans into a worldbuild means that they have a single society. In other words, essentially, all elves—or werewolves, dwarves, vampires—are basically the same in terms of society. This was true to a certain extent for Tolkien. He presents three major elf societies, but all three are basically elves in the woods who are master archers and are governed by elf-lords. Likewise, Tolkien dwarves are basically dwarves whether from Lonely Mountain or the Iron Hills and, in terms of society, orcs are orcs regardless of their origins (Mordor or Isengard). Probably because of the inspiration from Tolkien, the same held true for decades in the RPG industry. This uniformity of culture even holds true when members of the species are taken out of that society and live among other species, in many cases. In recent decades, especially since 2000, this has been changing to varying degrees.

One way to avoid this particular issue is to present or create multiple, distinct, societies of each species. In this way, nationality or ethnicity has more impact than species as such, as it does with humans, who typically have many very different societies even in secondary world fantasies. Humanity usually gets dozens of unique cultures in a world, but other species typically do not, so this can be a place to address that issue. We can also take into account the effects of immigration. Considering our own world, immigrants adapt over time to their new society. Some little traditions survive—favorite foods, holiday traditions, maybe some language—but over the course of a few to several generations, less of the "home" culture remains. This is true even down to language, unless something (like religious use) prevents deterioration—it is common for first- and second-generation immigrants to be fluent in the pre-immigration language, the third generation less so, and the fourth onward to maybe have a few words. The original culture may survive longer for immigrants of long-lived species, like most elves, but is likely to fade fairly quickly for those with human-like lifespans. Elements of the "home" culture may be picked up again to some degree by later generations, as the fourth, fifth, or sixth generations become interested in family roots.

Developing multiple cultures for a species also opens opportunities to play with stereotypes (and break them). It can be used to explore new variations on old clichés and "standard" elements of the genres. Multiple cultures may even provide a source of conflict—as in the Silvanesti versus Qualinesti elf relations in the *Dragonlance* setting; even though both nations are essentially the same, they have a longstanding conflict over inheritance and philosophy. This, overall, is something that *D&D*, for example, started striving for at least in 5th edition, acknowledging that each species may have many different cultures on many different worlds.[7] Terry Pratchett also began to explore this idea through the immigration of dwarves and trolls (among others) from the mountains of Überwald and Llamedos to Ankh-Morpork and the consequent alterations to their culture.[8]

Biological Determinism

Before discussing biological determinism, it seems best to define the concept. So, biological determinism is "the idea that all human behavior is innate, determined by genes, brain size, or other biological attributes … [but has been] proven to be scientifically invalid in terms of racial categorization and racial meaning."[9] However, the concept is still alive in the fantasy genres. It is a major trap and issue that appears regularly when species are brought into a setting. Biological determinism, and its child racial determinism, are significant issues because they are essentially built on reinforcing (typically racist, in this context) stereotypes, whether consciously or not.

In terms of building societies, biological determinism can create flat, dull societies. It can also, potentially, lead to cultural appropriation (through real-world inspiration), which may in turn lead to unconscious (systemic) racism coming out or appearing to be present. This is especially true if the species is being used to approach or discuss real-world issues of race or morality. In the fantasy genres, Tolkien presents one of the clearest examples of biological determinism, as his elves are inherently (biologically and unalterably) good regardless of their actions or motives while orcs are inherently (biologically and unalterably) evil regardless of their actions or motives. Neither species can ever change. There are no evil elves or good orcs in Middle Earth. This view became the standard in early RPGs, although it is being challenged and rethought in many more recent editions of many game systems since the 1990s—from *Shadowrun* to *D&D* 5E. The change is also visible in game mechanics, for both TTRPGs and video games. For example, in *D&D*'s first to 3.5 editions, half-orcs had penalties for intelligence and charisma (as well as class and level restrictions in 1st edition, that were present for all non-humans). In 5th edition, attribute penalties for species have been removed and options have been presented for customizing racial attribute bonuses. Playtest material for the forthcoming *One D&D* (2024) indicates that attribute modifiers will be tied to character background rather than species in the future. Conversely, in the video game *Everquest II*, species are categorized as "good," "neutral," and "evil." There is a mechanism for switching characters between the good/evil alignments, but it can be difficult and certain species (elves, dwarves, trolls, ogres) must start in their assigned moral category (but without any attribute bonuses or penalties).

To avoid biological determinism, it seems best to discuss species (elves, dwarves, orcs) in terms of tendencies rather than absolutes. For example, saying most elves tend to be graceful and prefer forested areas (tendencies) versus elves are graceful forest dwellers (absolutes). Combining such language with the creation of multiple cultures and societies, as discussed above, can make each group or appearance of the species unique and different rather than stereotyped. It can also implicitly acknowledge the impact of culture and surroundings on individual development, alongside biological factors, rather than ignoring them. Another option may be to base fantastic species on different roots from myth and legend. For instance, elves could be built on the Nordic alvar/alfar, the Celtic Sidhe, or the "little people," among others from many cultures, all of which are very different (and none of which are quite like Tolkien's elves).

Tokenism

The issue of tokenism[10] is also a major potential pitfall when we bring multiple species into a fantasy worldbuild. The issue is especially problematic if the fictional species is used as a stand-in for a real-world race or ethnicity. For example, Rowling presents only two werewolves (one on each side of her conflict) and, arguably, her goblins are tokens as only one of them gets developed or appears in a meaningful way over the course of seven books (and his portrayal is not exactly positive or neutral). In fiction, tokenism becomes a problem in large part because the one individual becomes the audience's idea of what that entire species is like. The single character becomes representative of the entire species or people. Often, that individual is caricatured in some way, too, though not necessarily. This is present to some degree in *The Lord of the Rings*, through Legolas and Gimli (single representatives traveling with and fighting alongside multiple humans—Aragorn, Boromir, Éomer, Théoden—and multiple hobbits). It is more visible in the *Dragonlance Chronicles* trilogy—with a party made up of six very different humans, one dwarf, one half-elf, and one kender. Steven Brust does this to some degree with the cat-centaurs (who only appear once or twice in twenty books).

The problem can be easily avoided by presenting a fully populated world, with representatives of any included species throughout the setting or narrative as appropriate. For example, scanning the background in a major trade city, coming across others on a road, maybe part of a trade caravan or travelling troupe, or ambassadors at socio-political events (also a good way to introduce multiple cultures/societies for a given species). Obviously, tokenism is easier to avoid when there are fewer species involved in the setting. If there are only humans and one or two other species (ex. *Underworld*, Markus Heitz's *The Dwarves*), more representatives of each species can be developed and shown, thereby giving the audience a broader view of the people. If there is a plethora of species (ex. Lisa Shearin's *SPI Files*, Ilona Andrews's *Kate Daniels*, *D&D*, or most FRPG video games), it becomes much more difficult to avoid without being distracting.

A Case for Multiple Species

Despite the potential problems, including species other than humans can be useful in the fantasy genres. On the simplest level, their popularity makes it clear that we as creators and audience members are drawn to the idea of not being alone in the world. Our societies have spent millennia telling stories of giants, ogres, blemmyae, elves, goblins, cynocephali, centaurs, satyrs, nymphs, oni, dragons, menehune, and thousands of other sentient, sapient species of beings. Virtually every culture throughout our world's history has such tales. Some of these stories exist to explain natural phenomena, some are cautionary and told to enforce social mores, but others seem to fill a deep psychological need to not be alone.

Introducing and writing other species also presents the matter of perspective. It is an opportunity to imagine and adopt another, often totally alien, point of view outside ourselves. This can, of course, be done with different races or ethnicities in our own world. However, that can be too problematic, in some cases, as biases, stereotypes, and false representations based on various media (news, entertainment, literary) and cultural biases can seep in, or be actively avoided (potentially producing an equally biased perspective). For many, adopting real racial/ethnic perspectives is best done by reading and playing in a world created by a person of that background, who is best able to portray it authentically.[11] This is the thought behind the Rick Riordan Presents imprint and the works of Roshani Chokshi, Yoon Ha Lee, and Carlos Hernandez that it publishes. Conversely, adopting the persona and thoughts of a frost giant, oni, or thousand-year-old dragon is both more truly alien and is significantly less likely to introduce bias, stereotyping, or offense. This can be a good way of exploring and commenting on the idea of self, humanity, and society from a temporarily outside perspective. That said, even with other species (in a fantasy sense) there is still the potential for stereotyping: the mopey immortal, the self-loathing vampire, or the arrogant elf that have all been done to death. But, even then, the stereotyping, while arguably lazy on a creative level, is not insulting since the typed character is not of a real race/ethnicity (and, hopefully, does not stand in for one).

Different species, beyond human, can also prove useful for thought experiments and cultural experiments. They can be employed to play with and explore different kinds of cultures and cultural evolutions not found in our world. These may be hidden societies or out in the open, depending on the setting. They may also be used to examine or emphasize particular elements of the creator's culture (as often happened with *Star Trek* societies and aliens). Vampires, for instance, have long been used in UF/PNR to explore the effects of immortality (or long lifespans) on society as well as to consider the ethics of feeding on other animal species. Elves have fulfilled a similar role regarding longevity in secondary worlds and some UF. Werebeasts, particularly the monstrous variety of werewolves (as opposed to the sympathetic variety), have been used throughout the classical to early modern through modern eras to project the worst elements of the human psyche and claim them as "the beast." Ironically, most beast species do not display the traits that werebeasts are often used to blame them for—ex. violence for the sake of violence, the "alpha" concept. Overall, species can be an option to explore how people and societies might develop in geographical environments not found on Earth (see Chapter 12's section on exotic geography), in magical environments, or in historical conditions that are significantly different from our own.

Finally, in the fantasy genres, species are also a way to introduce the audience to real-world folklore, legend, and myth. Most fantasy, and UF, species are at least inspired by our deep body of global folklore and myth. Originally, many of these species—elves, cynocephali, menehune, oni—were probably used to represent outsiders, foreigners, exotic places, and/or societal fears. Today, they can be interesting and entertaining to play with. Traditional depictions may be subverted or old stories played with (see Rick Riordan's body of work). New variations may be founded on and developed from the old sources, or one might return to old sources and thereby subvert genre clichés. The genres have created some assumptions that can be subverted. For example, Rowling's house elves are based on the folklore of brownies and other household fae, subverting Tolkien-based expectations of fantasy elves being tall, beautiful, majestic, lords of nature (by being small, servile, and urban). Still, they can be quite powerful (as household fae may be). Ilona Andrews does something similar with their vampires in the *Kate Daniels* series—vampires are mindless undead driven by a hunger for blood, unless mentally controlled by a "navigator" (a.k.a. necromancer) who can also speak through them—a significant subversion of the usual, post–Anne Rice, urban fantasy "suave and sexy" vampires.

Applying Species to Society Building

Once we decide to include any species beyond humans in a world, more questions arise, even before determining how to incorporate them into the world and its societies.

First, we ask: what species? Here we have three major options: traditional fantasy, traditional Earth lore, or entirely original (or a mix of the three). Traditional fantasy, and many traditional Earth (folklore, myth, legend), species have definite pros in that they are instantly recognizable to audiences and there is no need for major exposition to describe them. On the other side, they carry considerable baggage made up of preconceptions, so standing out can be more difficult, but possible. Traditional Earth lore could also, to stand out, draw from more obscure or non–Western myths and legends, probably with some explanation (see Ilona Andrews's *Kate Daniels*, Graci Kim's *Gifted Clans*, and Roshani Chokshi's *Pandava* books). Andrews does a great job of making their "traditional" species stand out, as with the aforementioned vampires. Terry Pratchett does the same with his elves, as does Steven Brust (Dragaera). Naomi Novik does so with her dragons (*Temeraire*) by making them rather cat-like.

Comparatively, entirely original species can be difficult. The first difficulty is coming up with entirely original species. Then they need to be described and explained, with more work than traditional species. But, they can be very rewarding when well-done and make it fairly easy to stand out. They could also be loosely based on traditional Earth lore, especially from obscure variations on stories or lesser known beings.

The second big question is: how many species? The more there are, the more likely they are to become stereotyped and the more likely tokenism is to crop up. The fewer there are, the more likely they are to be well developed (see below).

The third major question is: how do we make the species stand out? There are thousands of different elves, dwarves, and vampires in the fantasy genres, between literature, film, tabletop games, and video games. So, how can ours stand out? Should they even stand out? A couple of relatively easy ways to make even "cliché" species stand out exist. First, the traits or other characteristics can be varied from the "standard." Steven Brust's elves (Dragaerans) are large, muscular, beings that mostly reside in cities and engage in imperial expansion, while his dwarves (Serioli) are isolationist, largely incomprehensible, seem to perceive the world entirely differently from anyone else, and are little more than legends for most Dragaerans and Easterners (humans). In addition to their piloted vampires (*Daniels*), Andrews's vampires in the *Innkeeper Chronicles* are an alien species from a very distant set of worlds that evolved into a quasi-religious militant society (the Holy Anocracy). Another option is to, as with the *Innkeeper* vampires, develop the species' society (or societies) in some compelling and interesting way(s) that differ from expectations. This makes them stand out as different and unusual, even if they are physically "standard." Another option is to consider what they call themselves (ex. both Brust's Dragaerans and Easterners call themselves "human") and what others call them (ex. Brust's Easterners call Dragaerans "elves" or "Dragaerans").[12]

Human Dominant or Not

Most settings and societies in the fantasy genres default to being human dominant with other species discussed in relation to humanity.[13] That is, humans make up the majority of the population and hold most or all of the political, social, and economic power. We see this in Middle Earth, the Potterverse, Discworld, Melniboné (as the Young Kingdoms, e.g., human kingdoms, ascendant), *The Witcher*, and most D&D and video game worlds. There are some logical reasons for this, most notably that the audience is entirely human so often finds humanity to be an easy entry point into the world. Humanity also tends to be the baseline, or average, when fantastic species are included—every other species tends to be faster, stronger, smarter, more magical, and such or has their traits measured in comparison to humanity.

Human-dominant settings create certain social and power structures in the world, ones that often mirror real-world power structures. Usually, human dominance is explained as humans reproducing faster than other species or being more adaptable than other species. As noted, this makes humanity a baseline and a familiar touchstone for entry to the setting. However, it also sets up a sort of implicit, systemic, base of human exceptionalism.[14] Human dominance does not have to be the only way for a setting or society. It can be difficult, but rewarding, to work with another dominant species, though the human perspective could still be the entry point. For example, Brust's Dragaera is an elf-dominant society (technically, they refer to themselves as human, but Easterners call themselves human, too, and call Dragaerans elves) that the audience sees from a human perspective, usually (that of Vlad Taltos). Likewise, Lisa Shearin's *Raine Benares* series is set in a world dominated by elves and goblins, with humans a minority. Technically, Narnia is not human dominant, in that talking beasts and other species vastly outnumber humanity, but that is complicated by the fact that the kings and queens are all human (and are the only humans, at first). In science fiction, C.J. Cherryh's *Foreigner* series and *Chanur* series are also good examples, the former in a non-human dominant world from a human perspective and the latter from an entirely alien perspective.

Flipping the narrative and focusing on a society and world where humans are not the dominant species can be exciting and interesting to explore. There are a number of possibilities and issues to work through in those cases. For instance, it opens discussions of power, status, social structures, and a host of other topics. It can also simply be fun to play with as entertainment or a thought experiment.

Species and Society

Perhaps the most daunting part of presenting many species is developing societies for them, especially multiple societies per species. As creators and audience members, we want developed cultures to know where characters in the new species are coming from. To do this, we simply create the culture the same way as any other society, for the species' home societies. However, there is no need to fully create and develop every society from the beginning. That tends to lead to doing more worldbuilding and less narrative. Instead, we can create a baseline initial concept that gets developed as it appears in the narrative or other elements of construction. This is how a number of authors and game creators work—for instance, in Discworld a species appeared, a couple of novels passed, then Pratchett expanded the species and developed their society (or societies) in a novel focused on the species. Back when he wrote *The Color of Magic*, he did not necessarily think about including orcs and igors in the Disc, but eventually they were introduced, developed, and woven in.

Discworld brings up another interesting aspect of species and society: introducing and incorporating new species into existing societies. This is something that Pratchett did continually over the 30 years he worked with Ankh-Morpork, largely slipping them into the city's society via the Watch. To do this, we need to determine how integrated the species is in society—whether it is new or established, keeps to itself or tries to become fully integrated. A new species could become integrated through cultural establishments—ex. education, law enforcement, organized crime, trade/craft guilds, and religious institutions—or politics, or economics—ex. founding restaurants and other businesses. It may be helpful to look at the patterns of immigration in the real world as inspiration. In the U.S., at least, immigrants often form(-ed) pocket communities or neighborhoods (Little Italy, Chinatown, Slavic Village), whether by choice, by being forced to, or by necessity. A lot of these communities were/are centered on the locations of religious buildings (churches, mosques, temples). In addition to the communities, many immigrants moved into society through law enforcement or firefighting (ex. Irish-Americans), transportation (busses, taxis), and menial labor (construction, sanitation, landscaping) to establish themselves. In some cases, they vigorously protected positions in the field from other ethnic groups (ex. the Irish dominance of police forces in New York, Boston, and Chicago for many decades), effectively monopolizing the field in some cities.

Basically, we should find the species' niche in society. Pratchett's Ankh-Morpork—particularly in *Feet of Clay, Jingo, The Fifth Elephant, Thud!, Snuff, Going Postal, Making Money, Raising Steam,* and *Unseen Academicals*—are especially instructive in how this might work. Determining how the dominant society views members of the species, which could depend on the niche they occupy, can also be important. Both might, of course, change over the course of time that they are involved with the dominant society, as they become more woven into the fabric of the city or nation (ex. Pratchett's dwarves and trolls especially). Thinking about both niche and views should lead to some ideas about how the species might find societal acceptance, eventually. It might also determine that the species may never find full acceptance—particularly possible with species like vampires that feed on other species.

Species and Government

Part of introducing other species to a setting, especially into established societies, is their relationship with the government of the society in question. In this case, the question is one of the legal status of the species and its role in government. There could be laws about employment, education, residences, and a host of other aspects of life and society. Some of these laws or rules could be clearly and officially stated in the legal code, while others could be implied or unspoken in a given society. In the latter case, a law might be enforced for one group but ignored for another, for instance. A government might even be involved in the relationships between members of different species, both social and marital/reproductive relationships (ex. laws may forbid human-elf marriages or relations, akin to Black-White relations in South Africa under apartheid or the U.S. before *Loving v. Virginia* [1967]). The legal status of a species and the laws could be openly discriminatory and openly based in bigotry, prejudice, and stereotypes. They could be based on history—ex. a society that overthrew the tyrannical rule of elves may have laws biased against elves. They could be, ostensibly, in place to protect the species (yet still, potentially, be discriminatory). All of this, of course, assumes direct contact between different species. Tolkien, for instance, by and large shows no contact between humans and other species (except in Bree and Laketown).

Brust's Dragaera is an excellent example here. In the empire, humans (Easterners) are treated as second class residents (not exactly citizens). They are unable to access legitimate social power and are legally barred from political power (with the exception of Imperial titles, though only two of those have ever been bestowed on a human in millennia). Humans in the empire have only limited access to financial power, and even that only through crime in most cases. They are legally peasants at best, except the few who manage to buy titles in House Jhereg (and are most often criminals).

Conversely, in Pratchett's Discworld, non-humans are basically the same as humans in their daily lives. They seem to have equal access to work and the Watch. However, no non-humans hold legitimate positions of recognized authority in the guilds, temples, noble families, Unseen University, or the government, beyond some Watch officers (several sergeants and a couple of captains). Only one is known to hold widespread significant power outside their species' community—Chrysoprase the troll, and the entire Breccia leadership—and that through organized crime.

Role of Species

On a more global level, there is the why of species in the fantasy genres—that is, why is the species present in the setting? There are many roles that species may play in the setting, society, and worldbuild. And each species may hold multiple roles. In this section, the goal is not to judge possible roles, but simply to briefly discuss them.

The simplest role of various species is Brust's "Cool Stuff Theory," that the creator thinks the species is cool. This is the most basic and "shallow" of roles, not in a denigrating way but as a statement. The species gets added to the world because the creator thinks werecats, elves, goblins, or whatever are cool and enjoys them. There is nothing wrong with this level, or even stopping at this level, if they are integrated well into the setting. If they are just thrown in without any thought, that can lead to problems, both of the sort discussed above and for suspending disbelief.

Moving a bit deeper, as noted above, species could be added to include a different perspective or a challenge in the process of creating. The idea of adopting, exploring, and working through the perspective of an entirely alien being, like an ancient elf, ogre, or dragon, is alluring to many writers and creators. For many, it is part of the reason that they became interested in the fantasy genres (or science fiction, for that matter). Working from this sort of perspective is, indeed, a challenge and can be rewarding. It can also be a sort of brainstorming used to figure out elements of the worldbuild and society, imagining how a species might think and perceive the world (potentially with extra senses) can help influence the creation of one or more societies for them.

Of course, thought and culture experiments are certainly a common role. However, we do need to ask, honestly, why the exploration is occurring with elves, orcs, or vampires rather than with humans. There are many possible reasons. There could be the perspective challenge noted previously. Conversely, there could be a relative ease of experimenting with tough topics through completely fictional beings. Playing with fictional species can also be a means of avoiding insult to others or sidestepping knee jerk reactions in order to open minds within the audience.

Many, especially in recent decades, incorporate different species to introduce audiences to the folklore and legends of their cultures or those of their ancestors. Good examples include Roshani Chokshi (Hindu), Yoon Ha Lee and Graci Kim (Korean), Lori Lee (Hmong), and Daniel José Older (using a mix of Caribbean traditions). This is often mixed with the "Cool Stuff Theory" because the creators clearly enjoy sharing and playing with these beings and traditions. However, this role must be done with care and a lot of research, if the creator does not share the culture, to avoid appropriation and stereotypes.

Finally, a species might be included in order to explore real-world issues, especially of race. This is one that many creators like and have used, with mixed results and some controversy. Handled well, it can be a good way to "sneak" in discussions of real-world racism, slavery, and other issues. That said, there is the aforementioned danger of dehumanizing the real experiences of real people who deal with racism, the legacy of slavery, and other such issues on a daily basis.

9

Language

Sindarin, Quenya, the High Speech of Melniboné, High Valyrian, the speech of the Old Ones, the words of magic, indecipherable etchings on a lost tomb's walls. Languages of various sorts have been present in the fantasy genres from their earliest, pre–Tolkien, days. Some languages are mentioned only. Some are described in brief by their sound. Some only have a few words made up by the creator. A rare few are fully detailed as if real and follow linguistic rules and theory. Regardless of the level of creation, the inclusion of languages in a society and worldbuild adds layers of depth and detail to the setting and its cultures. This brings an added degree of life to the world and those who inhabit it.

Why Use Languages?

It is certainly true that ignoring languages or having a single language for a setting makes things easier. So, why bother addressing multiple languages in a world, or in a single society?

Possibly the most obvious reason to include multiple languages is realism. Most cultures and societies develop at least one language. That language typically evolves over time into many versions and dialects. Usually, at least in our world, when multiple cultures share a language, it is because of imperialism (ex. Mandarin, Latin, Arabic, and English). Even then, the conquered region and society tends to try to keep its native language(s) as well, barring conscious and systematic attempts to destroy the native language (as in Ireland, the U.S., and Australia). This can lead to language shifts and even evolution into a new language (ex. Old English into Middle English) and cases of polyglot societies (ex. Hong Kong, China, and Kazakhstan) with multiple official languages or languages used for a variety of different purposes (ex. government, daily use, and religious use).

Introducing languages and knowledge (or lack thereof) of languages can also add to the challenge and plot of a narrative or game. Clues or other necessary information integral to the narrative may be presented in languages unknown to the protagonists or translation could be difficult, unclear, or lose meaning in a critical way (lost in translation). Some video games, for instance, require seeking out specific NPCs to translate such documents or clues. Others require learning the language, whether by visiting a merchant NPC to purchase a particular language book or by gathering a set number of examples of the language to "learn" from. Issues of language can create diplomatic situations or negotiation problems. They could even introduce puns and riddles (ex. Gandalf reading the elvish script outside Moria).

Types of Languages

Before developing languages for, or incorporating them into, society, it is probably a good idea to look at some different types of language and terminology. Briefly discussing some relationships between languages and very briefly addressing linguistic evolution seem helpful, too. Different types of language may serve different purposes in a society. Additionally, using the broadest sense of the term (language), we could even include professional or field specific jargon as nearly a separate language—for example two theoretical physicists speaking to each other versus speaking to a public audience.

Language Groups

Without delving into deep linguistic theory, the shallow end of language groups should be addressed as the grouping of languages can be useful for including multiple languages in a setting. In brief, language groups are collections of related languages. They are often all traced back to a common "parent" language (ex. Romance languages all come from Latin) or a theoretical "parent" (ex. Indo-European languages). Particularly in the 5th edition, *D&D* has attempted a basic form of groups with relations between languages based on shared written script (also lifted from Tolkien's elvish script for the language of Mordor). A given language may also be part of multiple language groups, much like species classification in biology—ex. Romance languages are a more specific branch of the Indo-European language group. Languages in a group, especially a narrow branch group, are likely to be close enough relations to have some similar, or even the same, words. This is often enough for speakers of one language in the group to at least get the gist of another—ex. the relationship between Italian, French, and Spanish.[1] Due to how populations tend to move, neighboring societies tend to have the same language group (ex. Spain, Portugal, France, Italy). Exceptions, of course, always exist (ex. Romanian, a Romance language surrounded by Slavic languages). Sometimes languages also become hybrids, such as modern English, effectively a Germanic-Romance hybrid. Others belong to no known living language group, ex. Basque, Sandawe, Nihali/Nahali, or Waorani.

Spoken versus Written

The written and spoken versions of a given language are usually related and connected, as the written form is created to represent the spoken with characters standing in for sounds, syllables, or words. Obviously, a pre-literate society will lack a written version of its spoken language. However, it may have other visual means of recording information or memory aids, whether in imagery, bead strings, knot systems, or a host of other possibilities. These means are, arguably, a language in themselves. Conversely, sometimes people stop using a language in its spoken form but continue to write in it, at least to some degree. Technically, most of these cases are "dead" languages, that is a language that is no longer the native language of any society.[2] It is very possible that the spoken form of a language dies out but the written form remains, whether for daily, government, religious, or academic use, ex. Latin. In some cases, it is also possible that only the written form ever existed, for, say, a species/people/society that is unable to vocalize, or a language of magic, a religious language, or a spy language. Magic, religious, and scientific/academic/scholarly languages that cross socio-cultural borders may be written only. Readers may know the inter-cultural symbols by the names their own spoken language gives them, similar to numerals (the symbol 1 is recognizable around the world, but has many different names) or scientific notation.

Linguistic States of Life

In simplified form, languages have basically four states of being (not counting revived or constructed—often fictional—languages): modern (or living), dormant, dead, and extinct. Modern languages have current, living, native speakers. Depending on the population of speakers, a modern language could be endangered, that is on the cusp of transitioning to dormant, dead, or extinct. Dormant languages are dead languages that still act as a symbol of an ethnic identity. There are no fully proficient users, but the language has some social uses although it is not used in daily life. Dead languages are languages that are no longer native to any society, but may be in written use for scientific, religious, or legal purposes. Examples include Latin, Biblical Hebrew, Sanskrit, and Aramaic. Extinct languages have no living speakers or writers, as in the case of most ancient Mesopotamian languages and many Native American languages.

Inhabitants of a setting's societies will regularly use modern languages as the official tongues of each society and possibly for trade or magic. Conquered or displaced peoples (for example, *The Witcher's* elves) may have a dormant language, being forced to use the dominant language as their own begins to fade. Clergy, scholars, magicians, even spies and diplomats, or guilds may employ dormant languages. This possibility is especially true if the temple, university, or guild operates across national and cultural borders, ex. historical European scholars and the Church or *Dragonlance*'s wizards. Characters may come across extinct languages on various artifacts, artwork, extant documents, ruins, or a host of other places. Translating, even identifying, the language could be a subplot or mini-adventure/quest in itself. Once identified and translated, further plots, quests, and adventures may ensue.

Modern versus Old

As, essentially, living things, languages constantly change and evolve. After a time, they evolve enough to become distinct and acquire a new name or split. English is an excellent example from our own world. It "began" as Old English until c. 1100 and became Middle English (c. 1150–1470). Eventually, further changes led to becoming Early Modern (or Elizabethan or Shakespearean) English (c. 1470–1700) and, finally, Modern English (c. 1700–Present). With practice, most people can follow Early Modern English. Some dialects of Middle English (Chaucer's mid-14th-century London dialect) are reasonably clear with minimal practice while other dialects (the *Gawain*-poet's mid-14th-century dialect) are significantly more difficult. But, Old English requires learning it like a foreign language to comprehend. Following this example, if we go back a few centuries in a fictional society, a language is probably still readable with some work for modern society. But, going back several centuries even the same language becomes the province of specially trained individuals.

Those seeking a degree of realism in their settings and societies can work with that pattern and basic idea, particularly if old texts and ruins exist. Of course, the pattern assumes human-like lifespans and "normal" events, like foreign contact, invasions, and such (ex. Old English became Middle English in large part due to the Norman invasion of England in 1066). In cases of isolated societies, language will likely change less—as of the 1990s, there were still some people in Appalachia (U.S.) who spoke

Early Middle English in isolated valleys. How an exceptionally long lived species, like classic elves, or an immortal one, like typical vampires, would affect language change as a society is anyone's guess. That said, given the changes that have occurred in the last 400 years with Modern English, it is unlikely that any language will remain completely static because the world changes and influences language change, as does foreign contact. That said, the elvish of Lothlórien, an isolated community of essentially immortal elves, is likely to see less change than the languages of Rohan or Gondor, but will still probably be somewhat different over several centuries.

Translation

The presence of multiple languages introduces the issue of translation. This is something that is often addressed in science fiction, or handwaved with a universal translator or Babel fish, but is often ignored in the fantasy genres. An important note is that translation is never straightforward, and there are many types of translation. A literal translation attempts an exact word to word conversion from one language to another. This can become wordy (some words translate as phrases) or lose meaning (such as euphemisms or slang). Translating for sense, on the other hand, is less concerned with the literal meaning of the words and more concerned with the sense of the words and phrasing. This sort of translation may interpret euphemisms, kennings (ex. Old English's hronrad is literally "whale road," but means the sea or ocean), and other sayings rather than being literal. In other cases, especially if speed is an important factor, we might translate for the gist, basically summarizing. Poets may attempt to retain rhyme, alliteration, and meter in translation, without losing the sense of the work.

Difficulties

Any time that translation occurs, difficulties arise. There are many possibilities here, but this section will cover some of the more common ones as inspiration.

Perhaps the most important, and definitely the first, hurdle is identifying the language and dialect. This can be rather difficult, even for experts. Knowing the era of the writing (for documents) and where the document was found or where the speaker is helps. This gives a basis to look and listen for key words or pronunciations that can help identify a dialect. But, this takes time. Unless we "Daniel Jackson" it.[3] Misidentifying the language or dialect can lead to minor or major mistranslations and misinterpreting euphemisms or other indirect sayings.

Another major difficulty is loss of sense. Any time we translate between languages, even modern ones or closely related ones, some meaning is lost. This could be major or extremely minor loss. No translation, regardless of its purpose or literalness, is ever 100 percent perfect, partly because in most cases translators find the closest word to the original. These words may not entirely match up or convey exactly the same meaning or sense as the original did. They may also carry socio-cultural baggage in the language of translation that is not in the original. Many words in modern languages that are translated as "witch" in English have this issue, in that the term "witch" carries centuries of (often negative) cultural baggage in Anglo-(North) American usage.

Especially in the cases of recorded language (whether audio, video, or written), parts may be missing or lost, damaged, or otherwise unavailable. This provides obvious limits to translation, that can cause significant issues for meaning and sense. While a difficulty in all situations, it is particularly problematic if the translators are seeking a location, directions, or a weakness, for instance. This is one of the more common plot points when language and translation appear in the fantasy genres, and the action/adventure genre, as a key piece of the document is lost and the missing information must be found to achieve the goals. *Indiana Jones and the Raiders of the Lost Ark* is an excellent example, in which the Nazis dig for the Ark of the Covenant in the wrong location because they are missing a key line of text that Jones and his partners have.

Finally, there needs to be a foundation for translation. All translation requires some base to start from. This is the reason the Rosetta Stone was so important, as it carries the same text in multiple languages. That gave linguists a point of comparison from which they could derive ideas about what words in some Greek and Egyptian scripts meant. In northern Europe, vernacular Bibles served essentially the same purpose for linguists trying to figure out Old English, since they could compare the Latin (and Modern English) versions of the Gospels and other books to the Old English versions to begin building a lexicon and translation dictionary.

Plot and Challenge

The idea of translation problems can be a basis for both plots and challenges for characters in a society or world. There are a whole host of potential applications and venues here, but a few will be addressed for inspirational purposes.

Any attempt at inter-cultural trade, from simply purchasing food to setting up trade agreements between countries, requires communication. Therefore, any such attempt can be fouled by inadvertent or purposeful translation issues, unless a common language is found. Such a language might be a pidgin tongue, an ad hoc half-language, an attempt at sign language, or a formal trade language (or even a language shared by the international temple of the trade deity, whose clergy happily conduct negotiations in return for a modest donation to the temple). An entertaining example is the Silver Horde's attempts to purchase fruit in Pratchett's *Interesting Times*.

Diplomatic discussions are a classic venue for translation and language fails. Mistranslations here, or identification of language or shared language, can lead to unintended insults, misunderstandings of agreements, and even outright wars. As with many language issues, this has been a staple of the science fiction genre, but seems to be under-utilized in the fantasy genres.

Another staple of science fiction that can be easily adapted to the fantasy genres is the first contact situation. Contact with a lost society or a new one has obvious language issues that lead to problems of understanding (ex. Kevin Hearne's *The Seven Kennings*). This can also be applied to new parts of the world and to new species of beings. The situation can be easily brought into UF/PNR as well, from normal, mundane society's contact with a hidden paranormal species to a paranormal community's discovery of a new species to a paranormal community's contact with extra-planar beings.

Mysteries are another facet of the genre that comes into play. Solving mysteries requires clues to piece together, and some clues, especially with various species involved, may require knowledge of specific languages. That may also require either translating or finding a translator. Problematic or difficult translations, such as ones that require greater context to figure out which of a few meanings is intended, can be interesting and fun to explore here.

In a similar vein, there is the treasure hunt. Whether the treasure is gold or knowledge, it very likely involves old documents and artifacts. These texts, paintings, carvings, and other recordings often need to be translated. Some translations may be unclear or require determinations about meaning. For instance, a document could give directions to a cursed crypt or a royal bedroom depending on context and era. Missteps could lead to false directions, traps, and curses at the very least.

Finally, curse breaking can be a fun language and translation situation. In many cases of folklore, legend, and real belief, curses rely on their exact wording. Consequently, so does curse breaking. So, what if the curse was cast in a language that no one has spoken in 1200 years?

Finding someone with the knowledge necessary to accurately translate and "defuse" the curse becomes very important. Mistranslations could have minor detrimental effects all the way up to potentially killing the victim.

Common, Hidden, and Secret Languages

Most societies and cultures have a mix of languages that involve some ratio of common, hidden, and secret languages. These include, and go beyond, the effects of a polyglot society or various uses of different common languages (see below). Most in society are aware of, or use, common languages, but secret or hidden languages are inherently limited in terms of who has access to them.

Common

Common languages are those that are normally used in society. Any official, or de facto "official," language of the society, any language spoken by neighboring societies, any language spoken by immigrants, or any language taught in schools is included here. This also includes any dead languages taught in schools and/or used by professions—ex. Latin. If a setting has a trade language (ex. RPGs' "Common," lifted from Tolkien), that would count as well. Basically any language an average person in the society could be expected to have heard of, could see or hear (even if they do not understand), or could easily find someone to learn from would fall into this category. In our world, and most fictional worlds, the majority of languages will be in this group.

Hidden and Secret

Hidden and secret languages are a staple of the fantasy genres, especially in secondary worlds, but also exist in our own world. For the purposes of this section, they will be divided into four classes: Trade/Organization Cant, Covert Cipher, Personal Cipher, Species Language.

Trade and organization cants are present in most secondary world settings. They may be the language of magic, spoken and written only by magic-users. Especially in *D&D* and its descendants, thieves often have a hidden language of words, hand signals, and symbols. Various guilds, such as the masons, may have something similar that is unique to journeymen and above. In our own world, itinerants/homeless in various countries developed a language of marks to communicate information to each other, such as whether a house was open to giving food or had a vicious dog. Often such languages include a mix of visual symbols, gestures, words, phrases, and other signs. They do not necessarily need to be written or entirely verbal.

Covert ciphers are shared by an organization, rather than being personal. Legal or official thieves (spies) may have their own language akin to a trade-speak, and most will have some degree of cipher to send secret messages. Diplomats may have their own ciphers and language as well, to send secure information or request emergency help without alerting their hosts. Diplomats may also serve as spies, depending on the culture or society. Religious organizations may also have a similar cipher, especially if they are international in reach, to send messages without lay authorities being aware. Often these languages will be almost entirely written, but could include symbols hidden in documents or elsewhere visible to others.

Personal ciphers are extremely limited languages known only to one or a small handful of people. Historically, alchemists often created their own personal ciphers and languages to protect their research from rivals. Alchemists and magicians in the fantasy genres may do the same, depending on how organized and cutthroat the communities are. This sort of language could be extended to paranoid inventors (ex. the Grishaverse's Ilya Morozova) and scholars as well, regardless of which fantasy genre they are in.

In any fantasy genre, it is possible that an entire species may possess a hidden language that other species do not even know of, much less speak or understand. Two good examples are the vampires of the *Blade* franchise with both glyphs and ancient texts as well as the werewolves of the *World of Darkness* RPG. Such languages could be ancient, dead, dormant, or modern languages, depending on the creator's desire and the use, intent, or purpose of the language. Regardless, to be hidden or secret, there needs to be some requirement that the language not be taught to those outside the species. In a UF/PNR setting, this could be put in place to preserve the secrecy of the species and maintain their concealment, and to secretly mark safe places.

Application

The application possibilities for languages were addressed briefly above, but there are other possible uses and methods that deserve some deeper discussion.

Languages can be tied to species in ways similar to societies discussed in the previous chapter. Gaming, both video and TTRPG, tends to default to the one species, one language pattern (like one species, one society). Even the "Common" tongue is typically associated most with humans. This is, of course, very simple and easy to work with, however unrealistic. In RPG situations, this oversimplifying can be avoided by treating the "species language" (ex. elvish, orcish, dwarven) as one version of the language group and enough to grasp the basics of other related (elf, orc, dwarf) languages and dialects. For TTRPGs, the GM could require checks with penalties for unusual, unique, or rare dialects and versions of the language, rather than the automatic understanding some systems (ex. *D&D*) assume. In writing, the easiest method is to assume that each culture of the species has its own language, that may be related to those spoken by other cultures of the species (or neighbors of other species).

In some cases, as alluded to above, a culture may use different languages for different situations and purposes. An excellent example from our own world is the Vai of Liberia.[4] The Vai use English for government documents and business, Arabic for religious situations (as they are predominantly Muslim), and Vy for personal correspondence and life. A fantasy society may add a fourth or fifth language for magic or scholarship, among other possibilities. In a society, this division could give a certain degree of power to different groups (magicians, priests, bureaucrats), or help them retain power.

Making use of languages can be a daunting consideration. However, including them can be as simple as "Bob spoke to the merchant in halting Andren Elvish." For those who wish more detail, the language's sound could be described as a character uses it, as "The harsh, back of the throat sound of Dwarven words passed Jane's lips." Another option is to make up and intersperse a few words that sound right for how the language is imagined. These are the three most common means used. In fact, Pratchett typically uses a combination of description and occasional words when he brings in Ankh-Morpork's dwarves (or their Copperhead and Uberwald relatives). At the furthest extreme, a small group of individuals have fully created languages from scratch with an even smaller number tracing the evolution of multiple languages across 3000 years of history (Tolkien). This is neither necessary, nor perhaps feasible, in most cases. Tolkien only did so because he was a linguist by training and thought it was fun to create grammar, syntax, cases, conjugations, and such for languages. Most creators, by contrast, limit languages to a name and brief description, maybe a few key words (particularly curses). It could help to have a rough tree of related languages, to clarify what a character might understand without fully learning each and every language on the list—ex. a *D&D* character who knows Dwarvish may have some chance of getting at least the gist of Gnomish and Giant (in 5E, the GM might reasonably allow an Intelligence check with a DC 10–20 depending on the obscurity of the dialect and how closely related they rule Gnomish, for instance, to be to Dwarvish).

10

Sex and Gender

In the earliest days of the fantasy genre, sex and gender were often either ignored for all intents and purposes (ex. Tolkien) or took a very simplistic and one-sided view. The latter tended to range from exclusionary to outright sexist in its approach and execution, with some exceptions. Regardless, both sex and gender have always been present in the genres, even more in the UF and PNR genres as both incorporated and focused on (respectively) relationships and romance elements. As "Forgotten Realms Guru" Ed Greenwood has noted, sex, gender, and transgenderism have always been part of the TTRPG industry, specifically *D&D*, as well, even if they were sometimes less obvious than others.

Before going too much further, it will be helpful to define both terms. According to *Medical News Today*, sex "refers to the physical differences between people who are male, female, or intersex. A person typically has their sex assigned at birth based on physiological characteristics, including their genitalia and chromosome composition."[1] Conversely, gender is how a person identifies. Moreover, gender is "a broad spectrum. A person may identify at any point within this spectrum or outside of it entirely. [...] Gender also exists as social constructs—as gender 'roles' or 'norms.'"[2] In a simple, perhaps overly simple, form, sex is biology while gender is a mix of psychology and social construct.

In the last few decades, there has been growing mainstream awareness and shifts in both society and the fantasy genres with regard to sex and gender. This has been especially true in many branches of UF/PNR and YA fantasy, with regard to LGBT+ existence, issues, inclusion, and diversity. On the whole, this awareness has been met with generally positive responses, even from some of the oldest in the community. For instance, Greenwood, who has been writing fantasy fiction since 1967 and has been involved in TTRPGs since 1979, stated, "But D&D has half-orcs and half-dragons, and half-elves, and has magic items that specifically change gender, right there in the rules. Surely if you can handle the basic notion of cross-SPECIES sex, having a full variety of gender roles should be something that doesn't blow your mind,"[3] in response to a small, and shrinking, block of vocal, disgruntled, gamers.

With that in mind, this chapter will look at sex and gender, as defined above, in relation to society, religion, and magic in worldbuilding.

Sex and Gender in Society

As seen in our own world, questions of sex and gender play a significant role in society. Even limited to Euro-American cultures, the twin concepts have a complex history that becomes even more complex when we look at global cultures. Remaining solely with European cultures, there is a long history of crossdressing that goes back to at least ancient Greece and Rome, especially on the stage (ex. Plautus, Aristophanes). This led, at times, to decrying the stage/theater as immoral (ex. the Elizabethan Puritans). It is also present in mythology (ex. Thor). Gender fluidity and transitioning are not unknown either, whether we look at Norse mythology with Loki moving fluidly between sexes and genders or Greek myth with Hermaphroditus. Various orientations have also been present at different points, for example the Sacred Bands of Thebes and various stories about Apollo. Regardless of the culture, views on sex and gender reflect and impact their society in myriad ways. Here, for brevity, they will be broken down into three areas: Social Views, Gender Roles, and Legal Standing.

Social Views

While some authors and worlds in the fantasy genres retain a more limited view, there has been an increasing awareness of a spectrum of views regarding sex and gender within societies in the genres over the last few decades. Sometimes this is treated well, other times it is beset by stereotypes and tokenism.

Many such societies present a variety of genders and openness regarding (biological) sex, whether the societies are positive or negative in their views. For example, Yoon Ha Lee's *Thousand Worlds* is open to all gender identifications, as witnessed by the use of pronoun identification pins on military uniforms aboard ship. Presumably, the society is also open to all orientations, based on inference. Comparatively, P. Djèlí Clark's *Dead Djinn Universe* presents characters of multiple genders and orientations, noting that they are accepted in some subcultures but not necessarily in the dominant culture. That said, the (Egyptian, female, lesbian) protagonist's decision to dress in English suits and ties tends to be seen as more of an eccentricity than an "abomination" by most. Similarly, Aiden Thomas's

Cemetery Boys presents a gay trans-boy, whose orientation is accepted by his community only (he thinks) because they still see him as female. Most within the community seem to remember not to use his dead name, but also skim over and avoid acknowledging his gender identification otherwise. Leigh Bardugo's Grishaverse presents a wider variety, simply because she works with multiple cultures. Ravka, particularly the grisha subculture, seems open to all sorts of identification and orientation (ex. Tamar and Nadia's marriage, Nina Zenik's bisexuality, and Hanne Brum's transgender identity). Likewise, both men and women fulfill most societal roles, including military service (both in and outside of the grisha). Kerch seems to be relatively open in terms of gender and orientation as well, as there seems no reason to hide Jesper and Wylan's relationship, though it certainly has fixed gender roles within certain social classes, such as the mercher families, with men conducting business and women being wives and child bearers. Conversely, Fjerda is extremely conservative on issues of both sex and gender.

Fictional societies may be, as seen above, as broad in their views as any real-world society. Some may take a more conservative, limited view of sex and gender, often conflating the terms. Others may take a more open view, acknowledging and accepting both traits as spectra with a host of variations and possibilities to be encouraged and incorporated into society.

Gender Roles

As we see around us daily, societies may overtly or implicitly impose gender and sex roles for professions, domestic situations, and a variety of other social interactions. In the fantasy genres, some of these rules may be imposed by natural laws, ex. laws of magic (see below), while others may be tradition or social constructs, as in our own world. Fantasy species may also have biological effects, in that different sexes may have wildly different physiologies. Or a species may have, or appear to have, one sex—ex. Greco-Roman nymphs (all female) or Tolkien's orcs (all male). While gender roles in real societies are almost entirely social constructs, in the fantasy genres there could be other causes.

In many cases, gender roles may be tied to questions of public versus private space, sometimes in seemingly odd ways. For example, in most Euro-American societies, women are expected to cook in the home, but professional chefs/cooks have typically been male (and males cooking at home have "traditionally" done so outdoors, grilling in a public space). The same happens with tailoring and sewing—women have historically been expected to do so in private space, while tailors (as a profession) have tended to be male dominated (also applies to the modern fashion industry). Other cases are more complex, and are influenced by many factors. For instance, traditionally kindergarten through high school education has been predominantly done by women, but collegiate-level education has been predominantly done by males—until the last 30 years or so, as more balance has been achieved, in some/most fields.

For the most part, gender roles in societies tend to be a form of control and simplified classification. Societies also attempt to justify such roles through references to biology and "tradition," with no examination of when or where the "tradition" came from. Of course, all classification systems, especially simplified ones, are prone to exceptions and flaws.

Many worldbuilds in the genres assume either contemporary gender roles of the creator's society (UF/PNR) or the creator's assumptions about historical roles (F and historical UF). Sometimes they are based on real, perceived, or believed, traits of different animal species as well, particularly for fantasy species, such as werewolves. This can be highly limiting in a set of genres that are supposed to set the imagination free. So, it is important to remember that creators are not limited to real-world gender and sex roles for fictional societies. This is true even with historical fantasy, as changes in history that are made to accommodate fantasy elements can also alter gender roles, sometimes drastically.

Legal Standing

The legal position of sex and gender can get tied up in many things. They could be influenced by religious views of both (see below) and any connections that exist between sex, gender, and magic. The obvious places that sex and gender come into legal standing are relationships (including marriages) and the legality thereof, reproductive rights and adoption (if covered by society's laws), and legal/social recognition of sexes and genders, as well as transitioning between them. Interesting cases may include species with shapeshifting abilities (like *D&D*'s doppelgangers) or deities, both of whom may be able to adopt and shift between sexes at will. As noted by Greenwood above, there may even be magic—whether spells or devices—that can alter a person's sex, or gender (see below).

Other places of legal standing for sex and gender include sumptuary laws (governing what people can wear or even eat, usually by social class and sex), military service and training, and inheritance laws. For example, in medieval France, women could not inherit titles or property, but in medieval England, they could (thus the excuse for the Hundred Years' War). In early modern Germany, women could sue their parents to secure dowries and other property.[4] Inheritance in particular can lead to major plot points and conflict, especially if it is muddled and played with for complexity. In Bardugo's Grishaverse, Ravkan men and women, particularly grisha, both train for military service, although women may be limited to non-combat roles in the First Army (non-magic) while all grisha train for combat. Conversely, in the same world, Fjerdan men train for military service, but women are forbidden from such training.[5]

In extreme cases, one or more sexes/genders may be legally considered property or an official underclass. Both of these have been commonly explored in the fantasy and science fiction genres with varying situations and results, and have some basis in our own world from several cultures. In other cases, societies may be completely egalitarian in terms of sex and gender, legally speaking. Of course, legal standing and social practice may not entirely match up. While sexes and genders may have, in theory, equal legal standing, there may still be judicial bias, social discrimination, wage gaps, and other such issues on a social level.

Sex and Gender in Religion

Questions of sex and gender in their relation to religion operate on several levels. A few stand out as particularly important for worldbuilding. First, there are the views of the faith regarding the roles of sexes and genders, and recognition of genders. Second, there are the faith's requirements for clergy. Third, there is the faith's impact on society at large. For primary world fantasies, obviously real-world religions and their views are "pre-created." There is the caveat that all organized religions have multiple sects, each of which has different views. Historical primary world fantasies will require greater research based on faith, region (ex. Buddhism in Japan is rather different than Buddhism in Tibet), and the specific era. Of course, the creator is not limited to actual, real religions and sects. They can create fictional "lost" or "hidden" religions and sects at will. On the other hand, secondary world fantasies have more obvious room for variation and tailoring. In those cases, it is more common to create religions from the deity on up, without historical or cultural baggage to address or otherwise deal with.

Religious Views

The religious views of sex and gender will vary, of course, by faith, deity, and the religion's politics. If the deities are active, the views are more likely to follow the deity's views—because the deity can directly (visitations, manifestations) or indirectly (withholding miracles) intervene. If the deities are inactive or do not exist, views are more likely to follow the politics of the religion's leaders. Additionally, depending on their relationship, secular political pressure may also influence the faith's views. For basic purposes and space, this section will discuss only some base views and the roles of sex and gender in the faith.

A given religion could fall anywhere on the spectrum from saying nothing on sex and gender to being heavily focused on both. It can also fall on a parallel spectrum ranging from being very rigid and closed on the subject to being exceptionally open. There is a lot of space between extremes on both spectra. As we might expect, the deities and their teachings will, theoretically, have the most influence here. Traditionally, we tend to think of deities favoring their own perceived sex/gender, but that is not always true. There are also many deities that break the binary view—ex. Hermaphroditus and Loki. The role of the deity may also play a part in the views expressed by its worshippers. A god of the state's followers will tend to follow the secular lead (or influence the secular lead to their view). A sex/gender swapping deity's followers will probably be very open to a full spectrum of sexes and genders. A deity focused on order may have followers who insist on binary classification (or may accept a somewhat rigid, yet non-binary, spectrum), but also have specific set roles for each sex/gender.

Any given religion may, or may not, expect certain sex and gender roles to be followed in the broader society. If a religion does have such expectations, those roles may change or be ignored by some, most, or all sects, over time. Of more immediate impact, the ability of the faith to enforce those roles in society depends on how much political and social influence it wields (see below). Fictional faiths and sects will likely be heavily impacted by the views and teachings of the deity (or deities) they follow, which offers a great opportunity to explore a wealth of options. While the religion may not be able to enforce its views of sex and gender roles on society, it can certainly control them within its own sacred sites and clergy. Typically, in the fantasy genres we tend to assume that a male deity favors males (and only male clergy) and female deities favor females (and only female clergy), but exceptions are not uncommon. For example, in Greek myth, Apollo's oracles were predominantly female, though their interpreters/attendants were typically male. This common assumption also does not account for sex/gender swapping and other non-binary deities. Presumably, a non-binary deity would be more open in its selection of faithful and the clergy, or may limit worshippers or clergypersons to non-binary mortals only. The sect of the faith matters, too. For example, Catholicism only allows male priests, but has male and female monastics, while the United Church of Christ ordains men and women (since 1853) and has no monastics.

Social Impact

The societal impact of a religion's views, or a deity's, depends on a variety of factors in this context. Key factors include how many faiths/deities exist, the relationship between the religion and government, and the legality and popularity of the religion.

The more religions and deities present in a society, the less impact each individual faith or deity is likely to have. This, of course, has exceptions for patron deities of the society, new religions moving into areas with well-established faiths, and other factors noted below. If a society only has one religion or deity, it is likely to have a greater impact on the social views of sex and gender. It is also more likely to shape socio-cultural views through its services—whether religious services or community outreach—as the solo voice of the divine. Minor faiths in a society will consequently tend to have less influence on the whole.

If a faith or deity has a close relationship with the government, it is more likely to have greater influence in society. If the religion is controlled by the government, or the state is a theocracy, then both will tend to have the same or similar views. The religion will be able to use the apparatus of the state, and the state that of the temple/church, to disseminate its views and positions on sex and gender. Both can also be used to enforce conformity as needed, depending on the type of both religion and state. If the religion and the government are opposed, or otherwise not working together, the religious influence may be lessened or concealed to some degree, especially if the faith is illegal in the eyes of the government.

The legality and popularity of a given religion also plays a key factor is how its views are adopted, or rejected, by society at large. If the faith or deity is popular in society, it will consequently be more influential in its views. If it is less popular, then there will be, obviously, less impact across the culture. If the religion is illegal, then practitioners may move around in secret, which may or may not impact its popularity. An illegal religion may have great influence among the common people, but little to no direct impact on laws and courts. For example, Catholicism is popular in Italy and Ireland, so it has had a great influence, in theory. In contrast, the Shakers never caught on (in the U.S.), leaving them effectively extinct for most of the last century.[6]

Sex and Gender in Magic

In some settings and magic systems, sex and gender may have an effect on magic, or magic may work differently by sex or gender. The relationship between magic and sex/gender is governed by two major factors in most settings (when it exists at all): social rules (changeable) and laws of magic (unchangeable, in theory). Most cases, at least those currently in use, assume or are built on a binary understanding of sex and gender, or rarely a trinary (including hermaphrodites). Only recently are some mainstream authors addressing a sex and gender spectrum in both social and natural rules of magic. Most seem to be tending toward non-gendered magic.

Social Rules

A given society may determine that magic is open to one sex or gender, but not others. Alternatively, it may limit legal training in magic to one sex or gender, as in the case of Trudi Canavan's Sachaka (*The Magicians Guild*). In these cases, there are no physical laws that limit magic, rather only the society is creating limits. Other variants have social rules that allow certain types of magic only for certain sexes or genders. For example, healing magic may be the province of males and necromancy that of females. This sort of structure will reflect societal views of sex/gender. It might also represent a hierarchy of magics, if the society has a hierarchy of genders or sexes.

Social rules about magic may arise organically in society or they could originate with government, religions/deities, or an organization of magicians. They could also be the result of history or a host of other potential causes. Regardless of origins, societal rules will ultimately be changeable. That is, since they lack natural laws as a foundation or requirement, they can be changed as the society changes or if they are challenged. They can also be subverted by those in society, whether openly or covertly. For instance, Sachaka's laws against women learning magic were subverted by a secret society of women illegally teaching other women (Canavan).

Laws of Magic

In some settings, the laws of magic, whether natural or divine, may have a sex/gender basis. Genetic magic may require XX chromosomes, for instance, or different magics may be linked to chromosomes. An example here is Tanya Huff's *Gale Women* series in which the women are spellcasters and the men in the family are essentially incarnations of Cernunnos. Deities, if they are the source of magic, may define gendered magic (ex. Aiden Thomas's *Cemetery Boys*) based on their tenets and positions or areas of influence. The laws of magic, if they are set by nature, are likely to be unchangeable and largely inviolate. Divine-based laws may be changed, if the god(s) can be convinced to do so, or to allow an exception. Divine intervention, or its equivalent may alter natural laws, too. In both cases, most applications retain binary sex/gender views and do not deal with a spectrum in either case. Even Thomas, who has a transgender protagonist, still defaults to binary gender for magic rules, which is an important part of the plot and a cultural element.

In some cases, it can be difficult to tell if gendered magic is based on natural laws or social rules. For example, on Discworld, the rule that witches are all female and wizards are all male seems to be based on natural laws (ex. wizards are the eighth son of an eighth son). However, there also seems to be a social element—both are resistant to including other sexes/genders—and The Lady (luck) occasionally throws a proverbial wrench in the works (as in *Equal Rites*, where a girl, the eighth child of an eighth son, inherits a wizard's staff and thereby becomes a wizard).

11

Organizations

Rangers, Jedi, Sith, Death Eaters, Order of the Phoenix, Harpers, Order of Merciful Aid, Knights of the Round Table, Bene Gesserit.

Iconic groups and organizations stand out and bring their world to mind alongside a host of other impressions and associations. Most settings are home to government and non-government organizations that may be limited to a single society or inter-society in nature. How a given society responds to each organization depends heavily on the purpose of the group and its connection to society as well as the type of society and government.

We may well ask: Why go through the trouble of creating and developing organizations? This is an especially likely question when we take into account that developing a group is essentially like creating an entirely new society, or sub-culture, depending on the depth of development. A few reasons, of many, seem most useful. First, an organization can provide structure and guidance for characters and the audience. This can help ease their entry into the world and setting by being stable and revealing information to the audience from authority figures, and as needed (as with Cassandra Clare and Holly Black's Magisterium). Second, organizations can serve as patrons for characters. The patron can give access to information, training, quests/missions, equipment, and protection. Good patron group examples include the Jedi (*Star Wars*), the Rangers (Middle-Earth), the Knights of Solamnia (*Dragonlance*), the Knights of the Round Table (Arthurian), and even the Bene Gesserit (*Dune*). Third, an organization can provide a unified, or semi-unified, collection of antagonists. This gives the protagonist and audience a focus, if the opposition shares goals and means. Notable examples include the Sith (*Star Wars*), the Death Eaters (*Harry Potter*), the Zhentarim (*Forgotten Realms*), and the Knights of Neraka (*Dragonlance*).

Organizations also often come to represent the entirety of the setting or world. They may encapsulate the setting, or have the setting built around them. The latter is particularly common if the organization is created first, then the creator asks, "What world would this group exist in?" Consider, for example, the *Star Wars* universe without the Jedi/Sith, Arthurian romances without the Knights of the Round Table, *Star Trek* without the Federation, Andrews's post–Shift Atlanta without the Pack and the People. In each case, the worlds would be completely different without the central organization(s) that so often drive the narratives. In many cases, the conflicts and tensions or juxtaposition of groups sets the tone and theme of the world or setting.

For every group in a setting, at least the major ones, the worldbuilder will want to know their beliefs and goals. A brief description of the organization as a whole, and possibly a description of typical individuals, possibly a rough idea of their resources, and a list of some major people can be helpful. In some cases, a motto (ex. the Ankh-Morpork Assassins' Guild's "Nil Mortifi, Sine Lucre"[1]) and/or ranks of membership may be appropriate.[2]

Organizations and Society

Every society is host to a variety of organizations. If we look solely to real-world history, we see religious, monastic, military, trade/craft, business, political, paramilitary, honorary, criminal, and scholarly organizations along with secret societies, among a host of others. The fantasy genres typically also add the possibilities of magic-based and species-based (elf, goblin, etc.) organizations of various sorts. Often one group will fit into multiple types—ex. the Knights Hospitaller were a religious, military, and, technically, monastic organization while most guilds mixed trade/craft, business, educational, political, and secret elements. For this section, the focus will be on the relationship between organizations and society. Specifically, it will discuss legal versus illicit groups and mono-society versus inter-society groups, along with the impact that groups have on a society.

Legal v. Illegal Groups

The relationship between an organization and society depends on many factors and is often complex. Factors could include the purpose of the organization, how it is funded, the founder(s), how involved the organization is in society, or what resources it controls and how it uses them. For the moment, what matters is whether the organization is legally accepted by society or has been deemed illegal.

Many societies will create definitions of legally acceptable groups and legislation that defines categories of groups, at certain points, such as non-profit groups. Organizations created by the society—ex. honorary orders of knighthood—will likely also be legislated, even if only by royal proclamation or edict. These groups may or may not have government involvement, but will certainly have at least tacit legal approval to the extent that governmental bodies will not (legally) be able to disband them. Some may have full government funding (ex. mercenary companies the government hires to protect a city-state) or may be created by the government of the society (ex. law enforcement). Most types of organizations fall into this group. There are odd situations where a seemingly illegal group is legal, such as Terry Pratchett's Ankh-Morpork that features fully legal Thieves and Assassins Guilds supported by the state. Legal groups will be those that a society sees as useful to itself, or profitable. They could be regulatory (guilds) or otherwise take on some of society's duties (ex. policing). They could be creations of the society to control dangerous activities (ex. magic, alchemy, crime), to educate people (ex. guilds), or to honor service (ex. modern knighthoods).

Legal organizations may have a place, or some influence, in the governing of society. They may have a less direct influence on steering the society as well, or instead. Some good examples here include the Order of the Garter (England), the Fools and Assassins Guilds (Ankh-Morpork), the Order of Merciful Aid and the Paranormal Activities Division (PAD) (*Kate Daniels*), the Drüskelle and Second Army (Grishaverse), and the Night's Watch and Kingsguard (*ASoIaF*). In each case, the organization will have a direct relationship with society, operate relatively to completely openly, and may have direct contact with government. They are likely to have publicly known "offices" or related holdings, even if the public is not allowed entry. They will definitely have a reputation in the society. For example, the Order of Merciful Aid is known as the last ones only the most desperate go to for help and the Ankh-Morpork Seamstresses Guild has its own reputation both as "ladies of negotiable affection"[3] and due to the "elderly" Agony Aunts (Sadie and Dotsie) who serve as their enforcers.

Likewise, some organizations will be legally banned in a society. There are a variety of reasons a society may ban certain groups: public safety (ex. a cult that practices human sacrifice), illegal activities (ex. a criminal organization), political affiliation (ex. a network supporting an antagonistic power), hate groups, or simply due to the ruler's whims or pressure applied by economic, political, religious, or other factors. Illegal groups in society will likely be smaller in number, unless the society has a particularly totalitarian or authoritarian government. Typically, any criminal organization is in this category, some religions may be (the classic human sacrifice cult), groups of terrorists/freedom fighters (depending on side and type of government), resistance groups in conquered/colonized territory, and related groups are likely to be here. What exactly counts as illegal depends heavily on the type of society and government.

Most societies will outlaw crime, though there are exceptions (Ankh-Morpork). Likewise, most societies will outlaw groups that are harmful to citizens, with exceptions (ex. state sponsored human sacrifice, as with the Aztecs). Legal religions that hold political sway may use their influence to make other faiths illegal. State-sponsored magic groups may cause others, or non-aligned magicians, to be illegal *(The Magicians Guild)*. Laws regarding the use of and training in magic may also lead to illicit groups of mages. In urban fantasy settings, people rejecting a species government or magic government may form such groups. A good example here is Slade's underworld nightclub, and Demon Fight Club, in Jaye Wells' *Sabina Kane* series. In some UF (and fantasy) cases, all magic groups may be illegal. Illicit groups may, however, wield power in society through wealth, threats of violence, fear, bribery (of political and/or religious leaders), control of desired goods and services, blackmail, or a host of other means. They might also be considered useful by the powers that be, due to their connections, ability to acquire information, ability to secretly cross borders, and ability to commit other acts that those in power can deny ordering. Some good examples of illicit groups, particularly ones with some power, include the Ketterdam gangs that provide services and feed tourism (Grishaverse), the cult of Morgion that uses the threat of plague to achieve its goals (*Dragonlance*), and the female magicians of Sachaka who teach illicit magic and run an underground railroad and resistance of sorts (Canavan).

Mono-society versus Inter-society

Some organizations are going to be unique to a given society, whether small society or large. Examples include the Jedi Temple Guards (*Star Wars*), the Kingsguard (*ASoIaF*), the PAD or Paranormal Activity Division (*Kate Daniels*), the Second Army (Grishaverse), or the FBI (U.S.). Such groups may be legal or illicit, but tend to be more accepted, or perhaps treated with greater contempt, by their home culture compared to foreign or inter-society groups. The reach and influence of such groups is necessarily limited to the boundaries of their society. However, within that society, they may, potentially, have a great deal of influence and power. At the very least, they are likely to have greater access to resources within and knowledge of the society. They will probably also tend to be viewed better by those in power, and may even be influenced by or controlled by those in power.

Other groups are going to be multi-national, or otherwise cross legal and political boundaries, in nature and reach. Good examples include the Wizards of High Sorcery (*Dragonlance*), the People (*Kate Daniels*), the Brotherhood of Sorcerers (*The Witcher*), or the Catholic Church (Earth). Such organizations move and operate across societal and national borders, beholden to no single society or government. That broadness gives them potentially great access to resources and a variety of facilities. However, it is also likely to evoke the ire of governments, and possibly the populace, of many societies—they may see the group as dangerous to their rule, lacking in loyalty to society, spreading foreign agendas, or otherwise threatening, even if it is not. Such groups will be especially reviled by isolationist and authoritarian societies and governments, as they are far less susceptible to governmental control. That said, even more open societies may not fully embrace such groups. In any case, the reasons that the group is cross-societal in nature should be explained. For instance, a crime group with an interest in smuggling or piracy needs access to networks outside the society (to acquire goods from or to hide their ships in). An international group created to regulate magic and prevent governments from controlling them is also a favorite in the fantasy genres.

Effects on Society

Like all elements of society, the organizations in a society have an impact on social development and other aspects of society. Due to the broad nature of possibilities, only a few will be discussed here, notably economics, politics, and technology.

Groups like guilds, companies, political organizations, and even religious, magic oriented, or secret groups can act to shape the economics of a society. Some are obvious. For instance, guilds, mercantile families, and companies will work to ensure prosperity for their members. Others may be less direct. Religious groups may expand, limit, or control trade depending on the faith. Some religious organizations, such as medieval European monastic orders, will own property and land, in some cases excessive amounts of land, that influence the society's economy. Magic-based organizations may control access to certain goods, including magical devices, that can boost or sink other trades. Criminal groups can also have economic effects, through the provision of illicit or cheap smuggled goods and services or moneylending (as Brust's House Jhereg). A guild might even make itself indispensable to society, so much so that it becomes effectively untouchable, that also allows them to heavily influence politics (ex. the Spacers Guild in *Dune*).

Depending on the society, groups from guilds to organized crime to magicians to monastic orders could exert a political influence.

Organizations of rebels have an obvious political impact, since politics is the very reason for their existence. Groups could have control or influence over elected leaders, royal counsellors, or other policy makers. Some might work through influencing public views, even to the point of rebellion or revolt. In some cases, groups may be able to have a hand in the selection of royals and other heads of state. Some organization leaders may even be the power behind the throne, as in the case of the Catholic Cardinal Richelieu for decades in France.

The influence of organizations can even impact and alter technological development, or the development of magic. If religious orders are the only writers, it is not in their best interests for printing presses to exist. If a magic guild is the only source of fast transit, it is not in their interests to allow the development of faster non-magical travel. In contrast, guilds and merchant families will likely seek cheaper writing, recording, and travel technology to rely less on the priests and magicians, and save money. This creates socio-political conflict, and therefore both plot and realism in the setting.

Purpose and History

Any organizations in a given society will form, or be formed, for a reason. They tend not to spontaneously appear "just because." The reason the group exists should be known, if only to the worldbuilder, though most purposes will also be known to their members and possibly others in the world. Likewise, any organization that has existed for more than a few days will have a history. There will be things it has done or participated in and a chain of leaders/organizers, or those who have claimed to lead it. These two factors guide the character of the organization

Purpose

Every organization exists for a reason. That reason can be as simple as socializing or as big as saving or protecting the multiverse. Regardless of the scope, every organization should have a reason for being.

The type of organization may determine its purpose, or the purpose may influence the type. This is a chicken or the egg question, in some ways. The purpose of the group may require a certain kind of organization. Alternately, the type of organization may be a simple tool toward a goal. And many, or most, organizations can have multiple purposes, whether each is equal or they exist in a hierarchy (primary, secondary). As an example, the Second Army of Ravka (Grishaverse) has three competing purposes: to protect grisha, to train grisha, to protect Ravka. Which is considered the most important depends heavily on who is being asked, and when. The Rangers of Middle-Earth have two purposes, both of which intersect: to protect the peoples of Middle-Earth from Sauron's forces and to keep the heir of Gondor alive and hidden. Comparatively, the Night's Watch of the Seven Kingdoms (*ASoIaF*) has a single official purpose: to protect the Kingdoms from denizens of the North beyond the Wall. Unofficially, they also serve as a place to dispose of criminals and potential claimants to the throne.

Depending on the age of the organization, it may be important to note whether the organization's purpose or goals have changed and why. In these cases, keep note of the original purpose and the current purpose or role—see the History section below for a discussion of causes of change. Any dynamic group in any world will shift over time. This is especially true of a group that exists for a couple of decades, even more so if it has been around for centuries or millennia. A good example is the Jedi (*Star Wars*); originally founded as a monastic organization to teach Force sensitives, it grew to become a special force of police and diplomats for the Republic, and finally turned into quasi-military officers in the final years of the Republic before becoming a monastic order again after Order 66. *Dragonlance*'s Solamnic Knights began as a group similar to the Knights Templar, a holy order of knighthood devoted to Paladine and two other gods of good. In time, the Knights became the rulers of Solamnia, which changed their purpose—instead of fighting the forces of evil, they largely tried to retain power. Their purpose shifted almost purely to survival after the Cataclysm tore the nation and continent apart. In contrast, Middle-Earth's Rangers remained largely unchanging in purpose for over 1000 years.

History

As noted, any group that exists for more than a few minutes will have a history. At the very least, it will have a history of leaders, fluctuating size of membership (or even membership requirements, see below), and events the organization has been involved in. There may be a history of meeting places, holdings, and uniforms or symbols that evolved over time as the group changed in its role, purpose, and goals. Events in the organization's history are similar to those of any society (see Chapter 2), so those can be adapted to the scale of the organization. The focus here will be on internal and external historic forces that may lead to an evolving organization.

Every organization is subject to internal forces that can alter the group. For example, changes in leadership often lead to an evolution of the group in new directions, both good and bad for the group and society. The ambitions of leadership, and members, may lead to the group being overextended or expanding and redefining the purpose and goals of the organization. Changing demographics of membership may also lead to shifts in an organization's purpose, symbols, and appearance. Attempts to boost shrinking membership, to avoid the demise of the group, can be another factor. As membership fluctuates, so do the funds available to the organization. A drop in funding may lead to shrinking goals and holdings, while an influx of funds may lead to expansions, or even overextending. In some cases, if the organization has a finite goal, it could be achieved. If an organization's goal is achieved, it can cause the group to dissolve or change its purpose, if the members choose to continue the association.

External forces that can alter organizations are equally present and broad. To follow the previous paragraph, the leaders of the society, or legislation created by them, can lead to changes in organizations. At the most extreme, they can turn a legal organization into an illegal one or can lead a group to become passive, go into hiding, or become active or open in its activities. Any wars that the society is engaged in that impact the entire society can change or add purposes, even temporarily, for an organization. Good examples from our own history include Jewish gangsters (organized crime) opposing American Nazi groups in Chicago, NYC, and Los Angeles in the late-1930s or Operation Underworld (1942–1945) in which the U.S. government worked with Italian and Jewish gangsters "to counter Axis spies and saboteurs along the U.S. northeastern seaboard ports, avoid wartime labor union strikes, and limit theft by black-marketeers of vital war supplies and equipment."[4] Pandemics, epidemics, and plagues, like wars, can cause an abrupt change in organizations of all sorts, especially if paranormals and magic are involved. Other organizations in opposition to, allied with, or even seemingly uninvolved with the group can alter it in various ways through their own actions, which could lead to or instigate internal causes. As an extreme example, apocalyptic events will obviously alter most groups. Any organizations that survive the apocalypse will be rather different, whether due to redirection or a complete upheaval depending on the type and effects of the apocalyptic event. In a hidden magic setting, revealing, or threatening to reveal, the organization could lead to change. This, of course, depends on if and how the threat can be nullified or if it is already enacted. A good example is the society and organization of vampires in the *Southern Vampire Mysteries* series (Charlaine Harris).

Members and Influence

Beyond the reasons for the group and its past, the next obvious questions are: How does someone join? and How big is the organization? Either may, probably will, affect what the group controls, both in terms of its influence and the physical places it controls. Both elements may easily become plot points, be matters of history, and be altered by changes to the organization, as well as (in RPG setups) goals for players, or characters.

Membership

A key element of all organizations is membership requirements. Who can join, who cannot, and what they must do to join are important determinants of organization size and demographics. Membership could be open to all, or it could require certain skills or natural talent (for a craft or magic). It could be limited by social class, species, ethnicity, gender, sex, age, or a host or combination of other factors. Some factors could limit how high an individual may rise in the organization, too, depending on internal rules. The aforementioned Second Army (Grishaverse) only requires an in-born magical talent to join, with most being young when they start (but not required). All sexes, classes, genders, orientations, and ethnicities are accepted. Conversely, the Witchers (*The Witcher*) require specific mutations, with a necessary method of creation, and virtually all (if not all) are male. As a third example, the Wizards of High Sorcery (*Dragonlance*) require natural talent, the recommendation of a member, and passing the Tests. Any sex or gender is accepted, but it is species limited to humans, elves, and half-elves (though this may change in the 5th edition version of *D&D* and *One D&D*, based on released playtest materials).

Once we know who can join and how, the size of the organization is helpful. It can be used to determine the organization's influence and spread throughout society, or across societies. With more members, the group will be spread widely. The influence of the group can be based on either or both the number and status of members. A small group of high status or wealthy individuals may have as much, or more, influence as a group with large numbers. The stricter the entry requirements, the smaller the group will be while fewer requirements tends to create larger organizations. To use the above examples, the Second Army was never huge, but it is the largest collection of grisha in the setting. Heavy losses in the Ravkan civil war dramatically shrank the group and led to a practice of aggressive recruitment among the survivors. Likewise, the Witchers were always small in number, simply because of their entry requirements and the mortality rate of the mutation process.

Control

For these purposes, control comes in two forms: physical holdings and influence. Individual groups may be strong, moderate, or weak, or whatever degrees, in one, the other, both, or neither area.

Physical holdings range from the crash spaces and bolt-holes of a criminal gang where thieves and assassins can lay low for a time to the fortresses of military orders to entire geographic regions. What holdings a group controls should fit the type, purpose, and membership of the group. It does not make sense for an order of knighthood to have secret bolt-holes, unless they operate spies in enemy territory. Likewise, a criminal organization is unlikely to have castles, unless they also possess wealth and military might. That said, historically in our own world, monastic organizations controlled farms, villages, breweries, mines, and a host of other such property gifted to them by members of the nobility. Places held by an organization can become iconic, especially if they are unique and associated solely with one group. For example, The Little Palace and the Second Army (Grishaverse), Kaer Morhen and the Witchers (*The Witcher*), and the Tower and Forest of Wayreth and the Wizards of High Sorcery (*Dragonlance*). Some of these places may also indicate, or grant, a degree of influence in society.

Influence can come in a variety of forms and from a host of directions. Most organizations, and their members or leaders, are likely to possess multiple types of influence. This can be exerted to steer society, whether covertly, subtly, or overtly. Organizations may acquire influence through finances, popular support, blackmail, political standing, physical force, threats, leadership (of other groups), family and friends relationships, bribery, favors/debts, or a host of other possibilities. Their influence may, also, come from a variety of elements of society including, but not limited to government (local to national), business (merchants, guilds), education (kindergarten to university), religious, criminal, military, law enforcement, magical/occult/paranormal, high society, entertainment (street performers to theaters, movies, music, sports), and news/media (from town criers to multinational TV platforms). As an example, a classic, archetypal, Thieves' Guild may have influence over non-member criminals; government via blackmail; law enforcement through bribery; business via threats; and entertainment by openly or quietly owning theaters, gambling dens, and such in a city.

12

Geography

"You can't map a sense of humor. Anyway, what is a fantasy map but a space beyond which There Be Dragons?"[1]

Many worldbuilding books and websites discuss geography. Most pay more attention to geology and the scientific aspects of how our world formed than they do to story/imagination.[2] This is fine, so far as it goes, but is rather limiting. As the setting of a narrative, character interaction, and history, geography is clearly important and affects the other aspects of the narrative and development. After all, nothing exists in a vacuum, at least not for long; action and life need a place to happen. Dimitri Halkidis reminds us to consider how the world influences the people who live there, from the frequency and type of natural disasters to the locations of rulers and other cultures (in both distance and accessibility).[3] To that end, geography ultimately shapes cultures, nations, the character of cities, ecologies, climates, and people. Without a sense of geography, some sort of map (mental or physical), or inspirational photos or art, suspending disbelief and connecting with the audience can be significantly more difficult. Even with the quotation above, Terry Pratchett discovered this necessity, noting that "the *City Mapp*, which was designed with the considerable help of Stephen Briggs, was of massive assistance. Instead of limiting my options, which I'd feared, it opened them up. I began to see the neighbourhoods, the villages that had been swallowed by the sprawl, the way the city had grown. We had to build in the evidence of past ages— street names that didn't mean anything now, odd lanes, streets that curved around city wall[s] that were moved centuries ago."[4]

Focus on Secondary Worlds

Secondary worlds are a seductive and often fun choice, but they involve considerable work depending on how large and deep the creator decides to develop them, in terms of scale. They are also the type of world in which creators have the ability to play with and customize geography the most. Secondary worlds offer vistas of creative freedom. Even so, we have seen shifts in the audience since the 1930s to 1960s toward expecting world geography to make logical sense, and away from massive cities with no visible means of support. Even so, there is still room for exotic environments. However, secondary worlds also allow for alteration and freedom of geography through the use of magic, divine intervention, and semi-divine alteration to shape and reshape the world, if done with creativity. This allows for some geographic hand waving to be done.

For these reasons and others, this chapter will predominantly focus on secondary worlds and the influence of geography on society. There is more variety in secondary worlds, in many ways, so there is more need to discuss them. Also, in secondary worlds, we need to build the geography from the ground up, literally. Conversely in primary worlds settings, we build atop the foundation of real-world geography.

Scale

For most societies, geography applies on three notable levels of scale: local, regional, and national. Regional refers to a space within a nation or around a nation, making it effectively two scales. Obviously, we can shrink geography to city neighborhoods. We can also expand geography to both the continental and global levels, but both are beyond the scope of this piece (since there are few continent or world spanning societies, at least in fantasy/UF).

Local geography could be a city's neighborhoods and the landforms they built around or on. It could also be the location of rivers, woods, fields, deserts, and such around a town or village. Regardless, the geography influences the local society and community on many levels. For instance, a desert oasis village is going to be very different, socially, from a mountain city.

Regional (small) geography asks what natural features exist around the local society. For instance, does the desert rise to mountains nearby or to scrub leading to a steppe? What other settlements are in the region, as other villages, towns, or fortresses will alter the society that we are building. Likewise, based on geography we may ask if there are regional nomadic or semi-nomadic societies—and how they move around (ex. desert camel trains, river/canal boats, on foot, in wagons). The regional geography can also include ruins (whether due to old civilizations, warfare, plague) or lairs of monsters (ex. Grendel or a dragon).

National geography tells us how the national society conducts and feeds itself. It answers what natural features form the borders of the nations—sea, river, mountains, forest, desert, marsh/swamp, steppes, or something else—and therefore how firm those borders may be—a river forms a more obvious border than an arbitrary line drawn through a forest, for example. National geography tells us what features define the nation and its internal regions. It also includes where cities, major towns, and other notable structures or settlements are located. The geographical location of cities and settlements may be due to resources (ex. water), history, or strategic value, among other reasons.

Regional (large) geography is similar to small regional, but bigger. It asks what nations are in the region, referring to this part of the continent. It explains what the dominant natural features of the part of the continent are—ex. southern European and north African societies are heavily influenced by the Mediterranean Sea. These features shape trade routes and methods of travel. They can also create obstacles to expansion or communication as well as strategic areas in the region.

Fantasy vs. Realism

The question of realism in geography is, almost paradoxically, raised in secondary world building with an odd degree of regularity. On one level, certainly cultures are and should be influenced by and reflect their geography in realistic ways. On another, it seems strange to discuss the "realism" of a fictitious place that is part of an imaginative world. Even so, it is often discussed, with Middle-Earth being a particular favorite—Mordor's U-shaped mountains are often cited as unrealistic and therefore an example of "bad" worldbuilding in this way. The impetus for learning is, of course, great and laudable. However, we cannot learn everything about geology, climatology, meteorology, chemistry, and physics (at the very least) and apply it all. For one thing, no reader wants all that information. For another, it would make for very dry reading and, even if not directly told to the audience, would make for extremely lengthy worldbuilding to no good purpose.

For secondary worlds, especially in the fantasy genre, it seems better to let imagination do its thing. Of course, we need to keep the desired society and culture in mind because a desert-based nomadic culture is not likely to develop in the middle of a rainforest. If it does, there better be a very good, and probably convoluted, reason for it. To imagination, we can add that our knowledge of the real universe is minuscule. We are not certain how "normal" or "anomalous" our own world and solar system are. Since the beginning of space programs worldwide, we have found extra-solar planets of diamond (in theory) and massive Earth-like worlds.[5]

In short, scientific exploration has discovered things in our own universe that go beyond the imagination, or confirm the imaginations of earlier writers.

Different Universe

An important consideration for "realism" is that secondary worlds are not necessarily in the same universe as Earth. Therefore, they are not restricted by our knowledge of physics, geology, and other sciences, to a certain extent. Much pre-1980s fantasy took the need of plot or Steven Brust's "Cool Stuff Theory of Literature"[6] as their guide. Others looked to mythology and mined myths from around the world—such as Pratchett's Discworld that combined both the needs of plot with Hindu tales of the world's creation/shape (a flat disc on top of four elephants on top of a turtle). Perhaps, as N.K. Jemisin has suggested with magic,[7] some sense of wonder has been lost in calls for "realism." Suspension of disbelief is, of course, important, but verisimilitude to Earth is less so. Internal consistency will cause a suspension of disbelief without reference to Earth. For example, magic may defy gravity, if it does so in a consistent fashion. That said, there are certain commonalities between secondary worlds, and Earth. All such worlds tend to have carbon-based life that breathes oxygen, the worlds have gravity, and generally obey basic physics. They also tend to share some species of animals—horses, cows, bears, ravens, wolves—and plants—wheat, oaks.

Altered Geography—Magic

As briefly noted above, in fantasy and UF worlds, magic may be used to alter geography, on a small or continental scale. These alterations may occur purposefully, as side effects of spellcasting, as inadvertent releases of energy (or due to drawing energy from the world), as accidents or miscast spells, due to dimensional gates, or a variety of other effects. For example, we can return to Mordor's U-shaped mountains. According to *The Silmarillion*, Morgoth and Sauron used their magic to create, or shape, the mountains to protect their stronghold.[8] Strong magic may alter the land, even inadvertently, as we see in *Avatar: The Last Airbender* (especially earth bending), Kevin Hearne's *Seven Kennings* (earth and plant especially), and Bardugo's Grishaverse (controlling the tides in the harbor of Ketterdam). Even the nature of magic itself could alter geography—ex. Andrews's post-Shift Atlanta where magic waves cause accelerated plant growth and cause entire old growth forests to rise overnight during surges—or feed on the world, leaving desolation behind—as in D&D's *Dark Sun* campaign world.

Magic can also result in "natural" or created geographical oddities, such as the Flying Forest in Fillory (Grossman, *The Magicians*), the Forest of Wayreth and Shoikan Grove in Krynn (Weis and Hickman, *Dragonlance*), or the Underchasm and earth motes of Toril (*The Forgotten Realms*). All of these possibilities alter and shape society, if they occur naturally or through inadvertent or uncontrollable means. If they occurred through controlled or purposeful creation (Hearne, Bardugo, *Avatar*), they present a non-technological means by which society shapes the land around it for its own benefit, one that may go beyond what our current technology is capable of.

Altered Geography—Divine

If a setting has deities, especially active or formerly active ones, then divine actions can reshape the world and alter geography. Weis and Hickman's Krynn is an extreme example, as the gods dropped a mountain on part of a continent, thereby creating two seas (wiping out at least one nation), making a massive desert, and splitting a nation (Ergoth) off into islands. The effects and results of a divine alteration are limited only by three things: the nature and power of the gods, the deity's sphere of influence (if only one is involved), and how many deities are involved. If all the deities are involved, and not in opposing camps, then the effect of divine alteration is likely to be global in nature. If individual deities are involved, they may only affect a given region, or related space of land (ex. forest, desert, island, part of sea, lake) and the effects may be tailored to an individual deity. The sphere of influence can also affect the effects— for example, the death of the goddess Mystra on Toril (*The Forgotten Realms*) led to the collapse and corruption of the Weave, the source of all magic in the world. In most cases, if the gods affect the geography of the world, they usually do so at the time of creation. If they alter the world later, it is generally accompanied by a catastrophe or apocalypse event (ex. Krynn's Cataclysm or *The Forgotten Realms'* First and Second Sunderings and Time of Troubles). If the gods alter geography, there should be a reason or purpose behind it. This could be a side effect of a divine conflict. It could be to punish, reward, or remind mortals of something. It could be the result of a chaos or trickster figure (and mythological or folk lore tricksters always have a purpose or lesson to their chaos). Likewise, myths and legends should accompany the event and the resulting features. The event should be memorialized and significant, not brushed off as a daily occurrence. The exception might be if the setting is a realm of chaos that constantly changes, but such a place is unlikely to be suitable for mortals.

Shaping Society

Saying that geography is a major factor in shaping the physical aspects of a society is a bit of a truism. But, it bears saying. Geography obviously affects the layout of settlements and the building materials used, but it also affects architecture, art, customs, and fashion. The physical area in which a society develops even shapes and alters a culture's religion, or creates regional variants based on local conditions, needs, and features. For example, Poseidon was not an especially important god to the Spartans, as they had a landlocked city-state and no navy to speak of, while he was very important to the Athenians. Likewise, Sobek was extremely important to many Egyptians, as the god who created the Nile upon which so much of Egyptian society was built. For this section, the focus will be on five major areas of influence, since covering every aspect of society would be tedious: resources, trade/travel, defense/expansion, culture (in broad terms), and history.

Resources

A society's geography affects the resources that are available to it. This, in turn, affects the society's relationships with others, the character or feel of the society, and the appearance of the society, as well as necessities like food and sanitation. For example, forested mountains yield hunting, fishing, lumber, mining, quarrying, and fur trading, while a coastal desert offers fishing, glassmaking, possibly mineral extraction, and ocean/sea/lake travel. The geography shapes the building materials and food that a society has. It determines whether building will be done with wood, adobe, stone, or hides. It also determines what plants grow or thrive (for food, clothing, rope, and other needs) and what proteins are available (beef, goat, fish, beans). Available resources influence a society's reputation, economics, politics and conflicts (over access to resources), and fashion (available clothing materials and dyes by region or trade). Depending on species, geography may also influence what non-humans are in or interact with the society (or the ratios in which they appear). For instance, Tolkien and Pratchett tie their dwarves to mountains (though Pratchett complicates this) and Tolkien and *D&D* tie their elves to forests for the most part.[9]

If magic requires natural tools—ex. gems, tree species, metals (as in Sanderson's *Mistborn*)—then societies with access to these resources will become centers of magic. As such, they will likely acquire significant strategic value, or may be vilified depending on how magic is viewed. If magic is viewed positively, such societies might accrue a great deal of wealth and power by trading in magic resources. They may also become targets, as neighboring societies try to take over the source of needed materials (ex. Fonda Lee's Kekon, the only source of a type of jade needed to perform magic, that was colonized and is a strategic target for the world's other nations). If magic requires ley lines, or other special land features, then ley lines become a geographic resource like rivers and lakes. Societies and cities are therefore likely to be built along ley lines or near the necessary land feature.

Trade and Travel

As with resources, geography heavily influences the need for trade and the methods of travel available to a society. In part, it determines what a society has in excess and what it needs. For comparison, in Earth history, societies built on coasts and by waterways whenever possible because these provided drinking water, sanitation, major transportation routes (that were faster and easier than walking), and water for pack beasts and foot travelers. Likewise, desert societies tended to build around oases, deep wells, and rivers; they also tended to avoid wheels until recently, except along rivers and roads, because wheels and loose sand are not as good as, for instance, camel feet and sand. The geography also affects the population density, thereby affecting the need for trade and travel. When a person travels, the geography determines the difficulty of travel, and therefore trade—20 miles in the mountains is very different from 20 miles on the steppes or 20 miles in the jungle.

Because of these factors, many societal economies are built around available means of travel and trade. This could be horse or camel breeding ranches to ship building companies. Entire trades and professions may come into being due to the society's geography—ex. shipwrights, animal breeders and trainers, blacksmiths (for shoeing). The presence of magic and technology will affect or mitigate these tendencies. Technological inventions like airships or motor vehicles allow some aspects of geography to be ignored (flown over, for instance). Irrigation allows for movement away from rivers for settlement, as well as the creation of canals and canal boats for trade. Magic may alter the resources and lines of trade, as noted with ley lines above. Common magical travel might hold a greater influence than access to waterways, especially if water can be magically transported. This might lead to non-contiguous societies, that is societies in which the cities or other territories are not necessarily next to or touching each other. That could make for some interesting social developments.

Defense and Expansion

The geography of the area in which a society is situated can be, and often is, a notable determinant of how and if the society expands as well as how it protects itself from other societies, or if it needs to. As a fictional example, we can consider Fonda Lee's Kekon. The island nation is loosely based on a mix of South East Asian nations, and Hong Kong. It is a predominantly mountainous jungle geography with a society that developed hit and run defensive tactics and strategies against colonizers. It is also the only location for a magic mineral needed to use powers, so it has a history of conflicts with foreign invasion. Even two societies with the same, broadly, basic geography—ex. island states—may develop differently due to other factors of geography. For instance, England has a relatively small channel dividing it from mainland Europe, so it eventually developed as a naval power for its own protection and expansion (as native resources proved unable to support the populace). In contrast, Japan, also an island state, is surrounded by larger bodies of water and was largely left alone by neighbors, so developed an insular society and tactics to prevent ships from landing or creating a beachhead (for a time). Both are, of course, very different from Switzerland, surrounded as it is by mountains, that remained non-expansionistic and developed a strategy of controlling narrow mountain passes that worked well into the 20th century.

The expansion of a society could be aided by geography—open land, easy movement—or hindered by it—impassable mountains, lack of water access. A society may expand by land, sea, tunnels, or air, depending on technology and magic access. For most of our own history, societies were limited to land and sea expansion, due to technology and where useful territory was located. However, in a fantasy setting, subterranean expansion could be a possibility with various species and societies developing in that realm—ex. Pratchett's Ankh-Morpork that spreads on the surface, while dwarf families and groups expand through tunnels beneath the city (and occasionally come into jurisdictional conflict with the surface government, as in *Thud!*). Likewise, the introduction of magic, or a certain level of technology, could allow for expansion of society via the air. Airships, flying castles, flying beasts capable of carrying people and goods, or magical flight could all open up new opportunities for a society to spread out (as well as defensive concerns—real world castles, a staple of inspiration for fantasy, were not designed to withstand aerial attack, since such a thing did not exist; a fantasy castle may need to consider that vulnerability). Depending on the source and types of magic, a society could also expand in a non-contiguous fashion, early in its development, as mentioned above. Conversely, geography that hinders expansion of a society—mountains, an ocean, desert—could also protect the society from expansionistic neighbors, even geography driven climate may work in this fashion.

Culture

Because geography determines weather, flora, fauna, and other physical factors of a region, it also affects culture and society. Since culture and society are a complex interaction of foods, fashions, traditions, and other elements, they are the result of what is available to the society. Geography determines, or heavily influences, what plants (food, dyes, building, clothing, tools), animals (food, dyes, clothing, tools), and minerals (dyes, building, tools) are available in a society without trade. It also influences what clothing, tools, and such are needed by the society. To see this influence, we need only look at a handful of real-world societies and their dominant geography (not to say that it is the only geographic feature) such as Taiwan (island), Austria (land-locked), Switzerland (mountain), Tunisia (desert), and Mongolia (steppes) to see how each is, partially, a product of its geography. Each of the listed societies has significant differences, historically, in building styles and materials, food and food preparation, clothing (style, quantity, coloration), and traditions. Even when cultures have a basic similarity, for example nomadic, their geography has a significant impact that creates differences— ex. Mongolian nomads (central Asian steppes) versus Bedouin (North African desert) versus Romany (European mountains and woods).

In constructing societies, we need to keep these differences in mind. A mountain region is not likely to produce a culture of great race horses, but rather is more likely to be a source of stout mules or ponies. In fantasy worlds, this also affects "monsters" such as dragons, unicorns, and manticores. It also affects the sentient species—forest centaurs are likely to be smaller (close trees, low branches) while plains centaurs are likely to be larger (open space, nothing overhead). This is one thing that Tolkien, for instance, excelled at. Each culture of Middle-Earth was tailored to its location from laconic hobbits in rolling hills and brooks to horse-born Rohirrim raised on the plains and steppes to solid dwarves in their mountain homes. Much of this was, admittedly, due to the sources he was inspired by, whether middle-class 19th-century England, Viking Age Norsemen, or Nordic-Saxon mythology. Many others in the genre, obviously, followed his lead and sources to the point of cliché in some cases, and to the point of trying to subvert or reverse his work.

History

In addition to everything above, the history of a society is also greatly affected by the geography of its location. To use our own history as examples, Switzerland's historic neutrality has been greatly aided by geography as the entire border is mountains, making it a difficult country to invade before the invention of flight. Likewise, Venice was built where it was due to a swamp. Escaped Roman slaves built in the swamp and lagoon for protection, which later affected the design of the city and its canals, and led to problems of sinking buildings today. Just from those examples, we can see that geography can help protect a region (as with Andorra as well) or open it to invasions (Poland). It can create cultural backwaters and protect a society from plague and external influence. Geography can also create a history of wealth (both resources and trade routes) or poverty (lack of resources and lack of easy trade routes). What a society does with its geography is part of its history, as are the limits of what can be done given geography. These two, of course, must also account for the presence and level of both technology and magic. A city or region could be a barren place that sits along a major trade route, thus relying on trade for its wealth and existence. It could, alternately, be a bread basket that floods annually (the Nile or Yellow-Yangtze Rivers plain), or anything in between.

As we apply geography to history, some societies may be more or less affected by events in the region or world. Plagues, wars, and distribution of technology or magic may be aided or hindered by geography. Some societies may be in places that are naturally secluded and become places where old elements of society, or magic, survive. They may be bustling areas where new changes are spawned, due to trade or resources, for instance. Geography can also affect what advances are likely to occur. For example, a printing press is unlikely to be invented on a barren rocky island (except possibly as a thought experiment by a visiting foreigner) because it needs paper (cotton or wood pulp), wood (frame), metal (copper, iron), and ink at the very least. Almost all of those are unavailable on a barren island without trade. But, the island will probably be safe from plague and war, unless it is a major trade site (e.g., located along an important sea trade route).

Exotic Geography

Fantasy, and UF/PNR, allow for the possibility of exotic features that defy known science, another application of Brust's "Cool Stuff" theory. If they exist in a primary world setting, they likely need to be hidden somehow, unless magic is openly known about in the world. Most secondary worlds that have exotic geography do so openly, since magic tends to be known, even if mysterious. Any sort of exotic geography will have a profound, and hopefully obvious, effect and impact on any society on, near, or sharing a world with it. Due to the presence of magic, there are a nearly infinite number of possibilities for exotic terrain, but five major ones will be covered here: sky worlds/flying land, wandering islands, broken worlds, lava/boiling seas, and flat/ring worlds.

Sky Worlds and Flying Land

Perhaps one of the most common examples of exotic geography is sky worlds or floating landmasses. Sky worlds are probably the lesser of the two in terms of commonality. Most sky worlds have anchored or drifting landmasses in an otherwise entirely air world. Some of those land masses may be flat discs, but most have some degree of "dirt" hanging beneath them, as in the case of Weis and Hickman's Arianus (*Deathgate Cycle*). If humanoid beings are present in the world, this is probably for the best. Worlds that are entirely air are likely to be uninhabitable by humans and related species, though they may visit by means of vehicles, mounts, or magic. Typically entirely sky worlds will tend to be elemental planes.

The idea of flying landmasses is the more common appearance of this exotic terrain. If most lands fly or float, then there needs to be some means of traveling between them—magic, flying mounts, airships—otherwise there is little to no possibility of contact between societies. That said, if the floating landmasses are mobile, they may come into contact. That mobility, of course, may be controlled or not depending on the mechanism of flight and the world. Floating landmasses are even more common as the flying castle or city, though. These tend to appear in otherwise "normal" worlds. Typically a flying castle has a chunk of dirt or land beneath, usually hanging as a rough cone. This most often occurs because the castle is built on the ground and ripped from the earth to fly/float. Good examples include Castle Black of Dragaera (Brust), Netheril's cities (*Forgotten Realms*), the Dragonarmy's flying castles (*Dragonlance*), parts of the *Chronicles of Amber* (Roger Zelazny), and the Endor College for Witches (*Mary and the Witch's Flower*). The flying castle or city allows for concealment from others. It can also be a mobile base of operations and allows for changes of scenery. They could also provide safety and security for residents, or be a great threat to opponents (*Dragonlance*). In some cases, a flying castle could be a means of addressing magical and aerial threats that could be present on a magically active world. They could even be simply symbols of power and status (Dragaera). A flying city could be a means of isolating a society from others. That could serve to preserve culture and language. It could also stunt the growth of the society, if they are unable to travel or contact others.

Regardless of the intent or effect, flying landmasses and sky worlds present some key societal questions. First and foremost are the concerns for acquiring resources (especially food and water) as well as sanitation. Depending on height, the issue of breathable versus thin air could become an issue. In some cases, that might be hand waved by use of a magic bubble around the city or landmass that maintains pressure and air density, while the air is refreshed by some means. Travel between such landmasses has been noted above, but there is also travel to and from the ground, if any ground exists (ex. Dragaerans teleport from the ground to the floating castles).

Wandering Islands

Wandering islands are one of the classic pieces of exotic geography in the myths and legends of our own world. In Western literature, they go back at least as far as Greek myth with the island of Delos—birthplace of Artemis and Apollo—possibly further. At least a few legends also speak of aspidochelones—giant turtles with islands on their backs. In legend, sailors would stop on the island to replenish their fresh water only to have the aspidochelone submerge, drowning them. In fantasy or UF, the aspidochelone could remain at a level where the island remains on the surface, or even form a migrating archipelago of apsidochelone islands. Basically, wandering islands serve as flying islands, but for the sea or ocean. Travel to and from them is significantly easier—boats—but tracking them could still be an issue due to the sheer size of most oceans.

Typically, islands move for one of three causes: natural, magical, or divine. Natural movement could be the result of aspidochelones or other massive beasts. Other reasons are also possible. How the island naturally moves is important, in order to determine whether the movement can be controlled by the inhabitants or not. Magical movement could be caused by a spell, object, or other means. What maintains the ability to move is important in that the question arises about whether it can be interrupted or needs to be maintained (whether continually or recast) and how often. The question of control still remains, but adds the question of why the magic was used to make the island move in the first place. That is, what is the purpose of the moving island. Perhaps more importantly, does the original purpose still apply today? A divine causation is similar to magical in that the questions of control and purpose remain. However, the added question of whether the deity can cause the movement ability to stop arises. If the deity can cause it to stop, then keeping the deity happy becomes important, or keeping it distracted (if it forgot about the island), or the movement may end when the purpose is fulfilled. For example, Delos moved around to protect the twins and their mortal mother from Hera and to get around Hera's curse. Once the twin gods were born, Delos became rooted to the sea floor in its current (real) position.

Wandering islands open up a number of societal questions and concerns. The availability of resources depends on the kind of island and how it came into being. Concerns about sanitation and other necessities are rather easier with a wandering island than with a flying one, but are still present. The question of population is a huge one, particularly for sustainability, which is also true of flying islands and stationary islands, but is more important when trade may not be as readily feasible. Contact with other societies may be increased or decreased depending on the purpose of the island's movement—if it moves "simply" to move, then there could be increased contact with a wider variety of societies; if it moves for concealment, then the point is to decrease contact. Regardless, the history of the island and its settlement is likely to be an interesting one—the first settlers, the original purpose (if any), later contact. The island could have been granted motion to protect the chosen people of a god. Magicians may have caused it to move to protect from a world hostile to magic. It could simply be that sailors found an aspidochelone and settled or were shipwrecked and settled down. Inhabitants could be exploiting, or be in a symbiotic relationship with, an aspidochelone. Or residents could be trapped by a curse, among many other possibilities.

Broken World

On a more exotic level, some fantasy worlds are broken apart and "destroyed." Typically, this separates the land of the world into many discrete parts, possibly even different "worlds." Generally, the parts are still linked magically, often by gates of a magical nature or sometimes through vehicular access. This sort of geography allows for, or creates, a degree of isolation of societies, over the long or short term. Societies could lose contact or means of contact for years or generations, depending on the cause. This makes contact, trade, and conflict interesting, if not impossible. For instance, it might be possible to bring small packages between parts of the world, but not in large enough quantities to make trade viable or profitable, or to bring armies. Weis and Hickman's *Deathgate Cycle* is a good example in which a nuclear holocaust led to new species, one of which magically broke the world into four elemental worlds linked by magical gates. The video game *Wizard101* has a similar idea in that the world was broken in an ancient war that resulted in a Great Spiral linking the various pieces. Each world is based on an Earth analog culture—19th-century Egypt, 19th-century London, Viking Age Scandinavia—with unique animal-based peoples and geography-based societies. Piers Anthony's *Apprentice Adept* series has a sort of variant mixed with a portal fantasy variation. In the series, there are two worlds—one science fiction, one fantasy—on which every resident has an analogue on the other world. People, some at least, are able to switch consciousnesses with their other world analogue—ex. Sci-Fi A and Fantasy A's bodies swap consciousnesses so Sci-Fi A's mind is in Fantasy A's body and vice versa.

Lava and Boiling Seas

Impassable, or seemingly so, geography is a staple of the fantasy genre. It is often used to contain the story's action to a smaller space or to explain a lack of contact. Other times, it simply creates obstacles for the protagonist(s) to overcome. What impassable mountains are to land, the boiling sea is to water travel. In the past, generally little to no explanation of how the sea came into existence is given (ex. The Boiling Sea in Michael Moorcock's *Elric* series). Regardless of origins, the sea serves to limit sea travel. It cuts off access to islands and continents, or makes accessing them a long and difficult process of sailing around the sea. Typically, these boiling seas are also marked by dense clouds of steam that both reduce visibility and potentially harm sailors. In some cases, land might exist in the boiling sea. This might take the form of an isolated island with a society adapted to life in the eye of the sea, whether the "eye" is "normal" or boiling. It certainly reduces the potential for contact with other nations and societies. A more extreme variant is the lava sea. This could be the result of a continually producing volcano or the creation of magic or the gods. Generally, it is impossible to pass without magic or sufficient technology (for insulated metal ships, magic vehicles, or airships). Many are also home to fire loving species, peoples, and monsters. Perhaps the best example here is the Burning Sea of Taladas (*Dragonlance*, a second continent detailed in 2nd edition AD&D's *Time of the Dragon* boxed set) associated with the evil god Hith (Hiddukel), as a result of the Cataclysm (that hit Ansalon, Krynn's primary continent).

Flat and Ring Worlds

Flat worlds are somewhat based in some ancient mythologies and archaic cosmologies that were largely dismissed by the late BCE to early CE period, though they rose again in the 19th century. Because of these myths, the idea of a disc or otherwise flat world is not uncommon in the fantasy genre. The concept provides some limits, an edge beyond which there is nothing. It forms a built in boundary to the entire world and causes interesting travel concerns. It also opens up the question of what exists at the edge of the world—sea, mountains, or something else. In some cases, the question of what happens if one goes over the edge arises. In other cases, the edge of the world is insurmountable mountains, so the question of passing beyond the rim does not occur. In many cases, a flat world is not likely to affect most societies in the world much. It might affect directions (ex. Discworld's hubward as a direction toward the center of the disc). Additionally, unique societies may be created on the edges of the world, such as Discworld's Krull, home to astrozoologists who study Great A'Tuin, the world turtle. Obviously, Discworld is a good example, along with the Hindu cosmology that inspired its creation—a flat disc on top of four elephants on top of a turtle "swimming" through space. C.S. Lewis's Narnia is another good example in that it is supposed to be flat, and also a disc. However, Narnia's flat nature is only remarked upon rarely and is not important except in one instance when the Dawn Treader nears and reaches the edge.[10]

The idea of ringworlds is a concept borrowed from science fiction, the most famous use of which is Larry Niven's *Ringworld* and its sequels. Ringworlds are usually constructed around a star or artificial light/heat source, a variant is an artificial ring of habitats around a sun or planet. This is not implemented in fantasy much, but can be easily adapted to cities, nations, or an entire world. The metaphysics of other dimensions/planes of existence, magic, magical misfires, and divine creation could all be potential sources of a ringworld or city. Perhaps the best example is the city of Sigil in D&D's *Planescape* setting. This ring, or torus, shaped city in the Outer Planes encircles the top of a massive spire. It is, possibly, the multiversal center, accessed by dimensional gates—the gates also bring air, water, and sanitation. The societal effects of a ringworld include access to resources at the most basic level. That will depend heavily on where the city is located. If it is on a planet, then regular trade can conceivably occur, among other sources of materials. On the other hand, if it is located on another plane, or out of phase with a world, then the issue becomes rather more difficult. Transportation along the ring is also a potential concern, especially as the ring could be fully open or sectioned by walls into habitats. The latter could cause the creation of various societies, each with its own habitat, along even a small ring. Keeping people on the surface of the ring is also a concern—in sci-fi ringworlds, there is generally a degree of spin that creates some level of gravity, or another form of artificial gravity; in a fantasy version, almost anything could be used, limited only by creativity, internal consistency, and suspension of disbelief.

Primary World Geography

Use of the primary world is, of course, a staple of the UF/PNR genres because most works in the genres are set on Earth. Their Earths are, however, ones that are slightly or majorly shifted and twisted from the one we know in some way. At the very least, they include the presence of magic or fantastic peoples, whether werewolves or elves. In some ways, using Earth as the setting for societies is easier than a secondary world. The geography is already there and has already shaped history, society, and other worldbuilding elements. Moreover, these are familiar to us as writers, creators, and readers, since we live in the world. Creators only need to address the changed or hidden parts of the world, depending on the direction chosen for the narrative or setting.

For the purposes of this section, four major sub-topics will be addressed: use of real places, use of fictional cities, use of fictional countries, and the use of portal fantasies.

Real Places

A relatively easy and common approach in all branches of fiction and worldbuilding from urban fantasy to mysteries, thrillers to romances is the use of actual, real places as the setting. This is so heavily used that movie goers and TV fans often ask "Why is it always New York/Los Angeles/London that the aliens/spies/supervillains attack?" This is a common approach simply because the cities chosen tend to be iconic and unique in some way. And the geography, as well as its effects on society, are already present so there is no need to create something new. However, using real places can become very research intensive to be effective and true to the setting. This could involve a significant outlay of time to find photos, get descriptions, or visit the place. Living in the setting helps, but still needs research, usually field research, in visiting locations—to pay attention to the area, take pictures and notes, and such. The creator needs to become aware of the foibles of the area, or they may lose suspension of disbelief in some or all of the audience. For example, the first *Halloween* movie is supposed to take place in the Midwest at Halloween, but the trick-or-treating kids are wearing warm (southern California) costumes. Every (northern at least) Midwestern kid knows that Halloween costumes have to be ready for cold wind and, potentially, snow. Likewise, New Orleans has above ground cemeteries and raised, above ground, (or no) basements with little to no underground construction, because it is built on a marshy delta. Without a certain depth of research, trouble can arise if the audience is familiar with the area.

Once we have the information, there is a temptation to include all the research, to pass all the information on to the audience. However, it is often better to mix the feel of the place with some of the details. As Harry Turtledove has stated, it is best to do 100 percent of the research, but only show readers 1 percent, despite the urge to show them everything.[11] Mixing the two gives a sense of the place with occasional details to support or create a sense of authority without being a tour book or treatise on the location. Even most treatises and tour books do not include all the details. Scattering details around is generally more effective than trying to force the research into the worldbuilding or narrative. Sometimes the details, or specific ones, need to hit the cutting room floor.

A variant on the use of real places is to use modified real places. This is most common in alternate history fiction and post-apocalyptic fiction. Alternate history changes the location and society at some point in the past. This leads to a different present, or could be set in the alternate past. Good examples include Philip Pullman's London and Oxbridge (*His Dark Materials*), Nalini Singh's California (*Psy/Changeling*), and Ilona Andrews's Dallas (*Hidden Legacy*). In each case, something occurred or appeared in the past that changed the city. The change could be caused by a natural disaster, magical act, publicly known paranormals (Singh), publicly known magic (Andrews), secret paranormals, or "simply" being a parallel universe (Pullman). Whatever the cause, the change in the world or land alters society and potentially even changes the landscape to one degree or another (Andrews, Singh). On the other hand, an apocalyptic event may change the location in the past, present, or near future. As a result, society changes to adapt to the new face of the world. The apocalyptic event could be natural, magical, or technological in nature. Good examples include Ilona Andrews's Atlanta (*Kate Daniels*), Faith Hunter's *Rogue Mage*, and Weis and Hickman's *Deathgate Cycle* (nuclear apocalypse triggers changes in Earth, that leads to the broken world described above). Apocalypses allow the creator to change geography and society as much or as little as they desire. They could leave large parts of the old world around or leave only vague hints surviving in ruins.

Fictional Cities

Another common primary worldbuilding approach is to create a fictional city in our world. Sometimes these have very specific locations—Bon Temps, LA (with exact distances to Shreveport and New Orleans) or Magellan, AZ (with distances to Las Vegas and the Hoover Dam)—while other times the location is vague—New Bedford (mix of Midwestern U.S. and Canada) or *Lost Girl*'s unnamed city (Canadian, but not clear where). Regardless of which choice we use, we need to keep in mind that the fictional city and land will affect both the city's society and the real societies that exist around it. This is also true for an alternate variation that involves increasing the size of a real location, ex. from a 30,000-person town to a

500,000-person city, that alters the society of the town and the surrounding area.

For specific locations, the creator should think about how the presence of the new city, and possibly county, affects the area that really exists in the state, county, and province. That includes what land is around the city, what the area is like, and what effects these have on the new society. Allyson James, for instance, adds an entire county to the state of Arizona. However, it has a low population density that minimizes the effect on politics and society in the state and neighboring, real, counties. It also has the same rough geography as the counties around it, as well as very similar cultural elements, albeit ones affected by a high density of paranormal elements—multiple werebeast, witch, mage, and dragon residents, as well as paranormal tourists.

Vaguely located cities have more leeway than ones with specific locations. Still, they need some idea of the region's or area's geography before they are inserted. Placing hundreds of miles of wheat fields around a city set in the center of the Rocky Mountains will stretch credulity somewhat. That said, a vague location is able to create rivers, small forests, maybe hills or marshes that impact the city but have little impact on the region or maps. This is even easier with hidden cities that are unknown to normal humanity, or are inaccessible to non-paranormals. In these cases, magic may be used to alter the landscape in more fanciful ways, such as concealed forests and oases in a desert.

Fictional Countries

Some worldbuilders take things a step further from fictional cities and create entire fictional countries on Earth. Why? Like cities, fictional countries give the creator room to play with geography and work with the feel of a place without being limited by the real place. They can reshape a beloved place as desired. As with use of real places and fictional cities, fictional countries appear in a wide range of genres. For the most part, this is probably easiest if the country is small—like an island state or a microstate—but bigger versions have been shown to work. However, smaller countries have less geographic impact on a region. This is even easier if the country is hidden from normal people. Excellent examples include Idris, a small European country bordered by France, Germany, and Switzerland (Cassandra Clare); Marvel's host of nations—ex. Sokovia, Wakanda, Latveria,Kun-Lun, and Madripoor; and Avram Davidson's many nations from British Hidalgo (Limekiller) to Ruritania and Graustark (Dr. Eszterhazy). With fictional countries, the society can be created to fit the builder's desires, using neighbors (if any) as inspiration.

Openly known fictional countries need to have a determined location. The creator also should answer how it exists (part of real countries or new land added to the continent/new island) and its effects on existing societies. Marvel did this with Wakanda by saying it was a small African nation with minimal agriculture, thus having minimal impact (obviously hidden by technology). Likewise, Marvel's Sokovia is a small Balkan or former Soviet state in an area where changes in nations occurred relatively quickly (at least in the 1990s). Hidden countries are easier in some ways, especially when they are smaller. But, we still should decide how the country is hidden from outsiders or others in the world. For example, Clare's Idris has magical wards that prevent entry, redirect travelers, and hide the country from satellites. Conversely, Kun-Lun is effectively out of phase with Earth, or on a pocket dimension, that can only be accessed at certain places and times. Since they are hidden, these countries have virtually no impact on regional societies, history, or geography, because no one knows they exist. There may be odd side effects to their presence, depending on the means of concealment, but non-magical people will think these effects are normal. This can also be a good way to hide exotic geography.

Portal Fantasies

Many primary world fantasies include connections to secondary worlds. These are generally referred to as "portal fantasies," and go through waxing and waning popularity cycles. Some of the most famous include Lewis Carroll (Wonderland), C.S. Lewis (Narnia), J.M. Barrie (Neverland), L. Frank Baum (Oz), Lev Grossman (*The Magicians*), Neil Gaiman (*Stardust*), Terri Windling (*Bordertown*), Kaziu Kibuishi (*Amulet*), Terry Brooks (*Landover*), Diana Wynne Jones (*Howl's Moving Castle*), and, arguably, Rick Riordan and the Riordan Presents authors (that often include travel between fantastic-mythological worlds). Portal fantasies allow for the best of both worlds in that the creator is able to use Earth as a touchstone alongside an entirely, or partially, fictional world.

There are a nearly infinite number of examples, but they all share certain traits. First, there must be some means of crossing between worlds—a rabbit hole, wardrobe, gap in a wall, town/city where the worlds connect, a basement door, spells, a teleport ability—otherwise the whole construct does not exist. Second, decisions need to be made about how, or if, technology and magic work across the divide. For example, can Earth technology be taken into the other world, and can magic work on both sides of the divide. Third, we should know if the ability to cross the boundary is public knowledge, limited knowledge, or secret. For instance, Bordertown is public knowledge that has an impact on North American society, as some degree of trade and crossing opens up. Gaiman, Riordan, and the Riordan Presents authors tend to keep the knowledge limited to a small group—the people of Wall (Gaiman) who keep the secret or the magical community (Riordan, et al.) who keep the knowledge as part of their hidden societies. Meanwhile, Lewis, Jones, Grossman, and Brooks decided that the knowledge is hidden, open to very few, so there is no impact on society. Fourth, and finally for these purposes, are the questions of whether movement between worlds is voluntary or involuntary and whether it can be controlled. In the cases of Carroll, Lewis, and Baum, travel between worlds is basically involuntary and uncontrolled (although Aslan may have some control over it in Lewis's case). Conversely, in Grossman, Gaiman, and Jones, travel is voluntary and controllable. Grossman's barrier requires a person with a special talent (basically teleporting). Jones requires magic and special doors. But, for Gaiman's *Stardust*, crossing between worlds is literally as simple as walking through a hole in a low stone wall (which is why the village posts a guard at the wall 24/7).

13

Places

Locations in a society, beyond cities, are important focal points and can speak to the character of the society. At the very least, they create a certain atmosphere and a place for action to occur, but they can also effectively become characters themselves. How we define places or locations depends heavily on our focus for the setting or narrative—ex. large scale versus small scale. Here, we will be looking at the components of cities and places beyond the city limits. However, the same ideas could be applied to places within a given structure that alter the atmosphere and feel of the place and could operate on multiple levels at once. For example, Hogwarts is a distinct location in relation to Diagon Alley and Hogsmeade but it is also host to the Potions dungeon, the Astronomy Tower, the Greenhouses, and Hagrid's Hut while Diagon is home to Olivander's, Flourish and Blott's, and Gringotts, all of which are also distinct locations.

The level of detail provided about a place can affect how memorable the site is, but there are exceptions. Some places stand out due to detail, others because of their importance, and some due to their mystery. In Brust's Dragaera, the Imperial Palace is relatively detailed and very important, Castle Black is used fairly often and in pivotal ways, Vlad's office is very a common site with a fair amount of detail, but Dzur Mountain is often vaguely described (while individual rooms may get some detail) with legend and mystery forming its greatest draw. In Pratchett's Ankh-Morpork, the Unseen University Tower of Art stands above everything in the city and is visible everywhere (while being essentially a ruin), Pseudopolis Yard is pretty well described because many Watch novels use it, conversely Mr. Hong's Three Jolly Luck Takeaway Fish Bar[1] is never described, but is known solely as a cautionary tale because of what happened to it[2] and is highly memorable. The same can be done with Middle-Earth using Bag End, the Prancing Pony, Weathertop, and Amon Hen, among other places.

Location can even be the primary introduction to a setting, as with Bag End (*The Hobbit*) and Privet Drive (*Harry Potter*). Using those examples, consider Bag End's bucolic comfortableness that is broken by the dwarf party and juxtaposed with the privation and adventure of the rest of the narrative (and much of the world). Likewise, Privet Drive's inherent and aggressive mundanity serves to belie Harry's magic and is juxtaposed against Hogwarts and Diagon Alley's borderline crazy "magic-ness," while also setting up the Dursleys' atmosphere and character. These set ups give readers a false sense of what to expect, or perhaps a good idea since they are the very opposite of the narrative and world they lead us to enter.

Often locations are reflective of the history of the setting. In many secondary worlds, "there are buildings in strange places, antechambers built at a later date, layers upon layers of structures and aesthetic styles."[3] This can be seen well in Pratchett's Ankh-Morpork, in which residents have been building the city atop the city for many generations, leaving an underside of the city made up of layers of cellars that are former ground and upper stories of homes and businesses. It can also be seen in Moorcock's *Elric* books, with structures, and even entire cities, located in seemingly random, often currently inhospitable, places that were one lush and vibrant regions.

For the purposes of this chapter, six sections will be used: places of need, places of note, places of veneration, ruins, oddities, and the human element of place.

Places of Need

Certain types or classes of place are necessities for a society. The exact location or place, and its connection to the role, could be formal or informal, concrete and continual or floating[4] and temporary. Places of need are separated from places of note because they are necessary for society to continue, while "of note" are often bonus or leisure places rather than ones of necessity. They are different from places of veneration because "holy sites" are not required by society, though many have them. For these purposes, there are three types of necessary site, and one that straddles the need/note line: food, government, education, and trade.

Places devoted to food can range from the dull (granaries) to inns to restaurants. For these purposes, pubs and taverns are being left to "of Note" because their purpose is of a more social nature. People need to eat and most societies above a certain size will have specialty places where people can get food made for them, from street vendors to full restaurants. Some food places become points of focus while others stand out and become recognizable for the characters present, their appearance, or their oddity. Food places can be good sites for meeting others or notable patrons, resting, becoming involved in plots and jobs, and getting information. Brust's Valabar's (Dragaera) is a good example, known mostly by its reputation, menu, and use a couple of times as a meeting site between Vlad Taltos and members of House Jhereg's criminal branch. Comparatively, Gimlet's Hole Food Delicatessen (Ankh-Morpork; Pratchett) stands out for its characters and its menu (mostly rat-on-a-stick and rat curries) serving the city's ever growing dwarf population, including Carrot Ironfoundersson (who also uses the takeaway to gather information and gossip). CMOT Dibbler's traveling "stand" with his sausages-inna-bun becomes an unmistakable feature of Ankh-Morpork, as well as a test, a source of humor, and a cautionary tale.

Government places tend to be more noticeable in some ways. They can include judicial and law enforcement, as part of government. A government site can range from a village leader's home to a massive complex or network of buildings housing a large bureaucracy (ex. The Forbidden City in Beijing or The Tower of London). Basically, any government location is a place for the society's leadership to work, and sometimes live. The larger the nation or society, the larger the place will be or the more (and more specialized) places there will be. The massive Imperial Palace complex of Brust's Dragaera is a good example, with separate wings for each of the seventeen Houses surrounding an "imperial" core that houses the reigning imperial family. The maze of corridors and rooms, with courts and holding cells beneath the Iorich Wing (a House known for judgement and justice) and the guard barracks in the Dragon Wing, is a continual source of confusion. Rowling presents a rather simpler, and modern, Ministry of Magic with its awe-inspiring atrium and relatively easy navigation via labeled elevator buttons. A final good example is the Ice Court of Fjerda (Grishaverse) that mixes royal palace, elite military training center/base of operations, research facility, and prison in one massive, magically built, fortress.

Education places may range from the space under the village elder's favorite shade tree to a city unto itself (as in the largest modern universities). They could be formal places or they could move around, especially if education (or a specific type of learning) is illegal to all or some. They could be unified in one space, as in modern college and other school campuses, or they could be diffuse, as in many or most medieval universities or Oxford University today.[5] In each case, the location should provide access to the educator(s) and whatever tools the society deems necessary to teach. The fantasy genres are filled with examples of educational facilities from The School of Wizardry on Roke Island (Le Guin's *Earthsea*) to The Citadel (Martin's *ASoIaF*), Hogwarts (Rowling) to the University of Arcane Arts (Andrews's *Kate Daniels*). The Little Palace (Grishaverse) is an interesting example as it serves as both palatial residence and education center for an open elite, who are training for the military. Naomi Novik's Scholomance (*Scholomance*) is another interesting example, as a semi-sentient, possibly self-aware, school that serves as faculty as well as facility. Both Patrick Rothfuss's University (*Kingkiller Chronicles*) and Pratchett's Unseen University (Discworld) owe much of their appearance and character to Oxford and Cambridge Universities (a.k.a. Oxbridge), and Deborah Harkness's *A Discovery of Witches* uses Oxford directly, particularly the Bodleian Library. As we might expect, most of the educational places used in the fantasy genres are devoted to teaching magic in one form or another, but other, more mundane, schools exist (The Citadel and Rothfuss's University).

Places of trade can range from a cottage industry home-shop to a full-blown street or marketplace of shops and stalls. Arguably, places of trade are not strictly necessary for a society to exist, but they are certainly necessary for any society that has towns or cities and specialists. Obviously, trade has a lot of crossover with food, entertainment, social, and other sites, since many places serve multiple purposes and all categories are permeable. For these purposes, trade places can be the broad place (ex. a marketplace) and the component elements (ex. the shops within a marketplace). The Pork Futures Warehouse (Ankh-Morpork, Discworld) is a good crossover example, as it relates to both the trade (speculation or stock investment) and the food (literal sides of pork). The Exchange in Ketterdam (Grishaverse) is another good example of an important meeting place devoted to trade, speculation, and investment. Baha-Char, of *The Innkeeper Chronicles*, is a more complex example, inspired by Middle Eastern and North African markets, because of its component shops. Diagon Alley, and its component stores and stalls, may be one of the more recognizable examples in text, film, and amusement park forms. An extreme example is Asprin's Bazaar at Deva (*MythAdventures*), a dimension or world spanning marketplace with literally millions of shops, stalls, and other vendors.

Places of Note

Some places are not necessary for society to function, but we find them interesting or noteworthy for other reasons. They could be locations where plots begin or rest happens. They might be landmarks for directions or add character to a setting or larger location. Some may be visually interesting or mysterious. They could be a base of operations for characters, a

13. Places

source of rumors, or a source of impending or immediate danger. There are many possible types here, but this section will focus on four: social, arts and entertainment, residences, and landmarks. As above, the goal is to be inspirational rather than impossibly comprehensive.

Social places are those visited by people for the purposes of, well, socializing. In fiction and tabletop gaming, a lot of these are bars, pubs, taverns, and nightclubs. This may say something about the creators' cultures, or the genres' tropes.[6] The social place could, and does, overlap with arts/entertainment and food in many cases. Coffee shops and tea houses have, or had, stints of popularity here. Parks could be possibilities. Basically, anywhere people gather to socialize. Charlaine Harris's Fangtasia (*Southern Vampire Mysteries*), the vampire bar, works here and serves as a base of operations as well. The People's Casino in post–Shift Atlanta (*Kate Daniels*) is a good multi-use example as it is a social center on the surface and a training/education center (teaching new necromancers), governing center (offices of the People), and storage place (for vampires) beneath. Pratchett's Ankh-Morpork has a seemingly infinite amount of such places, from Biers to the Mended Drum[7] to the Cavern Club to the Pink Pussycat Club to the Bucket.[8] Although not much socializing goes on there, the Vulgar Unicorn (Asprin, *Thieves' World*) would also fit, if only as a starting place for many plots and place where Sanctuary's underworld does much of its business.

Arts and entertainment places are those sponsoring the arts or designed for entertaining patrons, whether the artists or entertainers are amateurs or professionals. This is, perhaps, one of the broader categories as it can include art galleries to museums, theaters to sports venues, pub/coffee shop stages to outdoor venues. In terms of usage, these are often places for characters to unwind, for character development (or to show off skills), building camaraderie, and possibly even introducing plots. The Ankh-Morpork Opera House (on wheels) is a rather large example that both hosted a parody of *The Phantom of the Opera* plotline and was booted and ticketed by the Watch for impeding traffic. Lisa Shearin's *SPI Files* brings in, at least for a few books, Bacchanalia, a goblin-owned sex club (and information/blackmail gathering place, as the owner is also a spy). On a smaller scale is the Camp Half-Blood Amphitheater, host to marshmallow roasts and amateur singing. Perhaps the most famous is the Hogwarts Quidditch Pitch, for sports primarily, but also for character development and plot. Another sporting venue is the Welters "auditorium" at Brakebills (*The Magicians*).

Residences may not seem especially noteworthy at first glance, but they can be important places to show character or to serve as a base of operations, either temporary or permanent, for a narrative. They can show the tastes and personalities of secondary characters and antagonists without having to info dump. The scope can run the gamut from a private cottage to a penthouse suite to a townhouse to a massive palace complex, with many other gradations. Rowling gives us many examples of notable residences including Number 4 Privet Drive, the Leaky Cauldron, the Burrow, 12 Grimmauld Place, Snape's home, and the Malfoy Mansion. Each reflects the personality and character of its resident(s) and serves a number of other purposes within the narrative. The Stackhouse home (*Southern Vampire Mysteries*) is another great example that serves as a base of operations for, and shows the character of, the series protagonist. Tolkien's Prancing Pony and Allyson James's Crossroads Inn provide temporary lodging for characters (whether protagonists or background), as well as a permanent home for James's protagonists. The Keep (*Kate Daniels*) is another that serves to reflect both its creators (post–Shift Atlanta's shapeshifters) and the world in which it was built (a dangerous place in which technology cannot be trusted and magical monsters may appear). For all its simplicity, Granny Weatherwax's cottage has become rather iconic for Pratchett's readers. In some cases, the residence becomes a character unto itself, as in the case of the Gertrude Hunt Bed and Breakfast (*Innkeeper Chronicles*), as the inn is both sentient to some degree and bonded to the protagonist.

Finally, landmarks are a sort of catch-all. They could be any notably visible location from a building to a park, a hill to a river. They can be man-made or entirely natural depending on the setting and locale. Some might be historically important. Others may be necessary for maps—ex. Caradhras or the Lonely Mountain in Middle-Earth. There could be a variety of other reasons the place stands out as a landmark. Perhaps the classic and most recognizable example is C.S. Lewis's Lamp-post in Narnia that marks the location at which the wardrobe deposits the Pevensies. For residents of Ankh-Morpork, the Unseen University's Tower of Art serves as a landmark, as the tallest building in the city. In Middle-Earth, Weathertop is a regional landmark for travelers.

Venerated Sites

Different places can become venerated for a whole host of reasons, and the level of veneration devoted to them can be on a sliding scale based on factors from importance to remoteness of the site. Some reasons a place could be venerated include birth (of a holy person or deity), death (of a holy person), ascension (briefly or permanently), a miracle performed, divine communication, divine manifestation, a sacred animal appearing on or

13. Places

leading to the site, a relic being found, a blessed natural feature (pool, well), or simply because it is a convenient place for a temple. Each reason can be applied to a god, prophet, teacher, wise person, or saint in the faith (as appropriate). For most deities, the site will probably include at least a small shrine, if not a full temple complex. This, of course, depends on the importance of the deity and site, the influence of the religion, and the remoteness of the site. For these purposes, a simple classification of sites is natural or man-made, and common or unique. Obviously, the first binary has a somewhat permeable definition, as man-made sites can be built on natural ones, and they commonly are as a place of worship built on or near the site, often with housing for clerical caretakers.

Natural sites covers sacred groves to springs, rivers to mountains. Basically, any natural feature deemed to be sacred or holy to a given deity, saint, or related figure. Our own world is full of such sites from springs dedicated to Christian saints to groves and pools said to house nymphs and minor gods to the Rock (Islam) to Uluru in Australia and Mount Fuji in Japan. Some, perhaps many or most, natural sites of veneration have man-made sites build atop them, especially in the Abrahamic faiths—ex. The Dome of the Rock—or nearby to protect the site and see to the needs of pilgrims, ex. shrines on the slopes of Mt. Fuji.

Man-made sites are basically any shrine, temple, mosque, church, cathedral, or other such site. Monasteries can be included as well, in many faiths and cases. These range from the tiniest of roadside shrines to the largest cathedral. Burial grounds fall into this category, too, assuming a constructed and consecrated space versus leaving corpses on a natural flat rock for scavengers to consume (which may be a natural venerated space). Typically, man-made sites will house clergy who care for the site and hold services, depending on the size and location. Depending on the nature of the deity, the site could have been chosen by the clergy or by the divinity. In many cases, the site will have some association with the deity, a saint, a prophet, or other such being (or an association of that sort will be invented).

Unique sites are those that cannot be copied or moved. Often these are natural sites of veneration that are connected to momentous events or specific beings. For example, the Rock (Mohammed's ascent into Heaven), Mt. Fuji (the kami Princess Konohanasakuya-hime), Uluru (many tales), Mount Sinai (delivery of the Ten Commandments), the Grove of Dodona (sacred oracle of Apollo), or the Island of Delos (birthplace of Artemis and Apollo). For obvious reasons, those who venerate the site may be extremely protective of it, perhaps even violently so. Believers' responses to the site, of course, depend on its specific reason for being sacred, its importance, and its location (the more remote it is from the society of believers, the less concerned they are likely to be about it in many cases). Unique sites could mix natural and man-made, as in the cases of the Dome of the Rock and the Parthenon. Other unique sites are entirely man-made and considered unique due to their role in the faith or their sheer size, as in the cases of the Hagia Sophia, the Vatican, and the Oracle at Delphi.

By contrast, common sites are mostly man-made for the majority of faiths. These are the common shrines, temples, and such that are erected by the faithful. They are likely to follow similar designs and patterns across the faith. Essentially, they are copies of a base structure made and constructed as needed by the religion.

Ruins

A staple of the fantasy genres pretty much from day one, ruins serve a lot of purposes in F/UF/PNR and are virtually omnipresent. Ruins connect to and remind characters and the audience of the past. They create a sense of depth and age to the fictitious world. They speak to destructive forces of nature, the gods, war, plague, and time. They hold the promise of adventure, discovery, and possibly riches (for business or adventurers). In some cases, ruins can be mysterious oddities. They can serve as homes, permanent or temporary, for those pushed out of everywhere else— whether due to poverty, species, mutation, or other reasons. They can hide antagonists and serve as lairs for monsters of all sorts.

Secondary worlds from Middle-Earth[9] to Eberron (*D&D*) to Faerun (*D&D*) to the Grishaverse (Bardugo) to Scadrial (Sanderson) are covered in ruins connected both to the past and to adventure for those willing to explore. Most are fairly mundane—farmhouses and chapels ruined in the wake of wars, or similar—but others are significant in terms of history, magic, and riches. Osgiliath (Tolkien) is a large example, as a city built to guard and watch Mordor that eventually fell to ruins and was abandoned under orc attacks from Mordor. Xak Tsaroth (Dragonlance) is another city, ruined by divine wrath (the Cataclysm), that became home to the dispossessed (gully dwarves) and eventually concealed antagonists (the Black Dragonlord/army of Takhisis). Caer Paravel is another famous example, the capital of Narnia that fell into ruins once the Pevensies left, before their return in *Prince Caspian*, to connect to the past and conceal the Pevensies' magic items. The flying castles of Steven Brust's Dragaera, built by House Dragon as a sign of power, fell into ruin during the magic-less Interregnum with ruins remaining as monuments to toppled pride and past glory. Finally, the remains of Old Valyria (Martin) recall ancient glory and indicate the ancient history of Westeros and nearby lands, while also seeming to be a source of plague.

The presence of ruins in primary world settings, however, tends to be post-apocalyptic or sometimes ancient ruins (ex. Greek, Egyptian, Mayan) tied to a focal culture of the narrative (as in the Riordan Presents line or Allyson James's *Stormwalker* series). Unicorn Lane in Ilona Andrews's post–Shift Atlanta is a good example, as home to the desperate in the city. Really, most of post–Shift Atlanta is ruins or is descending into ruins, and reclamation occurs for profit and rebuilding. Also from Andrews is The Pit in Dallas, TX (*Hidden Legacy*), formerly Jersey Village, now flooded, swamped, and home to the magically mutated and destitute. Rick Riordan brings ruins in from time to time, both in Greek and Egyptian sites—often as home to monsters or a connection to the past, occasionally for humor value (ex. ruined monster-themed amusement park in *The Sea of Monsters* [film version at least]). As noted, Allyson James brings in ruins, in this case at Homol'ovi State Park in Arizona. These are primarily a place for the protagonist to take photos, her profession of choice, but also home to ancient spirits that occasionally attract other beings.

Overall, ruins are commonly used to begin or imply adventure. They may conceal MacGuffins,[10] hide antagonists, and represent both history and apocalyptic events that give character to a setting and society. In some cases, they may be incorporated into modern cities (as in many cities throughout Europe). Some societies may bury their ruins or reclaim them to build current structures, as was done in medieval Europe, when stones from Roman ruins were salvaged to build castles, bridges, and other structures. Other societies may seek to preserve ruins and learn from them, as with most of modern Europe and Egypt, or profit off them (through tourism). As such, ruins may speak to a society's "glorious" past or be representations of shameful events of the past.

Oddities

A classic in science fiction and weird fiction, odd places are also common enough in the fantasy genres to be a trope. These are locations and places that are surrounded by mysteries and/or about which people know little beyond rumor. Examples range from real places like the Sphinx to fictional features like Dzur Mountain (Brust) and the Shoikan Grove and Tower of High Sorcery in Palanthas (*Dragonlance*). These mysterious locations could be ruins, cities, fortresses, libraries, tombs, temples, or some combination of them, among other possibilities. They could be in a state of decay, abandoned, or currently inhabited. These are places that raise more questions than they answer or that are surrounded by nothing but rumor and legend, often lacking any solid information, and stand out in some way. Such places could be natural, semi-natural, or unnatural sites, as in the examples above, or the example of a random obsidian monolith in a field in Iowa. They could be relatively mundane or have powers and magical effects, whether activated by touch/contact or as a radiated aura.

There are many uses for oddity places. Mysterious oddities serve as a clear beginning for plots, a physical manifestation of the call to adventure by their very existence. They evoke the desire to explore and search for loot or knowledge. Such places can also be ideal homes for antagonists in the form of cults or other secret societies. They form excellent places for people who are trying to hide their actions or who seek out secrets and power. They could be a classic lair to monsters (some of the stranger "dungeons" of *Dungeons & Dragons*). These monsters could be undead, dragons, or beasts of all sorts depending on the location, region, and type of place. Odd places could be the resting places of lost artifacts and knowledge needed by the protagonists or society. The presence of artifacts of great power could be the reason for the place's oddity. The place could simply exist to inject a sense of mystery into the setting. That sense of the unknown, and unknowable, may also add to the mystery and reputation of a character such that both person and place acquire or reinforce a legendary stature in society.

To take the above examples in reverse, the Shoikan Grove and Tower of High Sorcery it surrounds are the subject of a centuries old curse, by the time of the *Chronicles* and *Legends* trilogies. That curse has left the tower unoccupied since shortly after the divine Cataclysm tore the continent asunder. Moreover, the Tower's association with the Black Robe order of wizards, noted as evil-aligned magic-wielders, adds to the mystery and odd things seen and heard around the site. Then, the Shoikan Grove comes into play, adding further layers with its undead denizens and aura of fear, that affects and keeps away even members of the normally fearless kender species. Similarly, Brust's Dzur Mountain is associated with sorcery, wizardry, and the undead through its resident, Sethra Lavode. The mountain itself has a reputation, based on its appearance (like the head of a dzur, a felinoid species), and various stories surrounding it. Once Sethra takes up residence, the stories only grow, as her reputation and legends are added atop the mountain's. Additionally, the gods, particularly Verra, and Sethra (among a few others) hint that the mountain has a key role to play in magics that protect the world from invasion. All this before we look at the possibility that the interior rooms and corridors of the mountain rearrange themselves (or are simply so extensive that no mere mortal can keep track of them all) and Sethra's servant, Tukko/Chaz, who might be a personification or human-like manifestation/avatar of the mountain itself (Tukko/Chaz's nature is very unclear).

The Human Element

Every place of need and note, many venerated places, and some ruins and oddities have a human element to them. Human here being defined as any intelligent, sapient, sentient, however we wish to define it, species. People use, reside in, work at, or take care of the place, for the most part. Without the people, the place is simply there. The people of every place are different, but all can be divided into two categories: People of Need and People of Note—that is, the necessary people and the other important or interesting people. To demonstrate, let's look at a few places.

The Prancing Pony (Tolkien) needs Barliman Butterbur (the owner, proprietor, and bartender) as well as Nob (general serving hobbit) and Bob (stable-hobbit), among others (ex. cook, housekeeper), in order to function. Although not necessary for the Pony's functioning, Aragorn and Bill Ferny are interesting and notable figures who hang out at the Pony.

The Unseen University (Pratchett) needs the Chancellor, the Bursar, the Librarian, the deans and department chairs, the cooks, caretakers, gardeners, bledlows (security), and housekeepers to function. There are few characters of note in the case of the University, except, arguably, Hex (the magic-AI) and maybe Death or Susan Sto-Helit who visit occasionally.

Gertrude Hunt (Andrews) has three "people of need": the Innkeeper (Dina DeMille and, eventually, Sean Evans), the chef (Orro), and the Inn itself. Not counting short term guests or temporary staff (a few assistant cooks), there are also a few people of note in the form of Caldenia ka ret Magren (permanent guest), Beast (Dina's dog), and Olasard (Dina's cat).

Finally, the Crossroads Inn (Allyson James) needs the owner (Janet Begay), manager (Cassandra Bryson), cook (Elena Williams), housekeeper, and handy-persons (Maya Medina and Fremont Hansen, both "on call"). For people of note, it also has Mick (dragon), Pamela Grant (werewolf), and Ansel (vampire).

The people of need are those who are required for the place to operate and continue to exist in its current form. Those who are "of note" are those who are regularly present and who stand out or are important in some way but lack an official position. For example, Aragorn and Ferny are not needed to operate the Pony, but standout in the crowd and are important. Caldenia is a permanent guest, but not part of the staff (though she is, effectively, necessary for the inn … it's complicated). Mick and Pamela are not needed by the Crossroads, but are both dating the owner and manager respectively while Ansel is a long term guest who is protected by the owner. All of these characters, these people, add depth to the place, as well as dynamics. They also reflect the place and add to its atmosphere and resources.

14

Finishing Touches

Many elements of worldbuilding and societies are notable, but not big enough, necessarily or arguably, for a whole chapter. They could potentially be combined, ex. holidays could be mixed with measures of time and conceptions of time, but time gets very theoretical and is not used too much in the fantasy genres, with the exception of time travel.[1] Virtually all of the elements discussed here are realism details that, used sparingly (or broadly in some cases) add depth and other levels to the setting and worldbuild. Some are more obvious and visual than others, for clear reasons. Many are typically dealt with in a cursory or generalized manner—ex. how many fantasy characters wear tunics or dresses with little to no other detail or options, beyond color; or how many fantasy settings use generic "gold and silver pieces" for currency, if money is discussed at all. These are elements that are not strictly necessary for worldbuilding, though they are important parts of societies, that serve as fine tuning and finishing touches. That said, some of their importance depends on context. For example, clothing and fashion are of huge importance in visual worldbuilding (film, TV, video games) while often less so in written forms. Conversely, currency and holidays are not too common in film/TV unless some plot point revolves around them, while they are more present in video games and written forms, where more detail can be narrated or more time is available.

The following is not a complete collection of finishing touches, and some may say that they are more important than I give them treatment of here, but this section will cover clothing, currency, entertainment, holidays, sayings, and longevity.

Clothing and Fashion

Clothing and everyday fashions are probably the most visible aspect of a society and its resources or values. Choices of attire, and their popularity, reflect values and views held by society, and its subcultures, in cut, coverage, style, and color palette. These may also be influenced by a society's religious views and laws (e.g., sumptuary). Subcultures within a society, as well as particular roles in society (like judges, scholars, magicians [or different types of magicians]), are likely to have special clothing as well—for example, judicial robes or collegiate faculty robes (now only worn for special occasions like graduations).

Fashions and styles inherently speak to the geography in which the society exists. Even broadly similar geography—ex. deserts—will have different styles due to climate factors—ex. the Sahara near the Equator versus the Gobi in north-central Asia. Geography also affects the materials available for clothing—linen, silk, wool, cotton—as well as the dyes that a society can access—most pre-20th century dyes being plant, mineral, or animal-based—depending on both trade opportunities and the level of technology available. The goal is "not to create clothing styles which exist in a vacuum, but rather clothing styles which seem appropriate to the climates, cultures, and technology levels from which they originate."[2]

Fashion and clothing can reflect or demonstrate socio-economic class in both obvious and subtle ways. For instance, there is a great difference in what is being said by ostentatious displays of wealth compared to a refined, understated, elegance used to display wealth. The use of materials, style, and color can achieve this effect, and may even be legislated, as in the European sumptuary laws that followed the first wave of the Plague. These laws regulated who could wear what colors, how long the points of the toes of shoes could be, and the size of ruffs, among other things, based on socio-economic class and status in an era in which the trade and mercantile classes were acquiring greater wealth than that held by the nobility. In some societies, clothing may even be determined by, or required by/for, certain ages. It can also be used to reflect species cultures—for example, in Peter Jackson's *The Hobbit*, compare the dwarves of the Iron Hills with the elves of Mirkwood in their clothing and armor.

The presence of magic in a society, and how common its use is, may also affect the availability of materials and what can be done with them. For example, magic might allow the creation of artificial silk at an early stage of technological development, or might allow the magical breeding of larger silkworms that thrive in a variety of climates, or the use of spider silk for clothing. Widespread magic, or even limited magic, can create new materials—for the whole of society or only magicians—as well as different colors of dyes and different patterns or styles. In some cases, the use of magic may even require certain types of clothing—ex. Riordan's *Kane Chronicles* notes that magicians need to be clad entirely in non-animal products, preferably linen, with Sadie Kane's boots being a sole exception that is commented on but never really explained.

Currency

The development and use of currencies is less common in literature (of any fantasy genre), but more common in TTRPGs and video games. Even in the latter cases, it tends to be generalized. Regardless, currency can be another way to add a level of verisimilitude and depth to a setting. As noted, most use currency in a very general way—gold, silver, and copper pieces/coins—that is common to RPGs in any medium. Sometimes this is combined with platinum coins, gemstones, and jewelry, the last two often converted into coins.[3] Some take a moderately specific approach, naming some coins and creating some sort of exchange system. A good example here is Travis Baldree's *Legends & Lattes*, with gold sovereigns and copper bits, plus platinum ingots and silver coins, with a simple 10:1 exchange from copper to silver to gold. Others get very specific, such as the shared world series *Liavek*, with gold ten-levar, five-levar, and levar coins, as well as silver half-, quarter-, and tenth-levars, and two-, one-, and half-coppers. Regardless of the form, Scott Hungerford recommends taking a few pages "to work out ... coins, currencies ... [and] relative prices for foods, materials, weapons, gifts, and services."[4] It can be a good idea to base the "relative prices" on an exchange rate between the fictional currency and modern currency. For example, a good quality steel longsword costs 15 gold in 5th ed. D&D or an average of US $200 in our world today, leaving a gold piece being equivalent to about US $13.50, rounded up, in purchasing power; this might vary by which commodity is chosen, so an average price or conversion of 5–10 items might be in order. On a related note, one might consider the role of, and currency's effects on, moneychangers in the society, if the culture is one that has regular contact with other cultures.[5]

Most examples of the fantasy genres that introduce a currency system—and many ignore money or use real-world currency (most UF/PNR)—use a basic 10 copper equals one silver, and upward system. This is the system used by Baldree above and is common to virtually all RPGs, whether tabletop or video game. Some get a little fancy, as in the example of Liavek noted above, where 100 coppers equal one gold levar, while 50 coppers equal a silver half-levar, and so on. The currency system, as befits a predominantly Canadian-American group of creators, mimics the U.S. and Canadian currency systems. A more complex example is J.K. Rowling's *Harry Potter*, in which she based the currency on the pre–1971 British currency system—so, 29 knuts equal a sickle, and 17 sickles equal a galleon. However, Rowling is (in-)famously inconsistent with the spending power and value of her currency—ex. the Weasleys remove one galleon from their Gringotts vault to get school things for four kids, and Rowling says that a galleon is equivalent to about US $7.50 as of a 2001 statement; meanwhile the Year Six *Advanced Potion Making* book is nine galleons (about US $68) and Disapparation training is twelve galleons (about US $90; both *Half-Blood Prince*), which causes some problems in following the math.[6] The currency system in this case seems to be based more on "needs of plot" than on internal consistency, but has caused consternation among readers. Perhaps the needs of magic override the issue.

In any society, the government tends to control the creation and design of currency. There are many reasons for this, with perhaps the most important being the avoidance of flooding the economy and devaluing currency, standardization of currency (including metal content), and establishing solid exchange rates between societies/countries. As a good real-world example, after the Revolution, the U.S. tried allowing every newly formed state to make its own currency. The results were messy, at best, and counterfeiting was relatively easy because of it. If magic is involved, the potential problems become even worse. So, if magic is present, there are a few things to determine: (1) Can magic make currency? If so, how and under what rules? (In some cases, it might vanish after a set time, like fairy gold or *Harry Potter's* leprechaun gold.) and (2) If magic can create currency or illusions of it, how is that prevented? If it cannot be prevented, how does the law work with the issue? This could be highly destabilizing, as could the magical production of precious metals—as mentioned briefly in Bardugo's *Crooked Kingdom* (Grishaverse). If magic can copy or create currency and is widespread, any government will certainly be concerned. Laws will necessarily be in place to control and prevent the illicit copy and manufacture of currency via magic, if the government is even vaguely competent. That said, if the government is corrupt, members of the nobility, legislators, or other officials may be involved, directly or indirectly, in the illegal counterfeiting.

Entertainment

How people in a society are entertained can speak to the type of society and its values as well as any policies, laws, clothing, art, or architecture can. Entertainment is also an important part of keeping people happy and how they use their downtime, which adds depth and layers to character. Characters who are always "on" can become flat or dull, but how they entertain themselves helps develop the character. Entertainment runs the gamut from music to theater, books to sports, movies to video games. It can be used to support and reinforce social structures or to subvert them through mockery or demonstrating fallibility. For instance, the street theater play, "The Bloody Hand," in *Game of Thrones* in which the ruling Lannisters are mocked, possibly along with Sansa Stark.[7]

Entertainment can also be used to add realism, as few people work 100 percent of the time. It can be employed to teach and show different skills or aspects of society as well. M.K. Tod asks about writing, painting, music, sports, and related entertainments.[8] Kevin J. Anderson adds architecture, building murals/frescos, decorations, and sculptures, as well as how artists make money.[9] We, as audiences, react differently to a society that has theater or gambling as its primary entertainment than one that has gladiators. The latter tends to be seen negatively, as brutal, but also as displaying current, or imagined/glorified past, militancy. Some of the entertainment does not even necessarily need to be specifically seen "on screen" as it were, it can simply be mentioned in passing. Good examples of fully described entertainment include matches of "foot-the-ball" in Ankh-Morpork (Discworld), gladiatorial bouts in Jennifer Estep's *Kill the Queen*, quidditch matches and the wizard wireless in *Harry Potter*, illicit prisoner fights in Kerch (Grishaverse), and welters matches in *The Magicians*. Mere mentions include the Ankh-Morpork opera house and street theater (Discworld), gobstones in *Harry Potter*, the Comedie Brute in Kerch (Grishaverse), and the Hermes cabin's video games (*Percy Jackson*).

Holidays

The use of holidays can be a way to polish a society and differentiate it from others. Holidays add societal flavor through secular and religiously based celebrations and can highlight subcultures in various ways. Some obvious holidays are birth dates and death dates of rulers and other major cultural figures. Religious feasts and holy days for whatever deity or deities the society worships are also clear options. Changes of seasons, memorials of battles or related events, and the founding days of different societies, cities, and groups also make good holidays. For example, Middle Earth has Durin's Day, for dwarves (*The Hobbit*). Denizens of the Discworld celebrate Hogswatch (a religious holiday turned secular) and Lilac Day (in Ankh-Morpork, remembering the short-lived Treacle Mine Road mini-revolution and those who died in the event). The Grishaverse has Hringkälla (Fjerda) and the Feast of Sankt Nikolai (Ravka), both religious festivals, with the first also being a coming of age/induction ceremony. Holidays present the opportunity to include days of celebration, create days off work for background characters, provide cover for heists, and are good times for threatening plots (ex. attacks or disasters). They can also provide timing for plots, to give time limits for the action, such as "This needs to be completed before the Festival of the Sun."

Sayings

An easy way to add color to a society is adding simple, often brief, sayings and introducing them occasionally to character speech or thoughts. Sometimes they might be longer, such as Conan's "What is best in life" or the Litany Against Fear from *Dune*, but longer utterances will typically be used and repeated less often.

Sayings can create a cultural flavor and distinguish one society from another. This type of saying can give clues to cultural or social values and serve as bonding within the group. For example, *The Mandalorian's* "This is the way" or the phrase "No mourners, no funerals" from the core group of Dregs (Grishaverse).

Sometimes, sayings demonstrate social influences—from geography, religion, magic, or history—that spawn the sayings. These get repeated and used regularly in a society. Like cultural flavor, they define members of a group and bind them together. A few good examples include Conan's Cimmerian "By Crom!," Kerch's "The deal is the deal" (Grishaverse), and "May the Force be with you" (*Star Wars*).

Finally, swearing and cursing is integral to all languages and societies. Expletives appear everywhere, sometimes they are so common that their original meaning is forgotten.[10] In some cases, the terms were created in fiction because early fantasy publishing and TV would not allow actual expletives to be used. Excellent examples include (dipping somewhat into sci-fi as well), "Crivens!" (Feagle, Discworld), "Frak" (*Battlestar Galactica*), "Frell" (*Farscape*), and "Poodoo" (*Star Wars*).

Longevity

Long lived and immortal beings are a staple of the fantasy genres from immortal elves (Tolkien) and vampires (most UF/PNR) to long lived dwarves (Tolkien) and others. However, the variety of options for both, and the impact or effects, are not often considered beyond relatively stereotyped forms—ex. the morose immortal (vampire, Timelord) whose mortal companions always die and therefore bemoans immortality as a curse. Due to the nature of creativity and imagination, there are many different types, sources, and effects in both cases.

First, it is helpful to establish the difference between extended life and immortality. A being with an extended lifespan will eventually die of old age because they continue to age and the body eventually begins to break down. For immortality, the body stops aging, so the individual will never die of old age, though they may or may not be vulnerable to diseases. So, an extended lifespan allows the individual to live longer, but still age. Slowed aging is an effect that is often attached to longer lives. In these cases, the individual ages, but at a much slower rate than others. For example, they might age one year for every five that pass. Unaging is another variation, in which the individual never ages beyond a certain point (or can change their apparent age), usually adulthood or whenever they were made immortal. This is the default form for undead and vampiric immortality.

But, how does one become immortal? There are thousands of specific possibilities, but they mostly come into eight broad types. Alchemical immortality is, probably, magic. It is common in both Western and Asian legend, especially alchemy and Taoism. Most often, it comes about through the creation of the elixir of life, which the creator needs to drink regularly. Good examples are Nicholas Flamel (Scott, Rowling) and the Taoist Immortals. Ascension is one that does not fit neatly into a category. The individual ascends to a non-corporeal plane of existence without death, usually through enlightenment. This is the method of the Buddhist bodhisattvas and the Ancients (*Stargate: SG-1*). Many cultures include tales of food-based immortality, usually stories of the gods eating foods that generate or maintain their immortality. Good examples include the Norse with Idun's apples and the Chinese Peaches of Immortality. Related to food-based is item-based immortality. In these cases, a magic item confers immortality or extended life, often with a curse or price. Usually, the item cannot be discarded, or is extremely difficult to set aside. Examples include the portrait of Dorian Grey and Tolkien's One Ring. Location-based immortality confers immortality so long as the individual remains within the boundaries of a given space. If they leave, then they typically age at an accelerated rate. The grail knight in *Indiana Jones and the Last Crusade* is a perfect example. "True" immortality is generally genetic, and requires nothing else. This is where Tolkien's elves fall in the categories. Undead immortality is arguable, in that we can debate whether existing between life and death counts as immortal. This is where we would place ghosts, FRPG liches, and Norse draugr. Finally, vampiric immortality is immortality that requires feeding on others. This could be ingesting blood, draining emotions, or a host of other possibilities. Most vampires fall into this group, including Scatty (Michael Scott) and the Velvets (Neil Gaiman, *Neverwhere*). There are, of course, hundreds of other methods. The goal here is to bring in the most common or broad possibilities.

14. Finishing Touches

Once we determine how immortality works, we should look at the effects on the individual and society. The former falls into physical and psychological, and will only be discussed briefly since the focus here is on societies. Of the physical effects of long lives and immortality, maturation is probably the most important, as well as its resulting skill set. Often RPGs, for example, say that a 20-year-old human and a 70-year-old elf are equally mature and have the same basic skill set, which seems off. Even if the elf matures at a slower rate, they spend a longer time at each age range and stage, so presumably should know more—if a human picks up languages best within their first four years of life, the elf has 14 years in that stage and should know more languages. This is something to consider and think about in worldbuilding (RPGs do "all are equal" regardless of maturation age for character balance, like so much else, but may not think it out too much beyond that). Psychological effects of longevity and immortality most often focus on memory and information processing. If the immortal, or extended life, individual is non-human, then we can simply say they evolved to their lifespan and there is no issue (e.g., the brain evolved to handle the increased memory requirements). If the individual started as human, there may be some trouble, unless the process alters the mind. Many worldbuilds have introduced the option of immortals hibernating (*Underworld, World of Darkness*) to protect the individual's mind and allow society to evolve.

The social effects of immortality and species longevity are much broader, so this part will focus on five key areas: governance, inheritance, reproduction, social climbing, and social influence. If a society has immortal governors, it will tend to become static, a staid society, unless there are artificial mechanisms in place to cause change. For example, Elrond and Galadriel specifically worked to ensure that their realms remained unchanging, which is one reason they had to leave Middle-Earth. Immortal governments will tend to look like many modern governments, in which the federal bodies are dominated by members of the oldest age blocks, but taken to an extreme. Instead of having a legislature effectively controlled by septuagenarians, Rivendell was controlled by multi-thousand-year-old leaders. On a related note, if people in a society never die of old age, or take centuries to die of old age, then do their descendants inherit property, or power? If they do, when and how? What mechanisms are in place, socially, to transfer goods and authority to younger generations? Are there any such mechanisms, or do the immortals retain power forever (or until a successful revolution happens)? In order to have inheritance issues, first there must be reproduction. If immortals reproduce rapidly, they are likely to overrun the world in short order. Therefore, the society may include laws about who may reproduce and when they may do so. For instance, most UF/PNR vampiric societies have rules about who can create new vampires and how they are allowed to do so (usually asking someone higher up in society's permission). On the other hand, a species that reproduces too slowly will eventually die out, from disease or other non-natural deaths (even most immortals can meet violent ends). In all such cases, a balance must be found.

A question of great importance when we work with extreme longevity and immortality is that of social climbing. Without natural death, or with centuries between deaths, we must ask if it is possible for people to move up in society. In mortal society, openings in the social structure are created by death and retirement, at least until the last 30–40 years as retirement became less common at all societal levels. If both death and retirement are gone, due to immortality, then society is gravely affected. Younger individuals will tend to become restless, perhaps forming rebellions, revolutions, civil wars, and shadow governments. So, such societies may evolve artificial methods to solve the issue, such as forced retirement, use of challenges (physical, mental, or otherwise), or assassination (whether sneaky or state accepted) to open positions in social leadership. Tied to social climbing is the question of social influence. The longer an individual lives, especially in a position of great social standing, the more influence they are likely to exert on society. This can lead to a greater degree of social stagnation. A good example here comes from *Star Wars* in which Yoda served on the Jedi Council for several centuries. In this role, he exerted a massive influence upon, and created a stagnation of, interpretations of the Jedi philosophy, Jedi training methods, and Jedi membership requirements and recruiting methods. One could feasibly argue that he effectively exerted sole control over the Council, given that many of the other Council members were his students or deferred to his age and perceived wisdom. Because of his role, Yoda also wielded a significant, albeit indirect, influence on the direction of the Republic through being an unofficial advisor to countless Supreme Chancellors. Some would argue, convincingly, that this influence is in large part what led to the ultimate fall of both the Jedi Order and the Galactic Republic.

Appendix A
Divine Spheres of Influence

- Agriculture
- Air
- Ancestor
- Animals (as a whole or specific species)
- Beauty
- Birth
- Blacksmiths/Forging
- Children
- Creator
- Culture Hero
- Dance
- The Dead
- Death
- Earth
- Engineering
- Fate
- Fertility
- Fire
- Fortune
- Guide of the Dead
- Handicrafts
- Healing
- Home/Hearth
- Hunting
- Judgement
- Justice
- Knowledge
- Law
- Light/Sun
- Literature
- Local Deities
- Love/Lust (of all sorts)
- Magic
- Marriage
- Mercy
- Messengers
- Moon
- Mother/Father
- Music
- Nature
- Night
- Oaths/Contracts
- Oracles
- Peace
- Plants
- Prosperity/Wealth
- Protection
- Purity
- Revenge
- River(s)
- Rulers/Kingship
- Sea/Ocean
- Season(s)
- Sexuality
- Sickness
- Sky
- State/Nation
- Storms
- Time

Appendix A

Trade
Travel
Tree/Forest
Truth
Underworld
Vegetation
Victory
War

Watchmen
Water
Weather
Wind
Wine/Beer/Alcohol
Wisdom
Writing

Appendix B
Recommended Resources

James D'Amato. *The Ultimate RPG Game Master's Worldbuilding Guide.* Adams Media, 2021.

This book contains a good set of tables that can be used as inspiration or for randomly creating setting information for many genres. Because it is relatively short and covers a range of genres, it is somewhat shallow, but a great resource for rolling up world elements, including societies, on the fly. That said, the random generators are based on the author's core assumptions (ex. magic needs a price) that may not be applicable to all creators' worlds or visions.

Matt Forbeck. *Redhurst Academy of Magic.* Human Head Studios, 2003. https://www.forbeck.com/downloads/RAMPG.pdf.

Forbeck presents a well-developed example of a self-contained society complete with brief discussions of economics and residents. The best developed aspects, though, are the places within the society and the society's relationship with education, social hierarchy, and magic (as expected from a school of magic).

Trent Hergenrader. *Collaborative Worldbuilding for Writers and Gamers.* Bloomsbury Academic, 2019.

Hergenrader has created an interesting "worldbuilding card deck" method and provided solid development examples for building a society. His method revolves around a system of four structures (Governance, Economics, Social Relations, and Cultural Influences) broken down into 14 substructures (incl. rule of law, social services, wealth distribution, agriculture, class relations, orientation relations, military influence, religious influence, arts and culture). A few elements are added to the end as pieces that do not fit into the four structures, including age, ableness, the natural world, and magic.

Evan Jamieson, Richard Meyer, and William Stoddard. *GURPS Low-Tech.* Steve Jackson Games, 2001.

Although designed with a particular RPG system in mind, like most GURPS books, it has a lot of system-neutral information of use to worldbuilders. There are many excellent examples of tools and ideas about technological developments at a range of different levels from Stone Age to just before Industrialization.

Connie Jasperson. "World Building Part 4: Questions to Consider When Creating a Society." *Life in the Realm of Fantasy.* 23 March 2015, https://conniejjasperson.com/2015/03/23/

world-building-part-4-questions-to-consider-when-creating-a-society/.

Jasperson has created an exhaustive list of categories and questions for building societies. Her categories include social organization (and who has power), language, currency, ethics, values, religion, gods, level of technology, government, crime, law, foreign relations, and waging war. This particular blog post is part of her series of lists and questions about various aspects of worldbuilding in the fantasy genres.

Sam Kassé. "Worldbuilding in a Novel: A Guide to Creating a Believable World." *Self-Publishing School*. 18 October 2022, https://self-publishingschool.com/worldbuilding/.

Kassé presents a good collection of questions about social rules, religion, history, magic, and people. Beyond societies, the questions also address geography and science fiction elements.

Phil Masters and Alison Brooks. *GURPS Places of Mystery*. Steve Jackson Games, 1996.

Masters and Brooks developed an excellent discussion of real-world locations "of mystery." The book also includes a collection of resources about odd and unusual places as well as a discussion of location-based magic. Each chapter includes some potential plots or plot hooks for different historical eras and continents. Like most GURPS books, it provides a wealth of system-neutral, and non-system, material that serves as fodder for inspiration.

Elizabeth McCoy and Walter Milliken. *GURPS IOU*. Steve Jackson Games, 2000.

McCoy and Milliken develop not only a wonderful example of a semi-self-contained society, complete with social classes and unique flora/fauna, but also present an example of society and education. The book, and setting, is developed in order to cover at least three different "modes" from Silly to "Darkly Illuminated" in style and concept.

Janet Naylor and Caroline Julian. *GURPS Religion*. Steve Jackson Games, 1994.

In addition to being a very detailed resource for creating fictional religions, Naylor and Julian include a single page checklist for developing religions and deities (with page references) at the end of the book (page 167).

Michael Schultheiss. "Stone Age to Star Age: World-Building Societies in Fiction." *Medium*. 1 June 2017, https://michael-schultheiss.medium.com/stone-age-to-star-age-world-building-societies-in-fiction-44bd259edaba.

Despite being a broad and rather generalized article, the author's discussion of what he calls broad "modalities" of societies could be helpful depending on how one approaches worldbuilding.

Amelia Wiens. "A Worldbuilding Guide to Crafting Diverse Cultures." *SFWA*. 31 January 2020, https://www.sfwa.org/2020/01/31/a-worldbuilding-guide-to-crafting-diverse-cultures/.

This is a good resource for cultural values and psychology based on the creator's study of both psychology and sociology. Her divisions include a number of binaries that represent spectra, including individualism vs. communitarianism, universalism vs. particularism, and achievement vs. ascription.

C.L. Wilson. "Worldbuilding 101—Structuring Your Society." *Clwilson.com*. 14 September 2013, https://clwilson.com/worldbuilding-101-structuring-your-society/.

Wilson's discussion of class systems, value of life, and family structure, among other things, in a society is part of a good series of blog posts on worldbuilding in general that is brief, thought-provoking, and includes a handful of real-world examples.

Appendix C
Selected Primary Texts and Series

Andrews, Ilona. *Hidden Legacy* series. Avon, 2014–.

———. *Innkeeper Chronicles* series. CreateSpace (Amazon), 2013–.

———. *Kate Daniels* series. Ace/Penguin, 2007–.[1]

Asprin, Robert. *MYTH Adventures* series. Ace,[2] 1978–2016.

Asprin, Robert, and Lynn Abbey, eds. *Thieves World* series. Ace & Tor, 1979–1989 and 2002–2004.

Baldree, Travis. *Legends & Lattes*. Tor, 2022.

Bardugo, Leigh. *Ninth House*. Flatiron Books, 2019.

———. *Shadow & Bone Trilogy*. Macmillan, 2012–2014.

———. *Six of Crows Duology*. Henry Holt, 2015–2016.

Brust, Steven. *Vlad Taltos* series. Ace/Tor, 1983–.

Canavan, Trudi. *The Black Magician* series. Orbit, 2001–2003.

Chokshi, Roshani. *Pandava Quintet*. Disney Hyperion, 2018–2022.

Clare, Cassandra. *The Mortal Instruments* series. Simon & Schuster, 2007–.[3]

Clare, Cassandra, and Holly Black. *The Magisterium* series. Scholastic, 2014–2019.

Clark, P. Djèlí. *Dead Djinn Universe* series. Tor, 2016–.

Clarke, Susanna. *Jonathan Strange and Mr. Norrell*. Bloomsbury, 2004.

Foglio, Kaja, and Phil Foglio. *Girl Genius*. Studio Foglio, 2001–.

Gaiman, Neil. *Stardust*. HarperTeen, 2009.

Gladstone, Max. *The Craft Sequence* series. Tor, 2012–2017.

Grossman, Lev. *The Magicians*. Viking, 2009.

Harkness, Deborah. *All Souls Trilogy*. Penguin, 2011–2014.

Harris, Charlaine. *The Southern Vampire* series. Ace/Orbit, 2001–2015.

Hearne, Kevin. *The Seven Kennings Trilogy*. Del Rey, 2017–.

Herbert, Frank. *Dune* series. Chilton/Putnam/Tor,[4] 1965–.

Howard, Robert E. *Conan* series. Del Rey,[5] 1932–.[6]

Huff, Tanya. *Gale Women* series. DAW, 2009–2014.

James, Allyson. *Stormwalker* series. Berkeley/JA/AG Publishing, 2010–2018.

Jemisin, N.K. *The Inheritance Trilogy*. Orbit Books, 2010–2011.

Kim, Graci. *Gifted Clans* series. Disney Hyperion, 2021–.

Kurtz, Katherine. *Deryni* series. Ballantine/Ace, 1970–2014.

Lee, Fonda. *Green Bone Saga*. Orbit, 2017–.

Lee, Lori. *Pahua and the Soul Stealer*. Disney Hyperion, 2021.

Lee, Yoon Ha. *Thousand Worlds* series. Rick Riordan Presents/Hyperion, 2019–.

LeGuin, Ursula K. *Earthsea* series. Parnassus/Athenaeum/Harcourt Brace, 1968–2018.[7]

Lewis, C.S. *Chronicles of Narnia*. HarperCollins,[8] 1950–1956.

Martin, George R.R. *A Song of Ice and Fire*. Bantam, 1996–.

Moorcock, Michael. *Elric* series. Victor Gollancz,[9] 1961–.

———. *The Eternal Champion*. Dell Books, 1970.

———. *Hawkmoon* series. DAW/Tor, 1967–1975.

Nix, Garth. *The Old Kingdom* series. HarperCollins, 1995–.

Novik, Naomi. *Scholomance* trilogy. Del Rey, 2020–2022.

Older, Daniel José. *Outlaw Saints* series. Disney Hyperion, 2022–.

Pratchett, Terry. *Discworld* series. Doubleday/Random House, 1983–2015.

Riordan, Rick. *The Kane Chronicles.* Disney Hyperion, 2010–2012.

———. *Percy Jackson and the Olympians*; *The Heroes of Olympus*; *The Trials of Apollo*. Disney Hyperion, 2005–2020.

Rothfuss, Patrick. *The Name of the Wind*. DAW, 2007.

Rowling, J.K. *Harry Potter* series. Scholastic, 1997–2007.

Sanderson, Brandon. *Mistborn* series. Tor, 2006–.

Sapkowski, Andrzej. *The Witcher* series. Orbit, 2007–2018.

Scott, Michael. *The Secrets of the Immortal Nicholas Flamel* series. Random House, 2007–2012.

Shearin, Lisa. *The SPI Files* series. Ace/NLA Digital LLC, 2013–.

Siddell, Tom. *Gunnerkregg Court*. Archaia Studios Press, 2005–.

Stroud, Jonathan. *The Bartimaeus Trilogy*. Random House, 2003–2010.

Thomas, Aiden. *Cemetery Boys*. Swoon Reads, 2020.

Tolkien, J.R.R. *The Lord of the Rings*. Ballantine Books/Houghton Mifflin, 1954–1955.

———. *The Silmarillion*. Del Rey,[10] 1977.

Turtledove, Harry. *The Videssos Cycle*. Del Rey, 1987.

Windling, Terri, ed. *Bordertown* series. Roc, 1986–1998.[11]

Chapter Notes

Introduction

1. Wolfgang Baur, "How to Design a City-State, Tribe, or Nation," in *The Kobold Guide to Worldbuilding*, ed. Janna Silverstein (Kobold Press, 2012), 53.
2. M.K. Tod, "Worldbuilding—Culture & Society," *A Writer of History*, Dec., 15, 2020, https://awriterofhistory.wordpress.com/2020/12/15/world-building-culture-society/.
3. Baur.
4. Connie Jasperson, "WorldBuilding Part 4: Questions to Consider When Creating a Society," *Life in the Realm of Fantasy*, March 23, 2015, https://conniejjasperson.com/2015/03/23/worldbuilding-part-4-questions-to-consider-when-creating-a-society/.
5. Baur.
6. Kevin J. Anderson, *Worldbuilding: From Small Towns to Entire Universes* (WordFire, 2015).
7. M.R. Johnson, "The Place of Culture, Society, and Politics in Video Game World-Building," in *World-Builders on World-Building*, ed. M.J.P. Wolf (Routledge, 2020), 110. Doi: 10.4324/9780429242861-7.
8. Ibid.
9. Emily Temple, "In Defense of Worldbuilding," *LitHub*, April 10, 2017, https://lithub.com/in-defense-of-worldbuilding/.
10. Ibid.
11. A worldview that centers on Western civilization and favors Western modes over non–Western civilizations.
12. Such as Octavia Butler's *Patternist* series.

Chapter 1

1. Eventually, in the *Six of Crows* duology, Kerch and Fjerda become developed because they are the central locations for that story.
2. Patricia C. Wrede and Pamela Dean, *Points of Departure: Liavek Stories* (Diversion Books, 2015).
3. Kirk Tate and Janet Naylor, *GURPS Fantasy*, 2nd ed. (Steve Jackson Games, 1990).
4. Wrede and Dean, 5.
5. Ibid.
6. *Dungeon Masters Guide*, 5th ed., Wizards of the Coast, 2014, 15–20.
7. Possibly the best question to ask in writing and worldbuilding.
8. Inky-duchess, "Worldbuilding: Societies," *Writerly*, April 27, 2019, https://www.tumblr.com/inky-duchess/184488124988/worldbuilding-societies.
9. Ibid.
10. C.L. Wilson, "Worldbuilding 101: Structuring Your Society," *clwilson.com*, Sept. 14, 2013, https://clwilson.com/worldbuilding-101-structuring-your-society/.
11. Wolfgang Baur, "How to Design a City-State, Tribe, or Nation," in *The Kobold Guide to Worldbuilding*, ed. Janna Silverstein (Kobold Press, 2012), 55–56.
12. Ibid., 56–57.
13. Monte Cook, "Different Kinds of Worldbuilding," in *The Kobold Guide to Worldbuilding*, ed. Janna Silverstein (Kobold Press, 2012), 17.
14. Ibid, 17–18.
15. M.R. Johnson, "The Place of Culture, Society, and Politics in Video Game World-Building," in *World-Builders on World-Building*, ed. M.J.P. Wolf (Routledge,

2020), 111. Doi: 10.4324/9780429242861-7.

16. Michael Stackpole, "They Do What Now? On Societies and Culture," in *The Kobold Guide to Worldbuilding*, ed. Janna Silverstein (Kobold Press, 2012), 59.

17. *Ibid.*, 61.

18. Trent Hergenrader, *Collaborative Worldbuilding for Writers and Gamers* (Bloomsbury Academic, 2019), 54–60.

19. *Dungeon Master's Guide* v. 3.5 (Wizards of the Coast, 2003), 135.

20. Kevin J. Anderson, *Worldbuilding: From Small Towns to Entire Universes* (WordFire, 2015), 27–28. Standing for Political, Economic, Religion, Society, Intellectual, Arts and Geography, Climate, Political, Economic, Society, Religion, Intellectual, Arts, History, respectively.

Chapter 2

1. Dimitri Halkidis, "Worldbuilding 101: Cultivating a Culture," *Writing Cooperative*, Dec. 5, 2019, https://writingcooperative.com/worldbuilding-101-cultivating-a-culture-ec0386caf35b.

2. M.R. Johnson, "The Place of Culture, Society, and Politics in Video Game World-Building," in *World-Builders on World-Building*, ed. M.J.P. Wolf (Routledge, 2020), 1. Doi: 10.4324/9780429242861-7.

3. *Ibid.*, 2.

4. The term *zanshin* from Japanese martial arts seems helpful here, in a variant application. The martial use of the term involves focusing on the opponent in front, while being aware of the potential for other opponents elsewhere and the situation in general.

5. Bordertown is an important example, as a seminal UF series, per both Tor's editors and Neil Gaiman: "some say, Urban Fantasy was born in Bordertown" ("An Introduction to Bordertown," *Tor*, May 5, 2011, https://www.tor.com/2011/05/05/an-introduction-to-bordertown/); "Bordertown is one of the most important places where Urban Fantasy began," Neil Gaiman quoted in Terri Windling, "The Borderland Series," *Terri Windling's Studio*, n.d., https://web.archive.org/web/20160601203403/http://windling.typepad.com/editing/borderland.html.

6. Wolfgang Baur, "What Is Setting Design?" in *The Kobold Guide to Worldbuilding*, ed. Janna Silverstein (Kobold Press, 2012), 14.

7. We know Tolkien shared his thoughts and drafts with C.S. Lewis and others, and Gaiman, Herbert, and Rowling likely did with friends or family. But the creation itself was exclusively or almost exclusively their own.

8. Kevin J. Anderson, *Worldbuilding: From Small Towns to Entire Universes* (Word Fire, 2015), 77.

9. *Ibid.*, 79.

10. Arguably the genre goes back to Homer and/or various mythologies, but the earliest non-religious examples are probably the medieval romances in the West. Chinese wuxia literature also fits as a parallel, non–Western source for the fantasy genres.

11. Myths here meaning stories that involve the society's deities and were once held as part of the society's religious beliefs. For example, Greek stories about Zeus were part of ancient Greece's religious beliefs and traditions.

12. Legends here meaning stories about non-divine, mortal agents that were not directly incorporated into religious belief. For example, the Arthurian legends, while evoking Christianity, were not part of the Christian faith.

13. Janet Naylor and Caroline Julian, *GURPS Religion* (Steve Jackson Games, 1994), 6–20.

14. Michael Stackpole, "They Do What Now? On Societies and Culture," in *The Kobold Guide to Worldbuilding*, ed. Janna Silverstein (Kobold Press, 2012).

15. Though Tolkien certainly tried his best.

16. Keith Baker, "Bringing History to Life," in *The Kobold Guide to Worldbuilding*, ed. Janna Silverstein (Kobold Press, 2012).

17. *Dungeon Master's Guide*, 5th ed. (Wizards of the Coast, 2014), 27–32.

18. Basically magic wielder, although they claim it as a science.

19. Johnson, 7.

20. *Ibid.*

Chapter 3

1. Dave Mech, "Wolf News and Information," *Dave Mech: Scientist and Wolf*

Researcher, http://davemech.org/wolf-news-and-information/; David L. Mech, "Alpha Status, Dominance, and Division of Labor in Wolf Packs," *Canadian Journal of Zoology* 77 (1999): 1196–203; Rafi Letzter, "There's No Such Thing as an Alpha Male," *Business Insider*, Oct. 12, 2016, https://www.businessinsider.com/no-such-thing-alpha-male-2016-10.
 2. *Dungeon Master's Guide (DMG)* v. 3.5 (Wizards of the Coast, 2003), 142.
 3. C.L. Wilson, "Worldbuilding 101—Structuring Your Society," *Clwilson.com*, Sept. 14, 2013, https://clwilson.com/worldbuilding-101-structuring-your-society/.
 4. Kevin J. Anderson, *Worldbuilding: From Small Towns to Entire Universes* (WordFire, 2015), 48.
 5. Ibid, 50.
 6. *Tithe*, *Valiant*, and *Ironside*.
 7. M.K. Tod, "Worldbuilding—Culture & Society," *A Writer of History*, Dec. 15, 2020, https://awriterofhistory.wordpress.com/2020/12/15/world-building-culture-society/.
 8. Anderson, 45–46.
 9. Steve Jackson, *GURPS: Basic Set*, 3rd ed. (Steve Jackson Games, 1991), 189.
 10. Ibid.
 11. Ibid.
 12. Ibid., 188; *DMG*, 141–42; such laws may also extend to offensive magic and magical devices.
 13. *DMG*, 141.

Chapter 4

 1. *Dungeon Masters Guide*, 5th ed. (Wizards of the Coast, 2014), 11.
 2. The National Day Calendar notes 4,000 active religions today ("World Religion Day," *National Day Calendar*, https://nationaldaycalendar.com/world-religion-day-third-sunday-in-january/), while *The Register* suggests the existence of 4,300 religions as of 2006 (Stephen Juan, "What Are the Most Widely Practiced Religions of the World?" *The Register*, Oct. 6, 2006, https://www.theregister.com/2006/10/06/the_odd_body_religion/).
 3. *DMG*, 5th ed., 12–13.
 4. Janet Naylor and Caroline Julian, *GURPS Religion* (Steve Jackson Games, 1994), 126–38.
 5. Ibid., 131.
 6. *DMG*, 5th ed., 10–11.
 7. A fantasy in which one or more persons are transported from one world (usually Earth) to another (usually fictional) via some type of magic (ex. Narnia or The Land of Stephen R. Donaldson's Thomas Covenant). Occasional examples have persons from a fictional world transported to Earth (ex. arguably, Roger Zelazny's *The Chronicles of Amber*).
 8. The Satanic Temple is a clear exception, in that they are registered as a non-theistic religion in the U.S. (Matt Miller, "Why the Satanic Temple is Opening its Doors to American Muslims," *Esquire*, Nov. 21, 2015, https://www.esquire.com/news-politics/news/a39904/satanic-temple-founder-interview-muslims/). Other arguable exceptions include Daoism, Confucianism, Jainism, Buddhism, and Paul Tillich's existentialist Christianity.
 9. Naylor and Julian, 22–44.
 10. *DMG*, 5th ed., 11.
 11. A clear Christ-figure.
 12. Who were, historically, secular. Miriam-Webster defines the term as simply a trusted military leader (as for a medieval prince) or a leading champion of a cause. Note the lack of religious attachment, as compared to the use in TTRPGs and MMORPGs.
 13. *Dungeon Masters Guide* v. 3.5 (Wizards of the Coast, 2003), 143.
 14. Further discussion of these elements can be found in Naylor and Julian, 98.
 15. Aside from a few that will do online ordination, from the 1990s to today.
 16. Although not fantasy as such, *Monty Python's The Life of Brian* presents an excellent and comedic example of sect formation (within 24 hours of the religion being founded) as followers of Brian argue over whether they should follow "the gourd" or "the shoe." The movie also brings the question of heresy into the burgeoning worship of Brian as messiah (within minutes of its creation).
 17. This is essentially what happened to form the Anglican/Episcopalian Church, as King Henry VIII desired more power over religious leaders/matters. Ultimately, the Anglican and Catholic Churches saw only a few notable lasting

differences—including the central authority (Pope v. King/Queen of England), clerical marriage, reproductive rights, lack of monastics (Anglican), and the ordination of women. However, their ceremonies and vestments appear virtually identical.

18. Seb Falk, *The Light Ages: The Surprising Story of Medieval Science* (W.W. Norton, 2020), 81–122.

19. Founded in 1070 and still active today as multiple organizations: the Sovereign Military Order of Malta, the Most Venerable Order of the Hospital of Saint John, the Bailiwick of Brandenburg of the Chivalric Order of Saint John, the Order of Saint John in the Netherlands, and the Order of Saint John in Sweden; "Knights Hospitaller," *Wikipedia*, Nov. 9, 2022, https://en.wikipedia.org/wiki/Knights_Hospitaller.

20. Although they claim to have started as militant-monastics (Hospitallers), they are currently laypersons.

21. For example, the respect many in the U.S. hold for the Satanic Temple, due to their actions to protect freedom of religion, the Establishment Clause, and separation of church and state through lawsuits and public displays at government buildings.

22. A classic example is a statue from Herculaneum, Campania, Italy, that depicts Hercules (patron god of the city) clearly drunk and relieving himself. DeAgostini Editorial, "Drunken Hercules, Statue from House of Deer," *Getty Images*, Sept. 27, 2015, https://www.gettyimages.com/detail/news-photo/drunken-hercules-statue-from-the-house-of-the-deer-news-photo/601427271.

23. Steve Jackson, *GURPS: Basic Set*, 3rd ed. (Steve Jackson Games, 1991), 195.

24. He became a bishop in 1607 and cardinal in 1622 and was succeeded in his post as First Minister of State by another cardinal upon his death in 1642; "Armand-Jean du Plessis de Richelieu Biography," *Notable Biographies*, https://www.notablebiographies.com/Pu-Ro/Richelieu-Armand-Jean-du-Plessis-de.html.

25. From 1965 to 2014, the archbishop delivered a speech at every mayoral inauguration in New York City, effectively "crowning" the mayor; "New York's Archbishops: How They Shaped the City and the Church," *New York Times*, March 9, 2017, https://www.nytimes.com/2017/03/09/nyregion/new-yorks-archbishops-how-they-shaped-the-city-and-the-church.html.

26. "History of Clergy in Congress," *Pew Research Center*, Jan. 5, 2015, https://www.pewresearch.org/religion/2015/01/05/history-of-clergy-in-congress/.

27. Greater detail can be found in brief in Naylor and Julian, 133.

28. Who stand around waiting for the hero/anti-hero to slaughter them.

Chapter 5

1. For more on creating magic systems, see Stypczynski, *A Worldbuilder's Guide to Magic* (McFarland, 2021). Other good resources include *Authentic Thaumaturgy* (Steve Jackson Games; Isaac Bonewits) as well as *GURPS Magic, Thaumatology*, and *Powers* (Steve Jackson Games).

2. Keith Baker, "How to Make a High Magic World," in *The Kobold Guide to Worldbuilding*, ed. Janna Silverstein (Kobold Press, 2012), 65–66.

3. Who do not necessarily need to, or choose to, follow guidelines set by the setting creators or the system creators, depending on the type and power level of game they want.

4. *Dungeon Masters Guide*, 5th ed. (Wizards of the Coast, 2014), 24.

5. This is the route that our own European societies ultimately took (mostly 14th through 19th centuries). The widespread claim that witches, and other non–Church magicians, learned magic from pacts with demons who taught them led to trials and executions.

6. For a fuller, but still incomplete, discussion of different types of magic, see the first three chapters of Stypczynski, *A Worldbuilder's Guide to Magic* (McFarland, 2021).

7. Dimitri Halkidis, "Worldbuilding 101: Cultivating a Culture," *Writing Cooperative*, Dec. 5, 2019, https://writingcooperative.com/worldbuilding-101-cultivating-a-culture-ec0386caf35b.

8. Steve Jackson, *GURPS Magic* (Steve Jackson Games, 1990), 109.

9. An in-world reason that explains AD&D game rules that restrict the weapons wizards can use.

10. Jackson, 108.

11. *Ibid.*, 109.

12. "Imperial Prisons," *Lyorn* Records, Jan. 22, 2013, https://dragaera.fandom.com/wiki/Imperial_Prisons.

13. Kirk Tate and Janet Naylor, *GURPS Fantasy*, 2nd ed. (Steve Jackson Games, 1990), 137–40.

14. As parodied in the *Epic NPC Man* YouTube series by Viva La Dirt League, "Forcing NPCs to Buy Your Stuff," "Forcing Poor NPCs to Pay," and "How Does All the Loot Get There?" episodes; Viva La Dirt League, "Forcing NPC's to Buy Your Stuff—Poor Merchant," *YouTube*, Jan. 29, 2020, https://youtu.be/mYsyTq8pF2g; Viva La Dirt League, "Forcing Poor NPCs to Pay—Payment," *YouTube*, Nov. 11, 2020, https://youtu.be/JXLV1SQhVhw; "How Does All the Loot Get There?" *YouTube*, Feb. 1, 2023. https://www.youtube.com/watch?v=tE73Ag07Rn8.

15. Terry Pratchett, *Reaper Man* (Harper, 1991), 28.

16. Terry Pratchett, *Witches Abroad* (ROC, 1991), 17.

17. Reginald Scot notes a distinction between evil magic (meant to harm; including poisons, battery of children and animals, curses, accident causing, and ailments) and good magic (meant to heal, find lost or stolen goods, love magic, protection). For most of the medieval and early modern eras, some simplified the division to miracles as good, true magic and wonders as bad, false magic. But, determining whether an event was a miracle or a wonder was often open to interpretation; Reginald Scot, *The Discouerie of Witchcraft* (London, 1584).

18. Deuteronomy, for instance, outlines what divination processes are forbidden, implicitly noting others that are acceptable under Jewish law. Likewise, the University of Paris issued numerous articles concerning the practice of magic in the 14th and 15th centuries—in 1322 the university Dominicans condemned alchemy, in 1398 the university condemned all of the magical arts, and in 1466 the university condemned magic books. Lynn Thorndyke, trans., *University Records and Life in the Middle Ages* (New York: W.W. Norton, 1975), 168, 261-66, 351-52.

Chapter 6

1. Wolfgang Baur, "Worlds and Technology," in *The Kobold Guide to Worldbuilding*, ed. Janna Silverstein (Kobold Press, 2012), 69.

2. "Steven Brust," *Wikipedia*, Oct. 12, 2022, https://en.wikipedia.org/wiki/Steven_Brust.

3. Evan Jamieson, Richard Meyer, and William H. Stoddard, *GURPS Low-Tech* (Steve Jackson Games, 2001), 6.

4. Page 18, available as a free PDF download from SJGames (Warehouse 23); Scott D. Haring and Sean Punch, *GURPS Lite*, 4th ed. (Steve Jackson Games, 2020).

5. Jamieson, Meyer, and Stoddard, 6.

6. "[S]ocieties may not have the same TL at the same time" (Jamieson, Meyer, and Stoddard, 6).

7. GURPS is useful here, in its game construct of tech levels (TL) noted as TL (X+n) compared to TL X to indicate divergent technologies, as found in clockpunk or steampunk settings. So, the real-world 19th century would be TL 5 (maybe early 6), but a steampunk setting might be TL (6+1) indicating some nuclear age tech via divergent/alternate tech; William H. Stoddard, *GURPS Steam-Tech* (Steve Jackson Games, 2001); Haring & Punch.

8. "At one point I became particularly intrigued by an old telescope, with which I would study the heavens. One night while looking at the moon I realized that there were shadows on its surface. I corralled my two main tutors to show them, because this was contrary to the ancient version of cosmology I had been taught, which held that the moon was a heavenly body that emitted its own light. But through my telescope the moon was clearly just a barren rock, pocked with craters. If the author of that fourth-century treatise were writing today, I'm sure he would write the chapter on cosmology differently. If science proves some belief of Buddhism wrong, then Buddhism will have to change"; Tenzin Gyatso, "Our Faith in Science," *Dalai Lama*, Dec. 1, 2005, https://www.dalailama.com/news/2005/our-faith-in-science.

9. *GURPS Low-Tech* presents a good brief on social organization and

technology for Stone Age to medieval technology levels; Jamieson, Meyer, and Stoddard.

10. Way back in 1991, *Dungeon Magazine* published an AD&D adventure written by Willie Walsh called "Mightier Than the Sword" (Issue 29) that centered on a murdered inventor who developed metal nibs for pens (resulting in anger from the goose farmers and the scribe's guild).

Chapter 7

1. See Renée Dickinson, "Harry Potter Pedagogy: What We Learn about Teaching and Learning from J.K. Rowling," *The Clearing House* 79, no. 6 (July–Aug. 2006), pp. 240–44; Linus Friberg, "Pedagogy at Hogwarts: A Literary Analysis of Teaching Methods and Theories at Hogwarts in the Harry Potter Books" (master's thesis, Linnaeus University, 2019); M'Balia Thomas, Alisa LaDean Russell and Hannah V. Warren, "The Good, the Bad, and the Ugly of Pedagogy in Harry Potter: An Inquiry Into the Personal Practical Knowledge of Remus Lupin, Rubeus Hagrid, and Severus Snape," *The Clearing House*, 2018, doi: 10.1080/00098655.2018.1483152; Marcie Panutsos Rovan and Melissa Wehler, eds., *Lessons from Hogwarts: Essays on the Pedagogy of Harry Potter* (McFarland, 2020).

2. At the University of Paris, for instance, faculty were required to secure their own classrooms, often in the back or second floors of taverns or in lodging houses; "Rules Concerning the Rental of Classrooms, Paris, 1245," *University Records and Life in the Middle Ages*, trans. Lynn Thorndyke (Columbia UP, 1972), 51–52.

3. J.K. Rowling, *Harry Potter and the Prisoner of Azkaban* (Scholastic, 1999), 346; J.K. Rowling, *Harry Potter and the Goblet of Fire* (Scholastic, 2000), 320.

4. Wolfgang Baur, "Worlds and Technology," in *The Kobold Guide to Worldbuilding*, ed. Janna Silverstein (Kobold Press, 2012), 71.

5. The Greek term utopia literally translates as "no place."

6. L.W.B. Brockliss, *The University of Oxford: A History* (Oxford UP, 2016).

7. Flipping that dynamic might make for an interesting worldbuild or narrative plot, though.

Chapter 8

1. Paul B. Sturtevant, "Race: The Original Sin of the Fantasy Genre," *The Public Medievalist*, Dec. 5, 2017, https://www.publicmedievalist.com/race-fantasy-genre; Mike Ruso, "The Word 'Race' in the Fantasy Genre," *MikeRuso.com*, May 12, 2014, https://www.mikeruso.com/blog/race-in-the-fantasy-genre/; Helen Young, *Race and Popular Fantasy Literature: Habits of Whiteness* (Routledge, 2016); Sable Whisper, "Rethinking Race in Fantasy: An Evidence-based Approach," *Medium*, Mar. 9, 2019, https://realsablewhisper.medium.com/rethinking-race-in-fantasy-an-evidence-based-approach-8341c98ab05.

2. The term "race" will be used here to refer to real-world issues/relationships (as in common usage), while "species" will be used to refer to elves, dwarves, giants, etc.

3. "Race," *Cambridge Dictionary*, https://dictionary.cambridge.org/us/dictionary/english/race.

4. "A large group of people with a shared culture, language, history, set of traditions, etc., or the fact of belonging to one of these groups."; "Ethnicity," *Cambridge Dictionary*, https://dictionary.cambridge.org/us/dictionary/english/ethnicity.

5. "AAA Statement on Race," *American Anthropological Association*, May 17, 1998, https://www.americananthro.org/ConnectWithAAA/Content.aspx?ItemNumber=2583.

6. Rashawn Ray and Nicole DeLoatch, "Race," *Oxford Bibliographies*, Nov. 13, 2018, https://www.oxfordbibliographies.com/view/document/obo-9780199756384/obo-9780199756384-0173.xml#:~:text=Race%20is%20a%20human%20classification,people%20who%20share%20phenotypical%20characteristics.

7. This was most strikingly illustrated with the drow. In the *Forgotten Realms*, drow are a race of evil elves (see biological determinism) devoted to the spider goddess Lloth. The fifth edition Players Handbook (PHB) errata in 2021 specifically states that drow on other

worlds are not necessarily beholden to Lloth and therefore not necessarily evil beings (shifting from biological determinism to cultural forces); Matthew Rossi, "According to the Player's Handbook, Drow No Longer Have to Be Evil in Your D&D Game," *Blizzard Watch*, Dec. 15, 2021, https://blizzardwatch.com/2021/12/15/dnd-drow-evil/.

8. A key novel showing this effect and the tension it creates is *Thud!*

9. "Determinism, Biological," *Encyclopedia.com*, June 27, 2018, https://www.encyclopedia.com/science-and-technology/biology-and-genetics/biology-general/biological-determinism.

10. "The practice of doing something (such as hiring a person who belongs to a minority group) only to prevent criticism and give the appearance that people are being treated fairly"; "Tokenism," *The Britannica Dictionary*, https://www.britannica.com/dictionary/tokenism.

11. This is, of course, not to say that white people cannot or should not write Black, Asian, or Latino characters, or vice versa. But it should be done carefully and with conscious intent. Or in cases where other factors come into play in shaping characters and society. Ilona Andrews, for example, presents a varied mix of character ethnicities in their *Kate Daniels* series; however, their characters are more directly impacted by the recent magic-apocalypse culture and the variety of previously mythological beings present than by pre-Shift culture and racial issues.

12. Dimitri Halkidis, "Worldbuilding 101: Cultivating a Culture," *Writing Cooperative*, Dec. 5, 2019, https://writingcooperative.com/worldbuilding-101-cultivating-a-culture-ec0386caf35b.

13. Kirk Tate and Janet Naylor, *GURPS Fantasy*, 2nd ed. (Steve Jackson Games, 1990), 141.

14. "Exceptionalism is the perception or belief that a species, country, society, institution, movement, individual, or time period is 'exceptional' (i.e., unusual or extraordinary). The term carries the implication, whether or not specified, that the referent is superior in some way"; "Exceptionalism," *Wikipedia*, Mar. 18, 2022, https://en.wikipedia.org/wiki/Exceptionalism.

Chapter 9

1. Of course, different versions, say, Mexican Spanish, or dialects, Parisian French, may be more or less difficult.

2. Arguably, Latin could be considered an exception here as it is the official language of the Vatican. It is used in all official documents and is technically the spoken language of the microstate. However, it is not a native language and Italian is the default "daily" language of the city-state, with French as its diplomatic language (and the Swiss Guard uses German for commands as well as French and Italian for other purposes); "Languages in the Holy See," *Study Country*, https://www.studycountry.com/guide/VA-language.htm.

3. In the *Stargate SG-1* episode "Demons" (season 3, episode 8), Daniel Jackson takes one glance at a carved stone marker and identifies the language (Middle English), era ("pre–Chaucerian"), and dialect despite having no prior background with the language, time period, or geographic region. (Although the language has been identified by fans as Early Modern English and it has also been noted that if the people had been present on the world for "a thousand years," they would be speaking Old English); "Demons," *SGCommand: Stargate Wiki*, Oct. 2, 2022, https://stargate.fandom.com/wiki/Demons.

4. The Vai have been heavily studied by linguists and scholars of literacy precisely because of how their culture uses the three languages; Adam Jones, "Who Were the Vai?" *The Journal of African History* 22, no. 2 (1981): 159–78; Colin Barras, "A West African Writing System Shows How Letters Evolve to Get Simpler," *New Scientist*, Jan. 11, 2022, https://www.newscientist.com/article/2303865-a-west-african-writing-system-shows-how-letters-evolve-to-get-simpler/; Olena Tykhostup and Piers Kelly, "A Diachronic Comparison of the Vai Script of Liberia (1834–2005)," *Journal of Open Humanities Data* 4, no. 2 (Feb. 12, 2018), http://doi.org/10.5334/johd.10.

Chapter 10

1. Tim Newman, "Sex and Gender: What Is the Difference?" *Medical

News Today, May 11, 2021, https://www.medicalnewstoday.com/articles/232363.
2. Ibid.
3. Paul Tamburro, "Forgotten Realms Creator Ed Greenwood Is 'Saddened' by Baldur's Gate Controversy," *Mandatory*, April 6, 2016, https://www.mandatory.com/culture/973847-forgotten-realms-creator-ed-greenwood-saddened-baldurs-gate-controversy.
4. Steven E. Ozment, *The Burgermeister's Daughter: Scandal in a Sixteenth-Century German Town* (St. Martin's Press, 1996).
5. Hanne Brum presents an exception on multiple levels: on one hand, she is a woman who learned to fight, hunt, and ride; on the other, she spends most of the narrative as a pre-transition transgender man (who, as a man, would be trained to fight, hunt, and ride).
6. There are an estimated two Shakers in the world as of 2017; Erin Blakemore, "There Are Only Two Shakers Left in the World," *Smithsonian Magazine*, Jan. 6, 2017, https://www.smithsonianmag.com/smart-news/there-are-only-two-shakers-left-world-180961701/.

Chapter 11

1. "No killing without pay."
2. *Dungeon Masters Guide*, 5th ed. (Wizards of the Coast, 2014), 21–22.
3. "Seamstresses' Guild," *L-Space*, Aug. 8, 2021, https://wiki.lspace.org/Seamstresses%27_Guild.
4. "Operation Underworld," *Wikipedia*, Sept. 1, 2022, https://en.wikipedia.org/wiki/Operation_Underworld.

Chapter 12

1. Terry Pratchett, *The Color of Magic* (Harper Paperbacks, 2000), Foreword.
2. For example, Stephen Gillet's *World-Building* (ed. Ben Bova, Writer's Digest Books, 1996) that focuses solely on scientific world creation, with a lot of crunchy math.
3. Dimitri Halkidis, "Worldbuilding 101: Cultivating a Culture," *Writing Cooperative*, Dec. 5, 2019, https://writingcooperative.com/worldbuilding-101-cultivating-a-culture-ec0386caf35b.
4. Terry Pratchett and Paul Kidby, *The Art of Discworld* (HarperCollins, 2004), 4.
5. "New Exoplanet Is Twice Earth's Size—And Made Largely of Diamond," *Wired*, Oct. 12, 2012, https://www.wired.com/2012/10/diamond-exoplanet/; Alisa Harvey and Elizabeth Howell, "The 10 Most Earth-Like Exoplanets," *Space*, Jan. 20, 2022, https://www.space.com/30172-six-most-earth-like-alien-planets.html.
6. "All literature consists of whatever the writer thinks is cool. The reader will like the book to the degree that he agrees with the writer about what's cool. And that works all the way from the external trappings to the level of metaphor, subtext, and the way one uses words. In other words, I happen not to think that full-plate armor and great big honking greatswords are cool. I don't like 'em. I like cloaks and rapiers. So I write stories with a lot of cloaks and rapiers in 'em, 'cause that's cool. Guys who like military hardware, who think advanced military hardware is cool, are not gonna jump all over my books, because they have other ideas about what's cool. [. . .] The novel should be understood as a structure built to accommodate the greatest possible amount of cool stuff" (as rendered in most quoted forms, including Brust's Wikipedia entry).
7. On her professional website: N.K. Jemisin, "But, But, But, Why Does Magic Have to Make Sense?" *nkjemisin.com*, June 15, 2012, nkjemisin.com/2012/06/but-but-but-why-does-magic-have-to-make-sense/.
8. As further explained by J.R.R. Tolkien in *The Peoples of Middle-Earth*, ed. Christopher Tolkien (Mariner Books, 1996), 390 (note 14).
9. D&D has, at various points, expanded out to sea elves, desert elves, subterranean elves, and such as well, but their baseline (high elves and wild elves) still tend to follow Tolkien's lead.
10. *The Voyage of the Dawn Treader*, chapter 15.
11. Harry Turtledove, "Harry Turtledove: Revisioning History," *Locus* 50, no. 2 (Feb. 2003): 6–7, 81–82; Also, Kevin J. Anderson's admonishment to "*convey* a sense of a lot more details and a lot more growth without necessarily including

every tiny nuance": *Worldbuilding: From Small Towns to Entire Universes* (WordFire, 2015), 22; Or Wolfgang Baur's statement, "The designer's instinct should be to provide only that which is relevant.... The goal is not an encyclopedic worldbuilding approach.... Climate charts and trade routes may be useful bits of worldbuilding, but they should be largely invisible to the [audience]": "What Is Setting Design," in *The Kobold Guide to Worldbuilding*, ed. Janna Silverstein (Kobold Press, 2012), 12.

Chapter 13

1. Set on the site of a former fish-god temple in Dagon Street, opened on the night of a full moon and a lunar eclipse at the winter solstice.

2. Summarized by Archchancellor Ridcully as "crack-crack-gristle-AAAARGH!" ("Three Jolly Luck," *L-space*, Dec. 31, 2017, https://wiki.lspace.org/Three_Jolly_Luck).

3. M.R. Johnson, "The Place of Culture, Society, and Politics in Video Game World-Building," in *World-Builders on World-Building*, ed. M.J.P. Wolf (Routledge, 2020), 116. Doi: 10.4324/9780429242861-7.

4. Floating here is in the sense of moving, potentially applied to a market (as in Gaiman's *Neverwhere*) or school, that can be held in a variety of places, rarely if ever the same place twice.

5. With its thirty colleges scattered around the city but linked under the Oxford University umbrella.

6. How many tabletop RPG campaigns begin with "You all meet in a tavern...."? So many that it has become a sort of inside joke and the source of multiple memes.

7. Formerly the Drum and the Broken Drum.

8. Favorite hangout for off-duty Watch personnel.

9. Technically an ancient version of Earth.

10. "An object, event, or character in a film or story that serves to set and keep the plot in motion despite usually lacking intrinsic importance" ("MacGuffin," *Merriam-Webster Dictionary*, https://www.merriam-webster.com/dictionary/MacGuffin).

Chapter 14

1. And the exception of Terry Pratchett's trolls, who believe time moves backwards, but even then that is only mentioned a couple of times, plus his use of time travel in *Night Watch* ("Trolls," *L-space*, Dec. 15, 2021, https://wiki.lspace.org/Trolls#Troll_Afterlife).

2. M.R. Johnson, "The Place of Culture, Society, and Politics in Video Game World-Building," in *World-Builders on World-Building*, ed. M.J.P. Wolf (Routledge, 2020), 121. Doi: 10.4324/9780429242861-7.

3. As Steve Jackson notes, currency can come in many forms, including adventuring loot. Steve Jackson, *GURPS: Basic Set*, 3rd ed. (Steve Jackson Games, 1991), 190–91.

4. Scott Hungerford, "How to Write a World Bible (or, How to Keep it All Straight)," in *The Kobold Guide to Worldbuilding*, ed. Janna Silverstein (Kobold Press, 2012), 107.

5. *Dungeon Masters Guide* v. 3.5 (Wizards of the Coast, 2003), 140.

6. "Wizarding Currency," *Harry Potter Wiki*, Nov. 4, 2022, https://harrypotter.fandom.com/wiki/Wizarding_currency#Exchange_rate.

7. *Game of Thrones*, season 6, episode 5, "The Door," HBO, 2016; *Game of Thrones*, season 6, episode 6, "Blood of My Blood," HBO, 2016.

8. M.K. Tod, "Worldbuilding—Culture & Society," *A Writer of History*, Dec. 15, 2020, https://awriterofhistory.wordpress.com/2020/12/15/world-building-culture-society/.

9. Kevin J. Anderson, *Worldbuilding: From Small Towns to Entire Universes* (WordFire, 2015).

10. For example, the common English phrase, "This/That sucks," that, unbeknownst to many/most users, refers to oral sex.

Appendix C

1. The last book in the series was published in 2018, but multiple spin-off books (including *Iron & Magic* and *Blood Heir*) are in print as of the time of this writing.

2. Most recent publisher of most of the series, but there have been several publishers.

3. The last book in the series was published in 2014, but numerous short stories and spin-off series continue.
4. Continued by Brian Herbert and Kevin J. Anderson.
5. Most recent of many publishers.
6. Continued after Howard's death by L. Sprague de Camp and Lin Carter, among others.
7. Including short stories.
8. Most recent of many.
9. Most recent of many.
10. Most recent of several.
11. Mark Alan Arnold and Delia Sherman co-edited some volumes. Revived for one book with both old and new authors by editors Holly Black and Ellen Kushner in 2011.

Bibliography

"AAA Statement on Race." *American Anthropological Association.* May 17, 1998. https://www.americananthro.org/ConnectWithAAA/Content.aspx?ItemNumber=2583.

Anderson, Kevin J. *Worldbuilding: From Small Towns to Entire Universes.* WordFire, 2015.

"Armand-Jean du Plessis de Richelieu Biography." *Notable Biographies.* n.d. https://www.notablebiographies.com/Pu-Ro/Richelieu-Armand-Jean-du-Plessis-de.html.

Baker, Keith. "Bringing History to Life." In *The Kobold Guide to Worldbuilding*, edited by Janna Silverstein, 35–38. Kobold Press, 2012.

———. "How to Make a High Magic World." In *The Kobold Guide to Worldbuilding*, edited by Janna Silverstein, 63–67. Kobold Press, 2012.

Barras, Colin. "A West African Writing System Shows How Letters Evolve to Get Simpler." *New Scientist.* Jan. 11, 2022. https://www.newscientist.com/article/2303865-a-west-african-writing-system-shows-how-letters-evolve-to-get-simpler/.

Baur, Wolfgang. "How to Design a City-State, Tribe, or Nation." In *The Kobold Guide to Worldbuilding*, edited by Janna Silverstein, 53–58. Kobold Press, 2012.

———. "What Is Setting Design?" In *The Kobold Guide to Worldbuilding*, edited by Janna Silverstein, 11–15. Kobold Press, 2012.

———. "Worlds and Technology." In *The Kobold Guide to Worldbuilding*, edited by Janna Silverstein, 69–75. Kobold Press, 2012.

Blakemore, Erin. "There Are Only Two Shazkers Left in the World." *Smithsonian Magazine.* Jan. 6, 2017. https://www.smithsonianmag.com/smart-news/there-are-only-two-shakers-left-world-180961701/.

Brockliss, L.W.B. *The University of Oxford: A History.* Oxford UP, 2016.

Cook, Monte. "Different Kinds of Worldbuilding." In *The Kobold Guide to Worldbuildzng*, edited by Janna Silverstein, 16–19. Kobold Press, 2012.

DeAgostini Editorial. "Drunken Hercules, Statue from House of Deer." *Getty Images.* Sept. 27, 2015. https://www.gettyimages.com/detail/news-photo/drunken-hercules-statue-from-the-house-of-the-deer-news-photo/601427271.

"Demons." *SGCommand: Stargate Wiki.* Oct. 2, 2022. https://stargate.fandom.com/wiki/Demons.

"Determinism, Biological." *Encyclopedia.com.* June 27, 2018. https://www.encyclopedia.com/science-and-technology/biology-and-genetics/biology-general/biologicaldeterminism.

Dungeon Masters Guide, 5th ed. Wizards of the Coast, 2014.

Dungeon Master's Guide v. 3.5. Wizards of the Coast, 2003.

"Ethnicity." *Cambridge Dictionary.* n.d. https://dictionary.cambridge.org/us/dictionary/english/ethnicity.

"Exceptionalism." *Wikipedia.* Mar. 18, 2022. https://en.wikipedia.org/wiki/Exceptionalism.

Falk, Seb. *The Light Ages: The Surprising Story of Medieval Science.* W.W. Norton, 2020.

Game of Thrones. Season 6, episode 5, "The Door." HBO. 2016.

———. Season 6, episode 6, "Blood of My Blood." HBO. 2016.

Gyatso, Tenzin. "Our Faith in Science." *Dalai Lama*. Dec. 1, 2005. https://www.dalailama.com/news/2005/our-faith-in-science.

Halkidis, Dimitri. "Worldbuilding 101: Cultivating a Culture." *Writing Cooperative*. Dec. 5, 2019. https://writingcooperative.com/worldbuilding-101-cultivating-a-culture-ec0386caf35b.

Haring, Scott D., and Sean Punch. *GURPS Lite*, 4th ed. Steve Jackson Games, 2020.

Harvey, Alisa, and Elizabeth Howell. "The 10 Most Earth-like Exoplanets." *Space*. Jan. 20, 2022. https://www.space.com/30172-six-most-earth-like-alien-planets.html.

Hergenrader, Trent. *Collaborative Worldbuilding for Writers and Gamers*. Bloomsbury Academic, 2019.

"History of Clergy in Congress." *Pew Research Center*. Jan. 5, 2015. https://www.pewresearch.org/religion/2015/01/05/history-of-clergy-in-congress/.

Hungerford, Scott. "How to Write a World Bible (or, How to Keep it All Straight)." In *The Kobold Guide to Worldbuilding*, edited by Janna Silverstein, 105–107. Kobold Press, 2012.

"Imperial Prisons." *Lyorn Records*. Jan. 22, 2013. https://dragaera.fandom.com/wiki/Imperial_Prisons.

Inky-duchess. "Worldbuilding: Societies." *Writerly*. April 27, 2019. https://www.tumblr.com/inky-duchess/184488124988/worldbuilding-societies.

"An Introduction to Bordertown." *Tor*. May 5, 2011. https://www.tor.com/2011/05/05/an-introduction-to-bordertown/.

Jackson, Steve. *GURPS Magic*. Steve Jackson Games, 1990.

———. *GURPS: Basic Set*, 3rd ed. Steve Jackson Games, 1991.

Jamieson, Evan, Richard Meyer, and William H. Stoddard. *GURPS Low-Tech*. Steve Jackson Games, 2001.

Jasperson, Connie. "WorldBuilding Part 4: Questions to Consider When Creating a Society." *Life in the Realm of Fantasy*. Mar. 23, 2015. https://conniejjasperson.com/2015/03/23/world-building-part-4-questions-to-consider-when-creating-a-society/.

Jemisin, N.K. "But, But, But, Why Does Magic Have to Make Sense?" *nkjemisin.com*. June 15, 2012. http://nkjemisin.com/2012/06/but-but-but-why-does-magic-have-to-make-sense.

Johnson, M.R. "The Place of Culture, Society, and Politics in Video Game World-Building." In *World-Builders on World-Building*, edited by M.J.P. Wolf, 110–131. Routledge, 2020. Doi: 10.4324/9780429242861-7.

Jones, Adam. "Who Were the Vai?" *The Journal of African History* 22, no. 2 (1981): 159–78.

Juan, Stephen. "What Are the Most Widely Practiced Religions of the World?" *The Register*. Oct. 6, 2006. https://www.theregister.com/2006/10/06/the_odd_body_religion/.

"Knights Hospitaller." *Wikipedia*. Nov. 9, 2022. https://en.wikipedia.org/wiki/Knights_Hospitaller.

"Languages in the Holy See." *Study Country*. n.d. https://www.studycountry.com/guide/VA-language.htm.

Letzter, Rafi. "There's No Such Thing as an Alpha Male." *Business Insider*. Oct. 12, 2016. https://www.businessinsider.com/no-such-thing-alpha-male-2016-10.

"MacGuffin." *Merriam-Webster Dictionary*. n.d. https://www.merriam-webster.com/dictionary/MacGuffin.

Mech, Dave. "Wolf News and Information." *Dave Mech: Scientist and Wolf Researcher*. n.d. http://davemech.org/wolf-news-and-information/.

Mech, L. David. "Alpha Status, Dominance, and Division of Labor in Wolf Packs." *Canadian Journal of Zoology* 77 (1999): 1196–203.

Miller, Matt. "Why the Satanic Temple is Opening its Doors to American Muslims." *Esquire*. Nov. 21, 2015. https://www.esquire.com/news-politics/news/a39904/satanic-temple-founder-interview-muslims/.

Naylor, Janet, and Caroline Julian. *GURPS Religion*. Steve Jackson Games, 1994.

"New Exoplanet Is Twice Earth's Size—And Made Largely of Diamond." *Wired*. Oct. 12, 2012. https://www.wired.com/2012/10/diamond-exoplanet/.

"New York's Archbishops: How They Shaped the City and the Church." *New York Times*. Mar. 9, 2017. https://www.nytimes.com/2017/03/09/nyregion/new-yorks-archbishops-how-they-shaped-the-city-and-the-church.html.

Newman, Time. "Sex and Gender: What is the Difference?" *Medical News Today.* May 11, 2021. https://www.medicalnewstoday.com/articles/232363.

"Operation Underworld." *Wikipedia.* Sept. 1, 2022. https://en.wikipedia.org/wiki/Operation_Underworld.

Ozment, Steven E. *The Burgermeister's Daughter: Scandal in a Sixteenth-Century German Town.* St. Martin's Press, 1996.

Pratchett, Terry. *The Color of Magic.* Harper Paperbacks, 2000.

———. *Reaper Man.* Harper, 1991.

———. *Witches Abroad.* ROC, 1991.

Pratchett, Terry, and Paul Kidby. *The Art of Discworld.* HarperCollins, 2004.

"Race." *Cambridge Dictionary.* n.d. https://dictionary.cambridge.org/us/dictionary/english/race.

Ray, Rashawn and Nicole DeLoatch. "Race." *Oxford Bibliographies.* Nov. 13, 2018. https://www.oxfordbibliographies.com/view/document/obo-9780199756384/obo-9780199756384-0173.xml#:~:text=Race%20is%20a%20human%20classification,people%20who%20share%20phenotypical%20characteristics.

Rossi, Matthew. "According to the Player's Handbook, Drow No Longer Have to Be Evil in Your D&D Game." *Blizzard Watch.* Dec. 15, 2021. https://blizzardwatch.com/2021/12/15/dnd-drow-evil/.

Rowling, J.K. *Harry Potter and the Goblet of Fire.* Scholastic, 2000.

———. *Harry Potter and the Prisoner of Azkaban.* Scholastic, 1999.

Ruso, Mike. "The Word 'Race' in the Fantasy Genre." *MikeRuso.com.* May 12, 2014. https://www.mikeruso.com/blog/race-in-the-fantasy-genre/.

Scot, Reginald. *The Discouerie of Witchcraft.* London, 1584.

"Seamstresses' Guild." *L-Space.* Aug. 8, 2021. https://wiki.lspace.org/Seamstresses%27_Guild.

Stackpole, Michael. "They Do What Now? On Societies and Culture." In *The Kobold Guide to Worldbuilding,* edited by Janna Silverstein, 59–62. Kobold Press, 2012.

"Steven Brust." *Wikipedia.* Oct. 12, 2022. https://en.wikipedia.org/wiki/Steven_Brust.

Stoddard, William H. *GURPS Steam-Tech.* Steve Jackson Games, 2001.

Sturtevant, Paul B. "Race: The Original Sin of the Fantasy Genre." *The Public Medievalist.* Dec. 5, 2017. https://www.publicmedievalist.com/race-fantasy-genre.

Tamburro, Paul. "Forgotten Realms Creator Ed Greenwood Is 'Saddened' by Baldur's Gate Controversy." *Mandatory.* April 6, 2016. https://www.mandatory.com/culture/973847-forgotten-realms-creator-ed-greenwood-saddened-baldurs-gate-controversy.

Tate, Kirk, and Janet Naylor. *GURPS Fantasy,* 2nd ed. Steve Jackson Games, 1990.

Temple, Emily. "In Defense of Worldbuilding." *LitHub.* April 10, 2017. https://lithub.com/in-defense-of-worldbuilding/.

"Three Jolly Luck." *L-space.* Dec. 31, 2017. https://wiki.lspace.org/Three_Jolly_Luck.

Tod, M.K. "Worldbuilding—Culture & Society." *A Writer of History.* Dec. 15, 2020. https://awriterofhistory.wordpress.com/2020/12/15/world-building-culture-society/.

"Tokenism." *The Britannica Dictionary.* n.d. https://www.britannica.com/dictionary/tokenism.

Tolkien, J.R.R. *The Peoples of Middle-Earth.* Edited by Christopher Tolkien. Mariner Books, 1996.

"Trolls." *L-space.* Dec. 15, 2021. https://wiki.lspace.org/Trolls#Troll_Afterlife.

Turtledove, Harry. "Harry Turtledove: Revisioning History." *Locus* 50, no. 2 (Feb. 2003): 6–7, 81–2.

Tykhostup, Olena, and Piers Kelly. "A Diachronic Comparison of the Vai Script of Liberia (1834–2005)." *Journal of Open Humanities Data* 4, no. 2 (12 Feb. 2018): http://doi.org/10.5334/johd.10.

University Records and Life in the Middle Ages. Translated by Lynn Thorndyke. W.W. Norton, 1975.

Viva La Dirt League. "Forcing NPC's to Buy Your Stuff—Poor Merchant." *YouTube.* Jan. 29, 2020. Video, 3:25. https://youtu.be/mYsyTq8pF2g.

———. "Forcing Poor NPCs to Pay—Payment." *YouTube.* Nov. 11, 2020. Video, 3:20. https://youtu.be/JXLV1SQhVhw.

———. "How Does All the Loot Get There?" *YouTube.* Feb. 1, 2023. Video, 4:21. https://www.youtube.com/watch?v=tE73Ag07Rn8.

Whisper, Sable. "Rethinking Race in Fantasy: An Evidence-Based Approach." *Medium*. Mar. 9, 2019. https://realsablewhisper.medium.com/rethinking-race-in-fantasy-an-evidence-based-approach-8341c98ab05.

Wilson, C.L. "Worldbuilding 101: Structuring Your Society." clwilson.com. Sept. 14, 2013. https://clwilson.com/worldbuilding-101-structuring-your-society/.

Windling, Terri. "The Borderland Series." *Terri Windling's Studio*. n.d. https://web.archive.org/web/20160601203403/http://windling.typepad.com/editing/borderland.html.

"Wizarding Currency." *Harry Potter Wiki*. 4 Nov. 2022. https://harrypotter.fandom.com/wiki/Wizarding_currency#Exchange_rate.

"World Religion Day." *National Day Calendar*. n.d. https://nationaldaycalendar.com/world-religion-day-third-sunday-in-january/.

Wrede, Patricia C., and Pamela Dean. *Points of Departure: Liavek Stories*. Diversion Books, 2015.

Young, Helen. *Race and Popular Fantasy Literature: Habits of Whiteness*. Routledge, 2016.

Index

Adeyemi, Tomi 6, 23
adulthood 7, 208
afterlife 29, 227, 231
aging 208
agricultural 64, 91, 100, 110, 189, 211, 213
aircraft 101, 102, 108, 109
airports 13
airship 13, 100, 177, 178, 181, 184
alchemy 82, 84, 114, 118, 149, 163, 208, 223
alien 3, 46, 60, 80, 133, 135, 136, 139, 186
alternate 2, 11, 15, 19, 21, 22, 28, 40, 44, 47, 91, 103, 107, 187, 223
anarchy 41, 43
Anderson, Kevin J. 3, 19, 42, 206, 219-21, 226-28
Andrews, Ilona 22, 23, 28, 34, 39, 40, 44-46, 53, 54, 57-60, 69, 80, 82, 83, 87, 88, 95, 98, 105, 120, 129, 132, 134, 135, 162, 174, 187, 194, 199, 201, 217, 225
Ankh-Morpork 2, 10, 11, 19, 48, 53, 56, 77, 98, 99, 130, 137, 150, 162-164, 178, 191-196, 206
anocracy 46, 135
Anthony, Piers 183
apocalypse 34, 168, 175, 187, 199
apprenticeship 67, 81, 93, 115-23, 183
architecture 13, 17, 36, 73, 94, 176, 205, 206
aristocracy 46
army 10, 75, 93, 95, 156, 163, 164, 166, 169, 170, 183, 198
Asimov, Isaac 107
Asprin, Robert 1, 82, 115, 120, 194, 195, 217
autocracy 43, 46

Baldree, Travis 57, 204
Baldur's Gate Controversy 231
Bardugo, Leigh 2, 9, 10, 14, 23, 26, 35, 39, 47, 50, 53, 59, 60, 62, 82, 101, 105, 108, 122, 154, 156, 174, 175, 198, 205, 217
Barrie, J.M. 189
Baum, L. Frank 189, 190
Baur, Wolfgang 16, 24, 219, 220, 223, 224, 227, 229
Bennett, Robert Jackson 5
biological determinism 225, 229
Blake, Olivie 112

border 7, 10, 34, 50, 72, 106, 108, 143, 144, 164, 165, 172, 173, 180, 189, 218, 220, 230
Bordertown 23, 105, 106, 189, 220, 232
Boroson, M.H. 67
Briggs, Patricia 171
Brooks, Terry 128, 189, 190
Brust, Steven 4, 23, 32, 39, 56, 59-61, 65, 89, 90, 93, 95, 97, 101, 103, 104, 123, 132, 134-36, 138, 139, 165, 180, 181, 191, 193, 198-200, 217, 223, 226, 231
bureaucracy 41, 44, 150, 193
Burroughs, Edgar Rice 104, 105
business 49, 97, 98, 115, 122, 137, 150, 154, 162, 170, 192, 195, 198, 221, 230

campaigns 7, 48, 174, 227
Canavan, Trudi 159, 164
Carroll, Lewis 189, 190
caste 65, 119, 123
Catholicism 36, 66, 68-71, 73-75, 77, 118, 157, 158, 165, 166
cells (prison) 90, 193
Cervantes, Jennifer 5
Chadda, Sarwat 6
Chakraborty, S.A. 6, 120, 123
Cherryh, C.J. 24, 107, 136
Chokshi, Roshani 1, 5, 133, 134, 139, 217
citizenship 44, 111, 122, 138, 164
city-state 37, 43, 225
Clare, Cassandra 6, 47, 57, 59, 60, 93, 112, 161, 188, 189, 217
Clark, P. Djèlí 153, 217
Clarke, Susanna 28, 217
clergy 31, 36, 55, 58, 60-73, 76-78, 97-99, 107, 111, 118, 122, 124, 144, 147, 156, 157, 197, 230
cleric 38, 64-70, 73, 75, 78, 82, 98, 197
climate 171, 173, 179, 203, 220, 227
coalition 33
Cole, Myke 52, 85, 87, 88
college 93, 112, 118, 155, 181, 193, 203, 227
colonization 33, 50, 126, 163, 177, 178
conclave 55, 85, 86, 90
confederation 46, 50
Confucianism 221

233

234 Index

Congress 77, 230
Cook, Monte 17, 19, 219, 229
corporatocratic 51
cosmology 67, 184, 185, 223
council 41, 42, 51, 53, 55, 71, 85, 210
currency 13, 18, 73, 96, 202, 204, 205, 214, 227, 232
cyberpunk 46

Daoism 72, 221
Davidson, Avram 6, 188
Dean, Pamela 10–12, 219
death 15, 29, 34, 36, 51, 56, 64, 69, 73, 110, 128, 133, 161, 175, 196, 201, 206, 208, 210, 211, 222
deities 38, 57–65, 67–76, 78, 81, 97, 98, 106, 107, 118, 147, 155–59, 175, 182, 196, 197, 206, 211, 214, 220
De Lint, Charles 105
democracy 36, 37, 42–46, 48, 51, 55
demographics 10, 13, 168, 169
despotism 49, 50, 54
dialects 17, 141, 144–46, 150, 151, 225
dictatorship 41, 42
diversity 5, 6, 27, 115, 152, 214
divinities 29, 30, 34, 35, 58, 60–63, 65–68, 73, 82, 96, 98, 118, 158–60, 172, 175, 182, 185, 196–98, 200, 211

Earth 1, 2, 11, 24, 26, 28, 30, 53, 57, 59, 62, 81, 83, 92, 94, 105, 106, 131, 133–35, 165, 174, 175, 177, 181, 183, 185–89, 206, 211, 221, 226, 227, 230, 231
economy 1, 4, 19, 34, 42, 46, 84, 95, 96, 100, 108, 110, 111, 121, 123, 135, 137, 163, 165, 176, 177, 205, 220
education 38, 50, 65–67, 81, 84, 92–94, 100, 112–25, 137, 138, 155, 162, 170, 192–95, 214
egalitarian 43, 86, 156
empire 2, 11, 25, 29, 36, 37, 41, 42, 44, 45, 50, 51, 138
entertainment 26, 121, 133, 136, 170, 194, 195, 202, 205, 206
environmental 1, 49, 92, 101, 120, 133, 134, 172
Estep, Jennifer 206
ethics 2, 15, 114, 133, 214
ethnicity 36, 121, 126, 127, 129, 132, 133, 137, 143, 169, 224, 229
etiquette 54
exceptionalism 117, 136, 225, 229
expansionistic 109, 179

faiths 57–59, 67, 76, 106, 107, 118, 127, 157, 158, 164, 197, 198
federation 43, 45, 46, 162
festival 12, 69, 206, 207
figurehead 36, 45
financial 70, 110, 115, 121, 123, 138
Foglio, Kaja 217
Foglio, Phil 217
food 10, 13, 16, 29, 74, 96, 130, 146, 149, 176, 179, 182, 192–95, 204, 208

foreign 50, 53, 144, 145, 164, 165, 178, 214
foreigners 50, 134, 180
Friesner, Esther 7

Gaiman, Neil 24, 39, 44, 105, 189, 190, 208, 217, 220, 227
gamemasters 4, 17, 80
gamers 153, 213
games 2, 4–7, 25, 62, 101, 102, 126, 132, 135, 142, 202, 204–6, 213, 214, 219–23, 225, 227, 230, 231
gaming 5, 6, 150, 195
gender 8, 12, 21, 42, 65, 76, 81, 117, 121–23, 125, 152–60, 169, 231
geography 1, 4, 8, 13, 21, 69, 71, 74, 133, 134, 170–89, 203, 207, 214, 220, 225
Gladstone, Max 5, 23, 31, 35, 61, 97, 217
gods 12, 29, 32, 34, 35, 37, 51, 58, 60–65, 68, 69, 76, 81, 97, 98, 167, 175, 182, 184, 197, 198, 200, 208, 214
governance 19, 41, 42, 53, 84, 86, 209, 213
governing 31, 42, 47, 50–52, 84–86, 88, 155, 163, 195
government 8, 11, 12, 18, 33–36, 41–55, 76, 77, 81, 84–89, 93, 94, 98–100, 108–11, 123, 138, 141, 143, 150, 158, 159, 161, 163–65, 168, 170, 178, 192, 193, 205, 209, 210, 214, 222
Greenwood, Ed 61, 152, 155, 226, 231
Grossman, Lev 82, 95, 112, 175, 189, 190, 217

habitat 185
Harkness, Deborah 194, 217
Harris, Charlaine 22, 23, 28, 39, 40, 54, 60, 80, 128, 168, 195, 217
healing 72, 73, 83, 84, 92, 95, 98, 99, 159, 211, 223
Hearne, Kevin 31, 59, 62, 65, 82, 85, 119, 147, 174, 175, 217
Heitz, Markus 132
Herbert, Frank 24, 25, 47, 103, 217, 220, 228
hereditary 36, 43, 44, 48, 51, 65, 66, 86, 118, 119
heresy 69, 71, 78, 107, 108, 221
Hernandez, Carlos 133
Hickman, Tracy 62, 85, 175, 181, 183, 187
hierarchy 18, 43, 54, 64, 66, 67, 69–71, 73, 75, 94, 95, 124, 159, 166, 213
historians 21, 26, 27, 48
history 1–4, 8, 11, 14, 15, 19–29, 31–40, 43–45, 49–52, 56, 61, 66, 71, 78, 81–83, 87, 92, 95, 109, 113–15, 118–25, 127, 128, 132, 138, 150, 153, 155, 159, 162, 166–69, 171, 173, 176–80, 183, 186, 187, 189, 192, 198, 199, 207, 214, 219–21, 224, 226, 227, 229–31
holidays 12, 29, 30, 69, 130, 202, 206
hospital 75, 222
hospitality 29, 32, 63
Howard, Robert E. 27, 30, 57, 217, 228
Huff, Tanya 81, 82, 91, 105, 159, 217

identity 2, 53, 54, 143, 154
illegal 12, 87, 89, 158, 162–64, 168, 193, 205

Index

illicit 76, 162, 164, 165, 205, 206
immigrants 130, 137, 148
immortality 22, 50, 60, 105, 120, 133, 145, 207–10, 218
imperial 50, 51, 89, 90, 135, 138, 141, 191, 193, 223, 230
industrialization 101, 110, 213
inheritance 71, 86, 119, 130, 155, 209
institutions 45, 46, 49, 119, 121, 125, 137, 225
instruction 56, 67, 68, 115–21, 123, 124
interdimensional 103
invention 34, 35, 102, 103, 177, 180
isolationism 35, 135, 165

Jainism 221
James, Allyson 22, 82, 95, 104, 105, 188, 196, 199, 201, 213, 217
Jemisin, N.K. 5, 23, 26, 31, 174, 217, 226, 230
Jesuit 1, 66
Jewish 59, 70, 126, 168, 223
Jones, Diana Wynne 189, 190
Jordan, Robert 44

Khan, Ausma Zehanat 5, 59
Kim, Graci 5, 95, 134, 139, 217
kingdom 11, 26, 30, 36, 42, 44, 46, 48, 51, 135, 167, 205, 218
kleptocracy 47
Kornbluth, C.M. 46
Kurtz, Katherine 42, 44, 65, 217

labor 49, 96, 137, 168, 221, 230
Lackey, Mercedes 23, 44, 105
lair 172, 198, 200
landmarks 194–96
landmasses 181, 182
landscape 187, 188
languages 1, 2, 7, 8, 10, 22, 38, 100, 106, 113, 115, 116, 118, 127, 130, 131, 141–51, 181, 207, 209, 214, 225, 230
laws 2, 11, 12, 25, 29, 48, 54–56, 78, 84, 87, 98, 99, 110, 111, 138, 154, 155, 158–60, 164, 203, 205, 209, 221, 222
learning 67, 74, 81, 107, 114, 116, 121, 142, 144, 151, 159, 173, 193, 224
Lee, Fonda 6, 82, 101, 177, 178, 217
legal 12, 56, 76, 80, 86, 87, 89, 99, 109, 138, 143, 149, 153, 155, 156, 158, 159, 162–64, 168
legend 3, 29–33, 37, 39, 57, 59, 82, 86, 101, 113, 116, 120, 125, 128, 131, 134, 135, 139, 147, 175, 182, 191, 199, 200, 204, 208, 217, 220
legislation 35, 48, 52, 54, 55, 108, 162, 163, 168, 203
legislature 36, 48, 205, 209
LeGuin, Ursula K. 112, 115, 120, 217
Leiber, Fritz 23, 26, 27, 57, 104, 107
Lewis, C.S. 44, 57, 59, 63, 104, 105, 185, 189, 190, 196, 217, 220
libraries 119, 121, 124, 194, 199
lifespan 51, 130, 133, 144, 208, 209
lineage 26, 29, 33, 63

linguistic 141–43
literacy 38, 92, 107, 121, 225
literature 17, 66, 90, 101, 112, 115, 118, 120, 135, 174, 182, 204, 211, 220, 224, 226, 232
location 1, 3, 11, 13, 72, 73, 117, 118, 137, 146, 171–73, 178, 179, 186–89, 191–94, 196, 197, 199, 200, 214, 219
long-lived 51, 130
longevity 133, 202, 207, 209, 210
Lynch, Scott 34, 42, 45

MacGuffin 199, 227, 230
magetech 91, 102–5, 110
magic-apocalypse 225
magocracy 42, 47–49, 86, 94
manufacturing 95, 96, 103, 110
marriage 69, 75, 138, 154, 155, 211, 222
Martin, Gail Z. 24, 86
Martin, George 9, 14, 26, 27, 30, 44, 45, 82, 217
Mbalia, Kwame 5
McClellan, Brian 42, 45
meritocracy 41, 42, 47–49
Miéville, China 47
migration 17, 22, 182
militancy 26, 36, 74, 75, 135, 206
military 29, 35, 42, 49–51, 71, 75, 84–86, 91, 93, 101, 108, 109, 112, 153–56, 162, 170, 193, 194, 213, 221, 222, 226
monarchy 36, 41–44, 48, 54, 55
monastic 1, 2, 10, 41, 64, 68–70, 73–75, 78, 95, 107, 157, 162, 165, 167, 170, 197
money 5, 48, 96, 137, 166, 202, 204, 206
moneychangers 204
moneylending 165
Monk, Devon 22
monotheism 58–60
monuments 198
Moorcock, Michael 26, 30, 44, 45, 80, 184, 192, 217
Moore, C.L. 26, 27
mortality 169
Muir, Tamsyn 84
multiverse 1, 44, 80, 166, 185
mythology 8, 29–32, 59, 60, 62, 63, 81, 83, 113, 134, 153, 174, 175, 179, 182, 184

nation 1, 2, 5, 6, 9, 10, 12, 14, 16, 30, 36, 37, 41, 47, 48, 50, 51, 56, 62, 65, 77, 80, 85, 86, 130, 137, 167, 171–73, 175, 177, 178, 184, 185, 188, 189, 193, 211, 219, 229
nationalism 117
nationality 129
native 141, 143, 144, 178, 225
nature 1, 23, 24, 27, 29, 39, 46, 58, 60, 61, 67, 68, 71, 74, 75, 80, 86, 91, 92, 97, 107, 119, 134, 159, 161, 165, 174, 175, 183, 185, 187, 192, 197, 198, 200, 207, 211
necromancy 24, 84, 86, 87, 123, 134, 159, 195
neighborhoods 1, 10, 73, 78, 137, 171, 172
Niven, Larry 185

Nix, Garth 39, 218
nomadic 109, 172, 173, 179
non-binary 157
non-gendered 159
non-hierarchical 42
Novik, Naomi 33, 39, 82, 93, 95, 104, 116, 120, 134, 194, 218
Nye, Jody Lynn 23, 223, 231

Okorafor, Nnedi 6
Older, Daniel José 139, 218
oligarchy 42, 44, 51
ordination 66, 221, 222
orientation (sexual) 121, 122, 153, 154, 169, 213

pacts 222
pagan 69
pandemic 34, 168
pantheistic 59, 118
pantheon 57, 58, 61, 67
Paolini, Christopher 44
patriarch 43, 55, 70, 71
philosophy 60, 66, 67, 70, 74, 115, 118, 130, 210
pilgrimage 66, 72, 74, 75, 197
plague 29, 34, 35, 37, 67, 164, 168, 172, 180, 198, 203
planes (of existence) 181, 185, 208
plutocracy 47, 48
Pohl, Frederik 46
police 55, 56, 78, 88, 90, 137, 163, 167
politics 1, 2, 4, 15, 28, 29, 34, 36, 46, 48, 64, 70, 75–77, 81, 84, 87, 98, 115, 120, 135, 137, 138, 156, 157, 162–66, 170, 176, 188, 219, 220, 227, 230
polytheists 58
post-apocalypse 2, 44, 45, 187, 199
Pratchett, Terry 4, 7, 10, 44, 96, 97, 105, 108, 110, 113, 120, 122, 129, 130, 134, 137, 138, 147, 150, 163, 171, 174, 176, 178, 191–96, 201, 218, 223, 226, 227, 231
prisons 90, 193, 223, 230
privacy 88, 89, 111
Pullman, Philip 187

race 4, 8, 121–23, 126, 127, 130–33, 139, 179, 224, 225, 231, 232
racism 27, 117, 130, 131, 140
rank 18, 43, 64, 65, 67, 69, 115, 162
rebellion 25, 34, 99, 166, 210
religion 1, 8, 13, 45, 56–59, 61–78, 96–100, 106, 107, 111, 117, 118, 122–24, 153, 156–59, 163, 164, 176, 197, 198, 207, 214, 220, 221, 230, 232
reproduction 12, 136, 138, 155, 209, 222
republic 36, 37, 42–45, 48, 50, 51, 55, 167, 210
Riggs, Ransom 15
Riordan, Rick 23, 39, 55, 57, 59, 62, 80, 83, 91, 92, 95, 103, 105, 107, 133, 134, 189, 190, 199, 203, 217, 218
rivers 13, 172, 173, 177, 180, 188, 196, 197, 211

roads 13, 74, 132, 145, 177, 206
Roanhorse, Rebecca 5
roleplaying 4, 80
Rothfuss, Patrick 26, 194, 218
Rowling, J.K. 23–26, 30, 38, 39, 42, 45, 47, 52, 79, 83, 90, 106, 112, 113, 120, 122, 126, 128, 132, 134, 193, 196, 204, 208, 218, 220, 224, 231
RPGs 17, 80, 95, 131, 148, 204, 209

sacred 66, 72, 75, 107, 153, 157, 196, 197
sacrifice 87, 163, 164
Sanderson, Brandon 23, 44, 45, 176, 198, 218
Sapkowski, Andrzej 44, 82, 83, 116, 218
sausages-inna-bun 193
scholars 119, 144, 149, 203, 225
school 1, 7, 10, 17–19, 25, 26, 31, 33, 34, 38, 41, 56, 67, 70, 74, 104, 112, 115–25, 148, 155, 193, 194, 204, 213, 227
science 2, 11, 21, 24, 35, 42, 45, 46, 53, 67, 68, 74, 89, 102–4, 107, 108, 114, 115, 117, 121, 136, 139, 143, 145, 147, 156, 171, 174, 180, 183, 185, 199, 214, 220, 222, 223, 226, 229, 230
Scott, Michael 82, 105, 120, 208, 218
sect 29, 58, 65, 66, 68, 71, 72, 78, 156, 157, 221
self-taught 93, 113, 114, 118-122
settlements 13, 30, 41, 172, 173, 176, 177, 183
sexes 12, 153–57, 159, 160, 169
sexism 27, 117, 152
sexuality 211
Shakespeare, William 3, 27, 83
shape-shifters 60, 155, 196
Shearin, Lisa 22, 88, 103, 105, 106, 136, 195, 218
Shiite 71
Shoikan 175, 199, 200
Singh, Nalini 22, 23, 128, 187
Smith, Clark Ashton 57
spies 144, 149, 168, 170, 186
sports 170, 195, 205, 206
steampunk 45, 100, 103, 104, 223
Stephenson, Neal 47
Stroud, Jonathan 42, 47, 83, 120, 218
swamp 173, 180

Taoism 208
taverns 192, 195, 224, 227
Tchaikovsky, Adrian 42, 45
technomagic 96, 102–4
temples 31, 34, 45, 56, 60, 63, 67, 68, 71–74, 78, 99, 137, 138, 144, 147, 158, 164, 197–99, 222, 227, 230
theater 118, 153, 170, 195, 205, 206
theocracy 36, 42, 45, 47–49, 51, 55, 76, 158
theology 66, 67, 70, 115, 118
Thomas, Aiden 153, 159, 218
tokenism 128, 129, 131, 132, 135, 153, 225, 231
Tolkien, J.R.R. 4, 7, 22–27, 30, 32, 44, 56, 57, 59, 61, 62, 83, 104, 113, 129, 131, 138, 142, 148, 150, 152, 154, 176, 179, 196, 198, 201, 207, 208, 218, 220, 226, 231

totalitarian 163
totemist 58
transgender 152, 154, 160, 226
translation 38, 113, 142, 145–47
transportation 10, 79, 83, 100–103, 137, 177, 185
TTRPG 4, 5, 7, 25, 42, 126, 131, 150, 152, 204, 221
Turtledove, Harry 4, 8, 9, 14, 186, 218, 226, 231
tutoring 81, 115–22, 124, 223
tyranny 31, 51, 138

unaging 208
undead 51, 84, 134, 200, 208
underworld (place) 164, 168, 195, 212, 226, 231
union 36, 45, 168
universe 79, 153, 162, 173, 174, 187, 217, 219–21, 227, 229
university 2, 10, 14, 74, 78, 85, 93, 98, 99, 112, 115, 116, 118, 120, 122, 124, 138, 144, 170, 191, 193, 194, 196, 201, 223, 224, 227, 229, 231

valley 13, 145
verisimilitude 59, 174, 204
vernacular 74, 146

vestments 64, 68, 70, 222
video games 5, 7, 17, 25, 82, 95, 96, 101, 108, 118, 126, 129, 131, 132, 135, 142, 146, 150, 183, 202, 204–6, 219, 220, 227, 230, 231
violence 36, 56, 64, 133, 164

warfare 67, 79, 87, 172
wars 34, 51, 129, 147, 161, 162, 164, 167, 168, 180, 198, 207, 210
water 10, 53, 81, 83, 92, 98, 103, 104, 173, 177, 178, 182, 184, 185, 212
waterways 177
Weis, Margaret 62, 85, 175, 181, 183, 187
Wexler, Django 42, 45
Wiccan 59
Williamson, Jack 104
Windling, Terri 7, 23, 105, 106, 189, 218, 220, 232
witch 23, 28, 30, 31, 41, 61, 83, 85, 89, 90, 98, 112, 116, 123, 146, 160, 181, 188, 194, 222, 223, 231
Wrede, Patricia C. 10–12, 47, 219, 232
wuxia 220

Yong, Jin 82

Zelazny, Roger 7, 181, 221

www.ingramcontent.com/pod-product-compliance
Ingram Content Group UK Ltd.
Pitfield, Milton Keynes, MK11 3LW, UK
UKHW041942140426
5217IPUK00014B/621